The World According to **Roy Peterson**
with the Gospel According to **Allan Fotheringham**

D1400319

Douglas & McIntyre

Vancouver

This book is dedicated to
Flying Officer Lawrence H. Peterson 1921-1942 and
Flying Officer Sidney G. Peterson 1922-1944

Text copyright © Allan Fotheringham, 1979
Drawings copyright © Roy Peterson, 1963, 1968, 1970, 1971,
1972, 1973, 1974, 1975, 1976, 1977, 1978, 1979.

Canadian Cataloguing in Publication Data

Peterson, Roy, 1936-
     The world according to Roy Peterson

     ISBN 0-88894-254-0
     ISBN 0-88894-246-X pa.

     1. Canadian wit and humor, Pictorial.
2. Editorial cartoons - Canada. I. Fotheringham,
Allan, 1932-   II. Title.
NC1449.P48A4 1979   741.5'971   C79-091189-2

Design by Nancy Legue-Grout
Typesetting by Frebo Studio Limited

Douglas & McIntyre Ltd.
1875 Welch Street
North Vancouver, British Columbia

Printed by Hemlock Printers Ltd.
Bound by Brunswick Binding Inc.

The World According to Roy Peterson

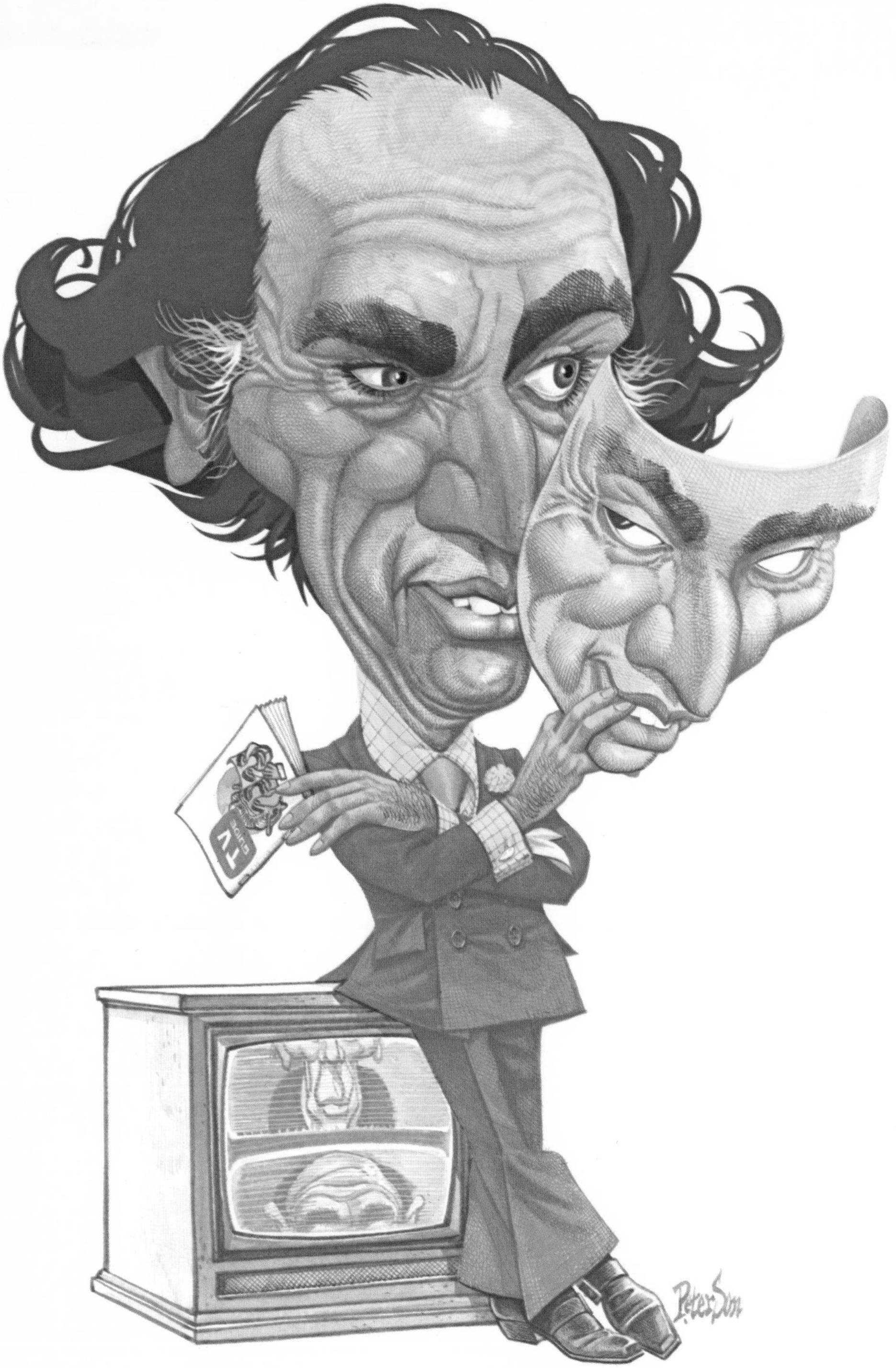

Pierre Trudeau

Contents

The Creator of the World

It has never, in my estimation, been fair. Cartoonists can hack and slash away, stab and bludgeon—reducing politicians and public figures to pygmies, fools and dolts. Character assassination of the most lurid form is permitted them. What is not fair is that when the lowly pencil press attempts the same type of personality analysis, we are vilified for being vicious, mean and guilty of exaggeration.

Why are the chaps brandishing pen and brush allowed the most extreme forms of satire and evisceration while the lowly typewriter jockey spends half his time in libel court, beating off lawyers, and reassuring nervous editors who allow their cartoonists to wield meat-axe and sledgehammer on the same victims? It is a mystery that, in a quarter-century of struggling through the underbrush of journalism, has always puzzled me.

I have watched at close hand, for a good portion of this tenure in purgatory, the merciless brush of Roy Peterson, who reduces major names to tiny blobs of ridicule on drawing paper. Mainly in the *Vancouver Sun* but also in *Maclean's* with excursions into the pages of *Punch*, *Spectator*, the *New York Times*, the *Washington Post*, *Weekend Magazine*, *Time*, *Saturday Night* and beyond. The great Duncan Macpherson, who towers over most of the world's cartoonists from his aerie at the *Toronto Star*, recently referred to Peterson as the top editorial cartoonist working in Canada. This retrospective collection provides the evidence for Macpherson's opinion.

More astute sociologists than this observer may in the future tell us why Canada supplies a disproportionate share of internationally ranked cartoonists. (I suspect it has something to do with reaction to the general mealy-mouthed nature of so much of Canadian life.) As well as Peterson and Macpherson, there are the mordant Aislin (a.k.a. Terry Mosher) of the *Montreal Gazette* and the puckish Len Norris, also of the *Vancouver Sun*, whose sly ridicule in the tradition of Giles has punctured policemen and politicians for years.

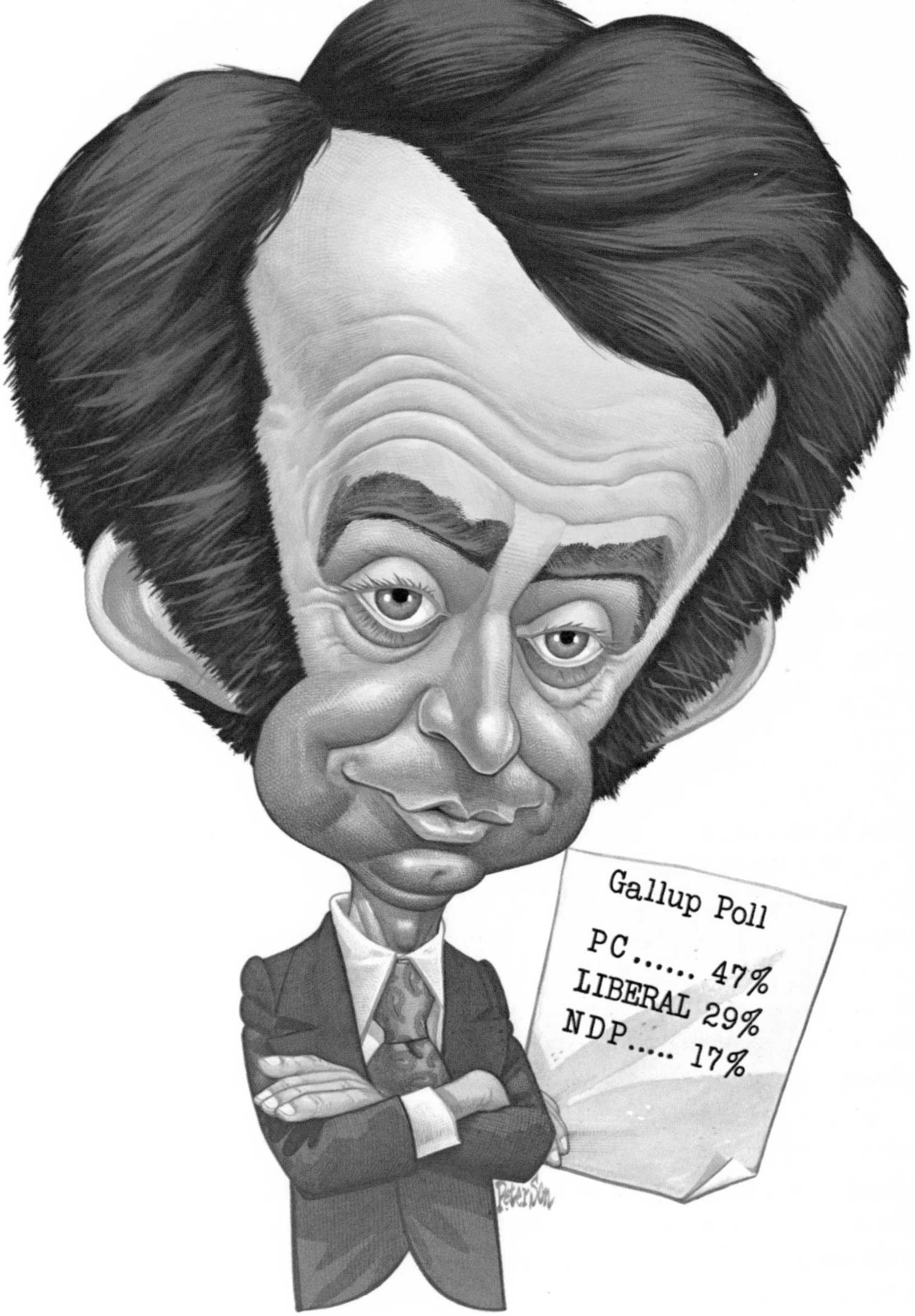
Gallup Poll
PC...... 47%
LIBERAL 29%
NDP..... 17%
Peterson

Joe Clark

There is also the eccentricity of our top cartoonists that links them. The hulking Macpherson is famous, in one of his Celtic rages, for attempting to hurl a manhole cover as a discus and hitting a police car, for demolishing press clubs and for plastering a slowly melting paste over a portrait of a newspaper proprietor that produced a Dorian Gray effect by morning. Aislin is celebrated for long and dark forays into the recesses of Montreal bistros. Sid Barron, who draws scenes of suburban Toronto bliss for the *Toronto Star*, in fact hates the city so much that for years he sent in his cartoons from Calgary. That apparently wasn't far enough away and now he draws Toronto from Victoria. There is the absolutely loony Ben Wicks, the Cockney refugee who has never mastered English and has yet to start on Canadian. Bob Bierman, the Victoria cartoonist who recently *was* the first cartoonist in Canada to be sued for libel, once grew so upset at a driver who was stealing his parking spot that he used his car as a battering ram and simply wrecked the offending vehicle. He's just as rough with a pen.

In contrast to all these wild men, Peterson is a mild-mannered assassin who saves his savagery for his drawing board. He lives on the gentle slope of a mountain in West Vancouver along with his tender wife, Margaret, five children, two badly trained dogs called Buddy and Blitz, a cat, a canary called Spot and a gerbil who answers to Mr. Bill. There are also two horses somewhere in the menagerie, and if he acquires one more specimen he's going to work out an even trade with the Stanley Park zoo. He is quiet, witty, stubborn, with facial foliage that reminds you of either Lister Sinclair or Lenin (depending on whether or not you've been skewered that day) and one drooping eyelid that places him in instant sympathy with Robert Stanfield. His charity towards the world stops there.

He was born in Winnipeg, a handicap he has been able largely to overcome, in 1936 of good Icelandic stock and has lived in the salubrious creative climate of Vancouver since 1948, forcing the art directors of the continent to come to his mountain all the while. His refusal to succumb to the lure of vulgar cash in Toronto and elsewhere—he prefers yearly forays to Washington or Berlin or Moscow, when he turns reporter as well as illustrator—has brought its rewards.

Six books, two National Newspaper Awards and first place in the International Salon of Cartoons among 565 artists from 56 countries provide ample evidence of his genius. His drawings are all the more remarkable because they are spread over such a spectrum of styles. Most cartoonists have one basic style and wisely stick to it. It seems to me that there are six different Petersons, and this collection is designed to show all six.

There are the regular editorial cartoons, the staple of all editorial pages; the powerful, uncaptioned "portfolios," in which Peterson sums up the week's news in one blow; the caricatures—surely of the calibre of New York's David Levine—of Norman Mailer, Trudeau, Stanfield, Bill Bennett and others. There are those which for want of a better term can be called the "social comment" cartoons—Peterson's wicked view of a hotline host or bureaucrat—a portion of humanity penned in acid. There are the artistic sketches arising from Peterson's travels abroad. And finally, there is the view of Canada as a Swamp, populated by frogs and beavers. This is sardonic Disney-with-a-bite, taken from Peterson's four books with Stanley Burke, that reduces all of us to the primate stage where we truly belong.

Peterson follows the best of traditions. We owe our insights into 18th-century Britain to Hogarth's lusty sketches of the gin-soaked wretches of London and of the Tories and the Whigs hauling the crippled, the insane and the criminal into the polling station. Hogarth's contemporary, Gillray, created caricatures—full of pockmarked, bloated ladies and slope-chinned aristocratic men—savage enough to delight a Peterson, a Macpherson or even a Wicks.

Thomas Nast, the father of American political cartooning, evolved from being a propagandist during the Civil War and the sentimental creator of the Santa Claus figure we know today into making blunt assaults on civic corruption epitomized by Boss Tweed and Tammany Hall. But it was Ronald Searle, the high priest of *Punch*, with his antic extensions of reality, who is really the godfather of modern cartooning. From Searle flowed Pat Oliphant, the Australian now at the *Washington Star*. Then Jeff MacNelly of the *Richmond News-Leader*, Mike Peters of the *Dayton News* and Don Wright of the *Miami News* — equals developing different areas of the new style. And then 120 clones, all trying the same trick.

Peterson is no clone. When he was just 20 he went to England and had the courage to phone Searle, then world-famous for his caricatures. Searle took the time to invite the young Canadian to his home and, once he had seen his work, offered the encouragement that pushed Peterson farther along the road to the vivisection, decapitation and emasculation of those deserving such treatment.

It should also be kept in mind that Peterson grew up in the golden age of *Mad* magazine, when Jack Davis, Wally Wood and Harvey Kurtzman

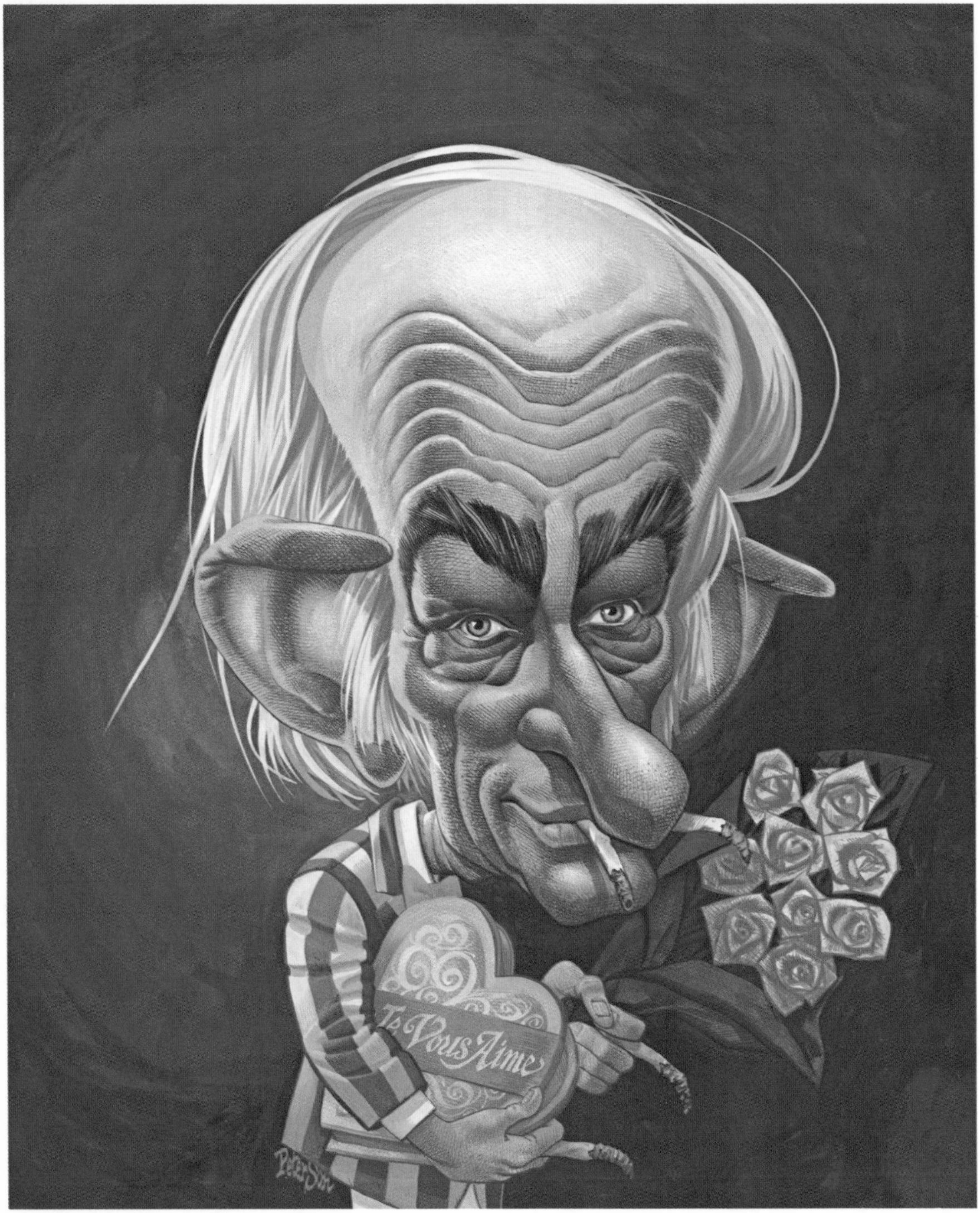
Je Vous Aime
PeterSon

René Lévesque

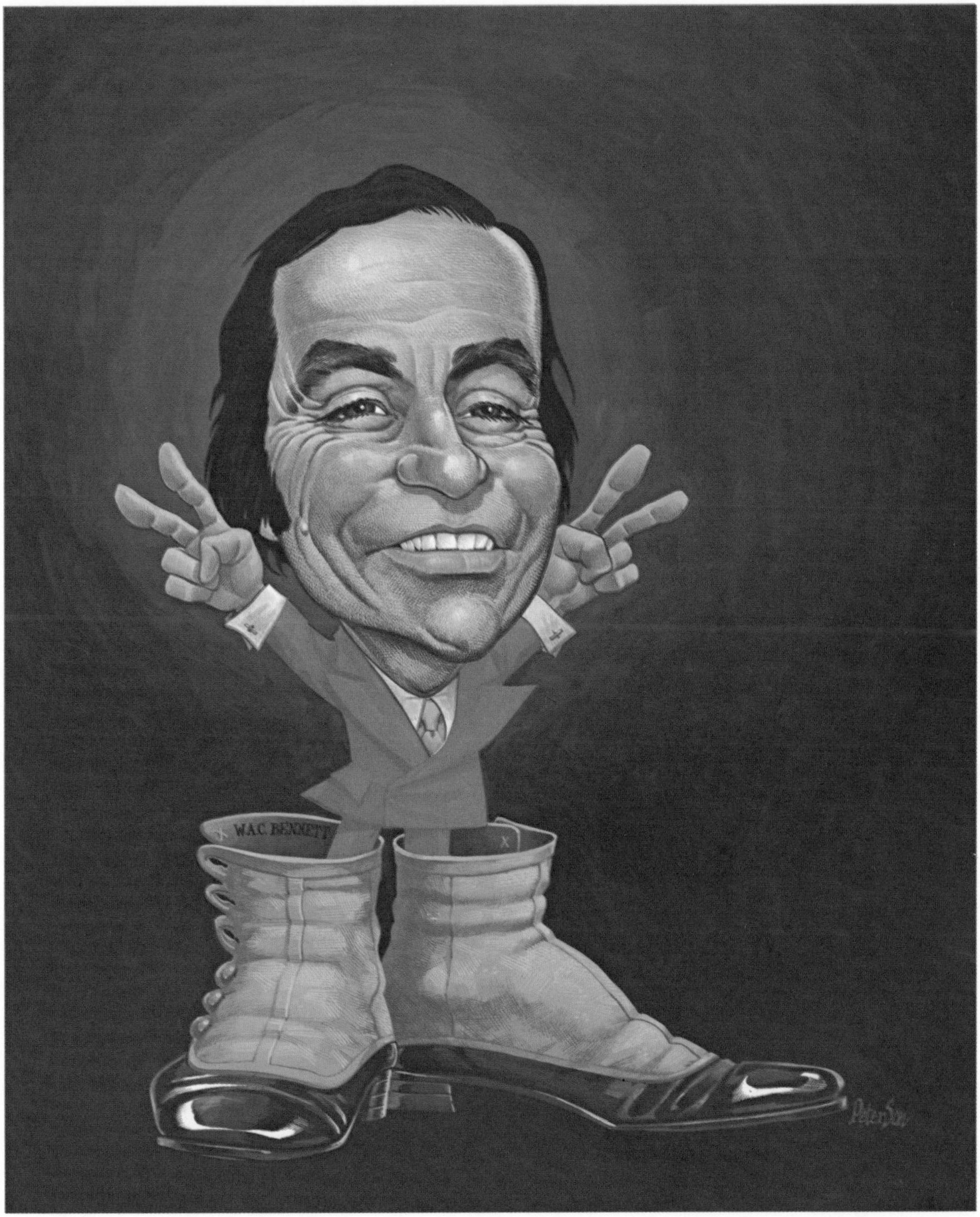
W.A.C. BENNETT
Peterson

Bill Bennett

were wending their manic way through the minds of North American teenagers. (So much has the world changed in its view of what is sane that Davis has recently been illustrating the occasional cover for *Time*. *Mad* comes to the middle class.)

I love Peterson in his most outrageous moments: the hotliner with the yawning yap half a hectare wide; Eugene Whelan and his Ottawa Dried Chicken (another Canadian turkey); the hockey agent pursuing King Kong; Phil Gaglardi as Phil Gaglardi; the Packaged Joe Clark; Trudeau as a dropout from Laugh-In, blasted by Ruth Buzzi.

It is interesting, in viewing the Peterson version of Pierre Trudeau that opens this book, to note the mask. It is a theme that appeared frequently in the 11 years that Trudeau confronted Peterson—and vice versa. It was, in the finale, the true analysis: the very private man who would not reveal himself to the public. It was why he was defeated: the voter could never really figure out who he was. He demanded our complete fealty to his concept of Canada but would not, in return, repay our trust by unveiling his soul. He left office the man in the mask.

Joe Clark, in Peterson's pen, emerges as more than somewhat bemused by it all, the indecisive mouth wavering between nervous humour and fake assertiveness. His head topples his body, his hair topples his head. Peterson detected early on that here is a man feeling his way through life.

René Lévesque, on the other hand, is a sly fox with hard eyes; a philanderer come to woo us and con us. Cartoonists love Lévesque's hair as a prop. (Aislin has had him holding it down with a barrette, then latterly with a paper clip. God save the current politician: *Globe and Mail* columnist William Johnson revealed that the reason for Lévesque's mercurial, now-you-see-it, now-you-don't smile is that he has bad teeth.) Peterson, ever the savage gentleman, simply increases the flow of the uncontrollable Lévesque mane until it resembles the spillway of the James Bay hydro dam and lets it ramble while the butts of Canada's most famous smoker crumble and droop. The butts, you'll note in all these Lévesque portraits, do not sizzle and threaten. They crumble and droop. Far be it from me to argue with a cartoonist's perceptive eye.

The Nixon-chinned Bill Bennett, alias MiniWac, is another matter, as provincial as Lévesque is worldly, as desperate for approval as René is bored with acclaim. One has seen too much of the world and regards Canada as parochial; the other has yet to penetrate the Canada beyond the mountains, and—drowning in his father's shoes — has a belligerent-while-wary tone to his approach. As the only premier in Canada who has never gone to university, he likes to think he is smarter than most of them—but is not quite sure.

The inscrutable Peter Newman, a Peterson fan who has been a patron of his work and who has helped make Canada safe for talented Canadian journalists and artists, was witness to an unusual cartooning controversy. Peterson is the only cartoonist that *Maclean's* commissions for covers. It was national news, therefore, when the phlegmatic Icelander produced for *Maclean's* debut as a weekly newsmagazine a cover so devastating that it wasn't used. The Peterson concept of a cornered Trudeau who had just jettisoned yet another election call struck *Maclean's* publisher Lloyd Hodgkinson as inappropriate for the launch issue—thus producing gleeful headlines from the considerable number of Canadian journalists who somehow felt that a fake-Canadian *Time* was preferable to a flawed-Canadian *Maclean's*. Of such inexplicable logic is this ill-confident country built. The crisis of the cover also lost Newman several top editors and reverberated for weeks in the Toronto media mafia, than which there is none more incestuous. It is a perverse sort of tribute to the troublemaking capabilities of the quiet chap in British Columbia, who has somehow wisely escaped ever working full time for anyone. (Newman, who detected the essential bittersweet irony of the whole episode when others couldn't, requested and now owns the original of a Peterson rejoinder in the *Vancouver Sun* showing Trudeau cowering in the same pose before the inaugural issue of *Maclean's*.)

Peterson has this problem with covers. Commissioned to do the cover for a biography of W.A.C. Bennett—so badly written by a Bennett flunkey that it almost won, unsubmitted, the Stephen Leacock Award for Humour—he presented the offering carried on page 74. It proved completely unacceptable to the sycophantic sponsors. Too truthful. Too mirthful. The book died; the caricature lives.

Because he persists on his West Vancouver mountain, it's a little-known fact that Roy Peterson ranks as one of the world's most talented cartoonists. He is not fully recognized—yet. Not until this work appears.

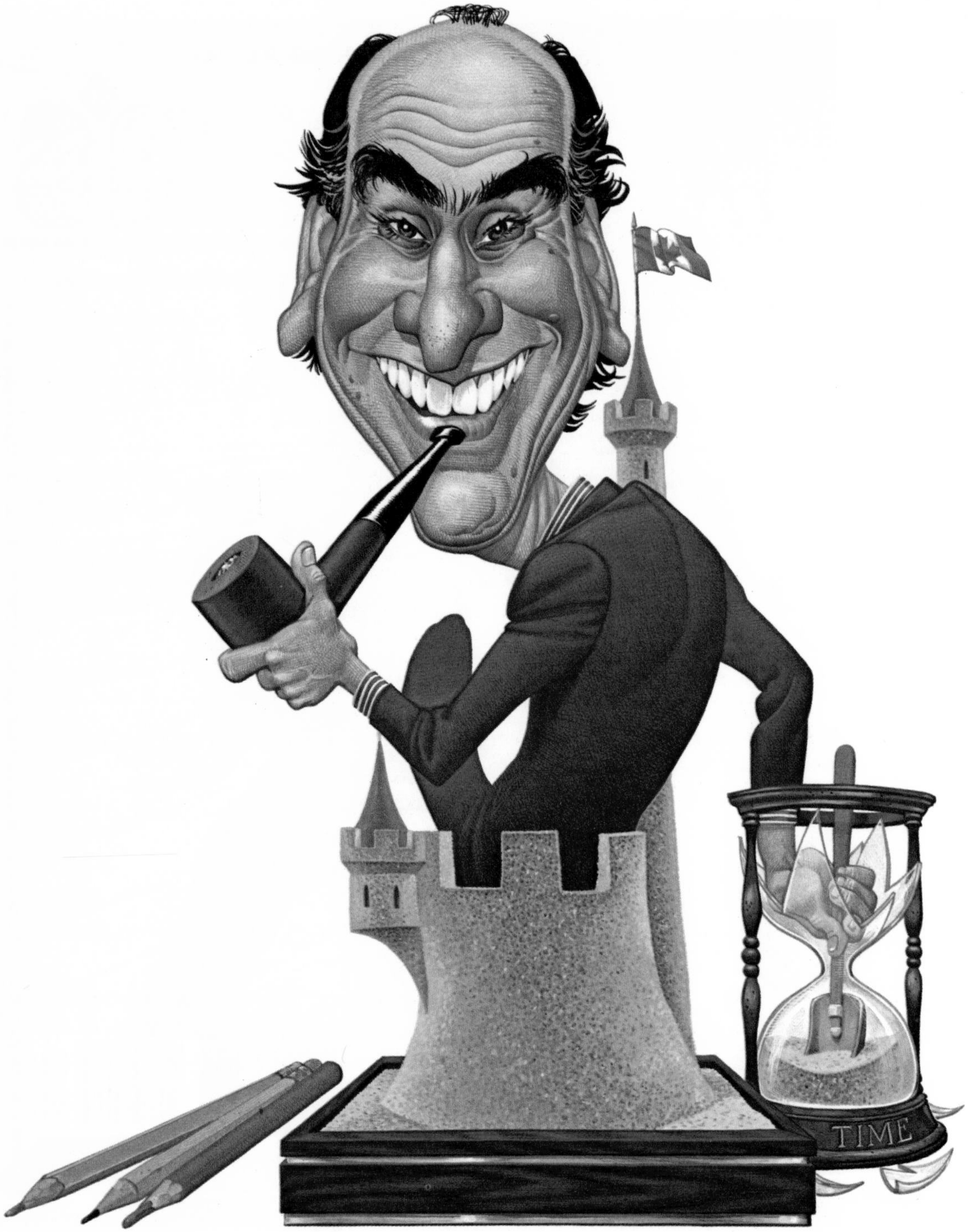
TIME

Peter Newman

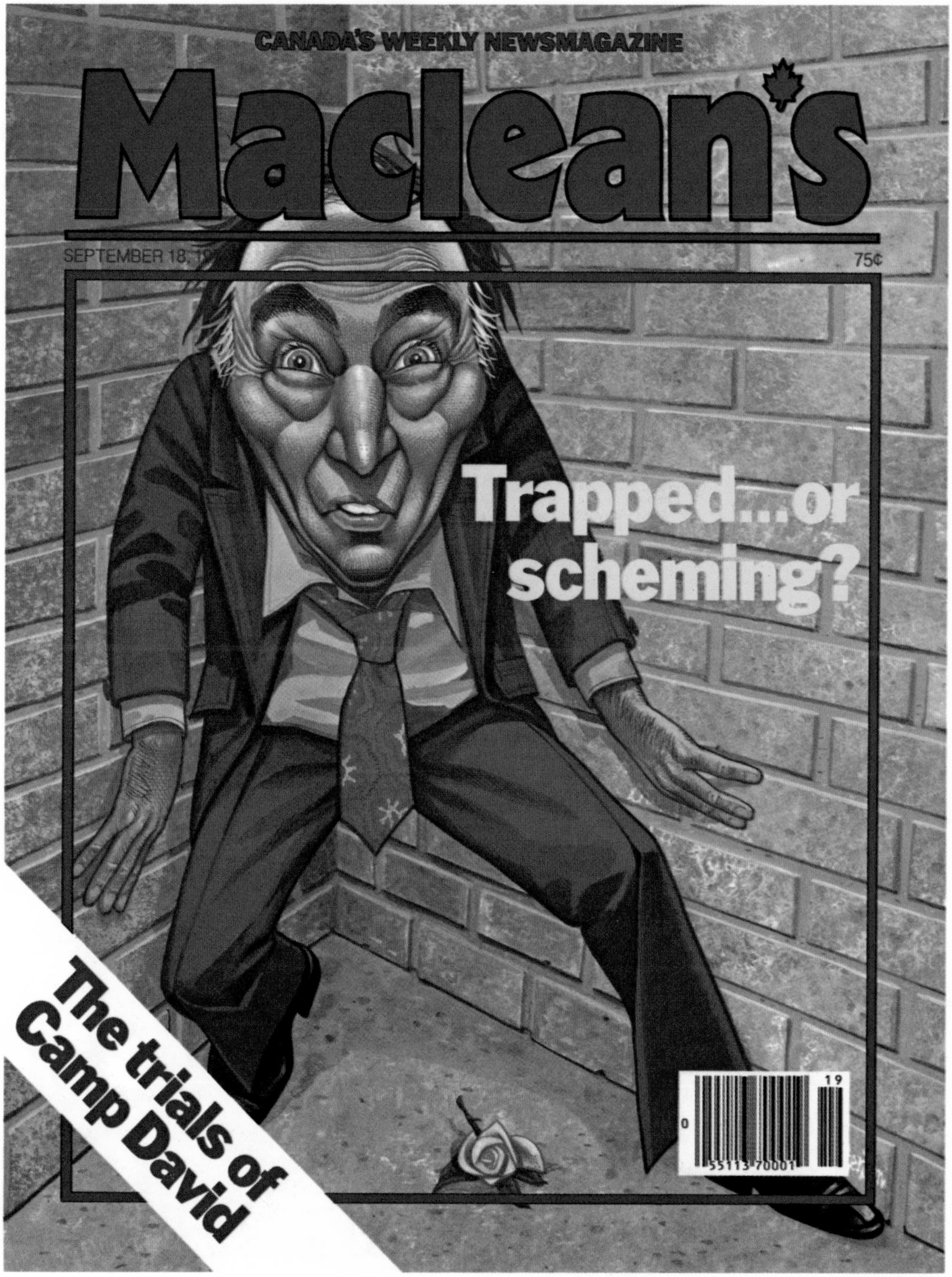
CANADA'S WEEKLY NEWSMAGAZINE
Maclean's
SEPTEMBER 18
75¢
Trapped...or scheming?
The trials of Camp David

Pierre Trudeau
Commissioned for *Maclean's* premier issue as a weekly, 18 September, 1978.

A Pen for All Seasons

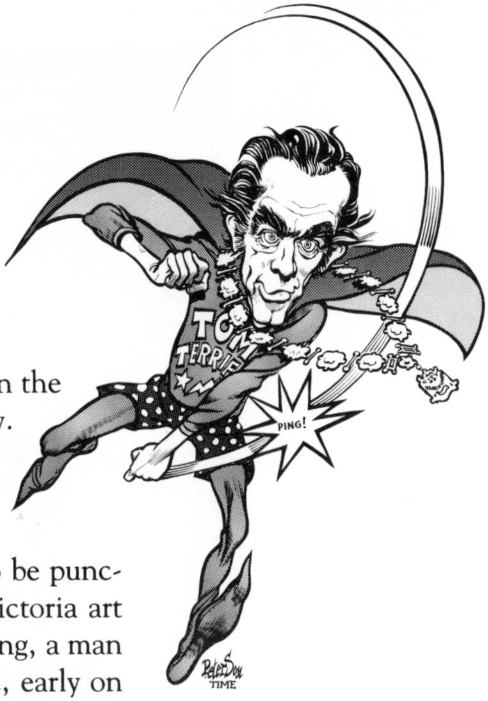
TOM
TERRIE
PING!
Peterson
TIME

The proof that the economical way to political vivisection lies in the artist's pen rather than the typewriter can be shown quite easily. Some of our most skilled surgeons of the pencil press tried first of all to do it the other way. Only when they failed did they resort to the more awkward form of the printed word.

Pierre Berton, that shrewd observer of balloons dying to be punctured, started out by attempting to become a cartoonist at a Victoria art school. Bruce Hutchison, the dean of Canadian political reporting, a man who can still operate on a victim without benefit of anaesthetic, early on sold cartoons to the *New York World*. Charles Templeton, in one of his many previous incarnations, was a newspaper cartoonist—before he found it was easier to become an evangelist, newspaper editor, politician, broadcaster and best-selling author.

A reporter can describe, endlessly, the inane patter of that dispenser of bubblegum-for-the-mind: the hotliner, this century's forgettable contribution to our culture. The yawning eye of the television camera can peer into the gullet of the open-mouth monster and record his mindless blatherings to the geritol set. But only the caricaturist, as Peterson here, can deliver the truth: the essential *jerk* encased in headphones, a prisoner of electronics, nicotine, ratings and ego. Only exaggeration will set us free.

The secret that Peterson is slipping to us, in his own subtle way, is this: we are being jobbed. If ever, in an outrageous burst of democracy, one tenth of one per cent of the Canadian population were able to travel to Ottawa to observe first-hand the shenanigans allowed to exist there on a daily basis, there would be riots in the streets and a general uprising of the unwashed. The amount of boondogglery, barefaced indolence and outright theft of public time that is committed on a gross scale would outrage a canal horse. Half the manpower of Canadian journalism over the past two decades has been bribed into flackery on behalf of the state: information officers paid by the taxpayer to tell the taxpayer why the government is doing so well. Neither print nor TV can deal adequately with such double-think. Nor has there been yet a cartoonist in Canada—or in any other country—guilty of overstating the case. Insiders always know that. It's why cabinet ministers' aides, and ministers themselves, always clamour to request a savage cartoon original. They know in their heart of hearts that even when Peterson, or any other cartoonist, comes *close*, he still doesn't realize how much he has overlooked. Their request as much as anything stems from relief.

Peterson doesn't overlook much. The Canadian rock group Bachman-Turner Overdrive, dutiful Mormons who tithe, pick up dollar bills with a scavenger's spike. Norman Mailer, a bus conductor's coin dispenser on his tie, exploits the puffy corpse of Marilyn Monroe. Charles de Gaulle, a disjointed Don Quixote, huddles under his halo. Peterson at the Poor People's March in Washington, the Berlin Wall or in Moscow is drawn to the brutal, the macabre, the bullies. In his selection is a message.

The key to his version of the world, one thinks, is the Tax Collector. Not the grim reaper. Not the sorrowing civil servant trudging about his appointed task, nor the grey technocrat carrying out his master's distasteful orders. Here we have a joyful harvester, the fat and jolly burden on top of society. What Peterson detects (while we can only suspect) is the glee and satisfaction in the flunkey's countenance and bearing. He is a perfect product of our system. He has forgotten who is supposed to be on top.

Peterson, in his own shy way, is just trying to even up the score.

Of two things we're sure, as we spin on our axis, the First be DEATH and the Last be TAXES R.I.P.

THE COLLECTOR

18

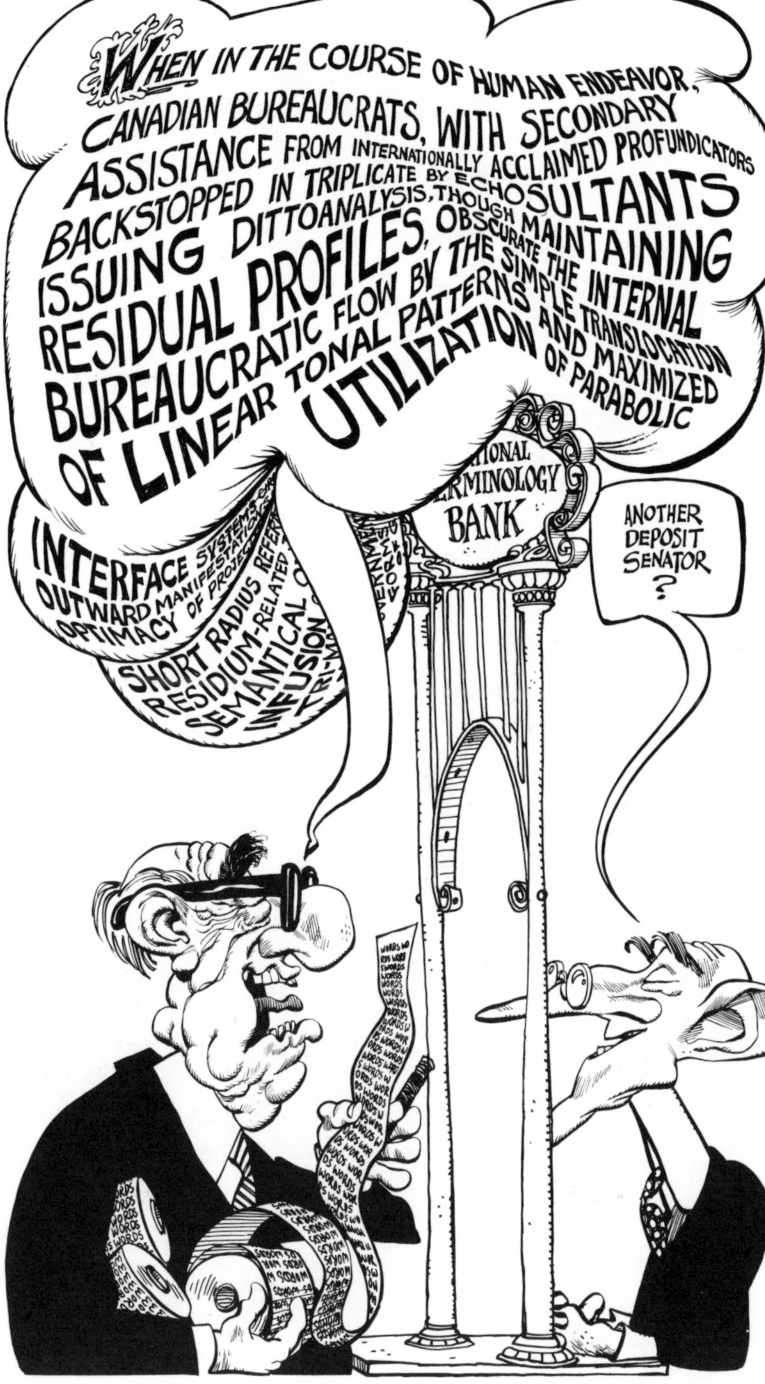
WHEN IN THE COURSE OF HUMAN ENDEAVOR, CANADIAN BUREAUCRATS, WITH SECONDARY ASSISTANCE FROM INTERNATIONALLY ACCLAIMED PROFUNDICATORS BACKSTOPPED IN TRIPLICATE BY ECHOSULTANTS ISSUING DITTOANALYSIS, THOUGH MAINTAINING RESIDUAL PROFILES, OBSCURATE THE INTERNAL BUREAUCRATIC FLOW BY THE SIMPLE TRANSLOCATION OF LINEAR TONAL PATTERNS AND MAXIMIZED UTILIZATION OF PARABOLIC
INTERFACE SYSTEMS
OUTWARD MANIFESTATION
OPTIMACY OF
SHORT RADIUS
RESIDIUM-RELATED
SEMANTICAL
INFUSION
BANK
ANOTHER DEPOSIT SENATOR ?

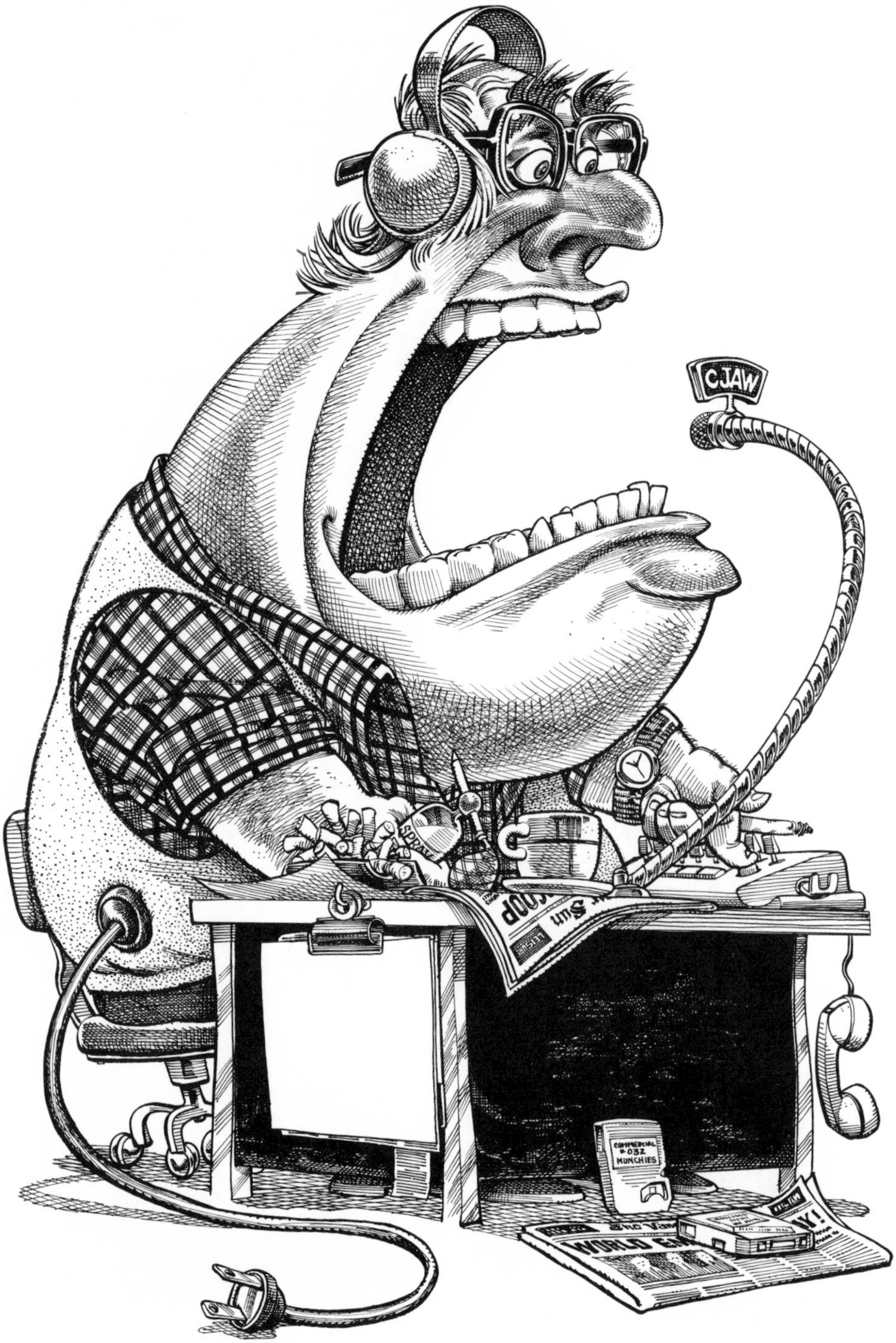
CJAW
COMMERCIAL #032 MUNCHIES

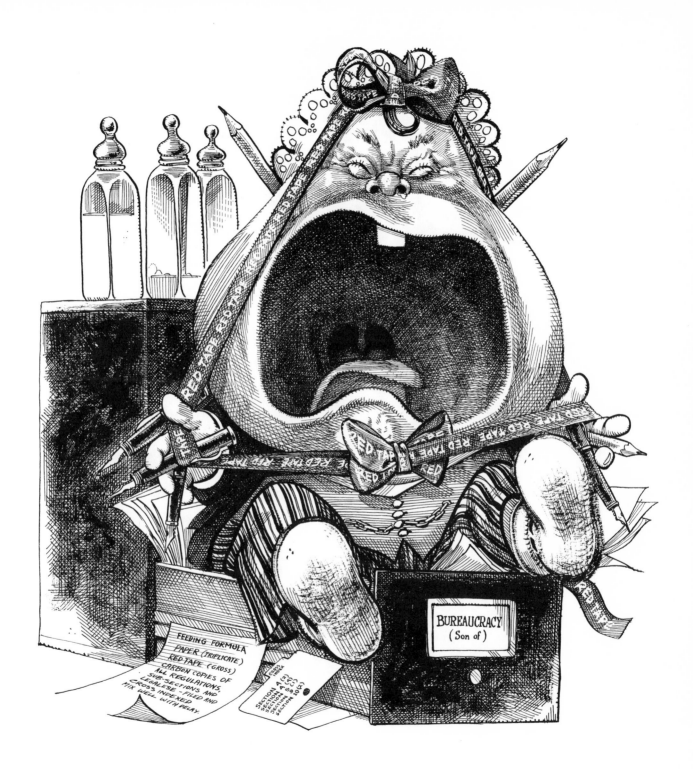

FEEDING FORMULA

PAPER (TRIPLICATE)
RED TAPE (GROSS)
CARBON COPIES OF
ALL REGULATIONS,
SUB-SECTIONS AND
LEGALESE - FILED AND
CROSS INDEXED
MIX WELL WITH DELAY.

SECTION 4 §32
SECTION 4 §33
SECTION 4 §98

BUREAUCRACY
(Son of)

RED TAPE

Pelé

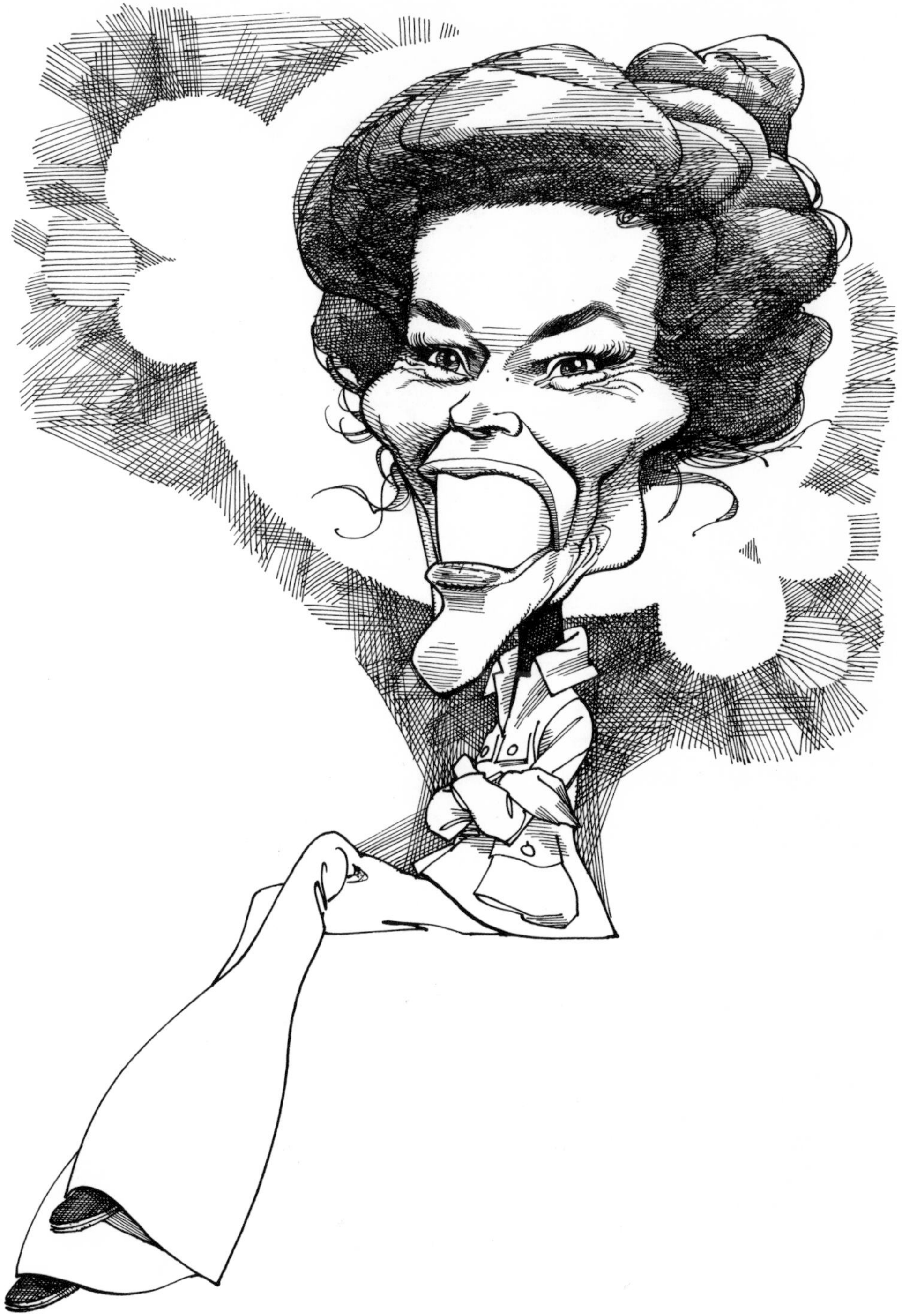

Katharine Hepburn

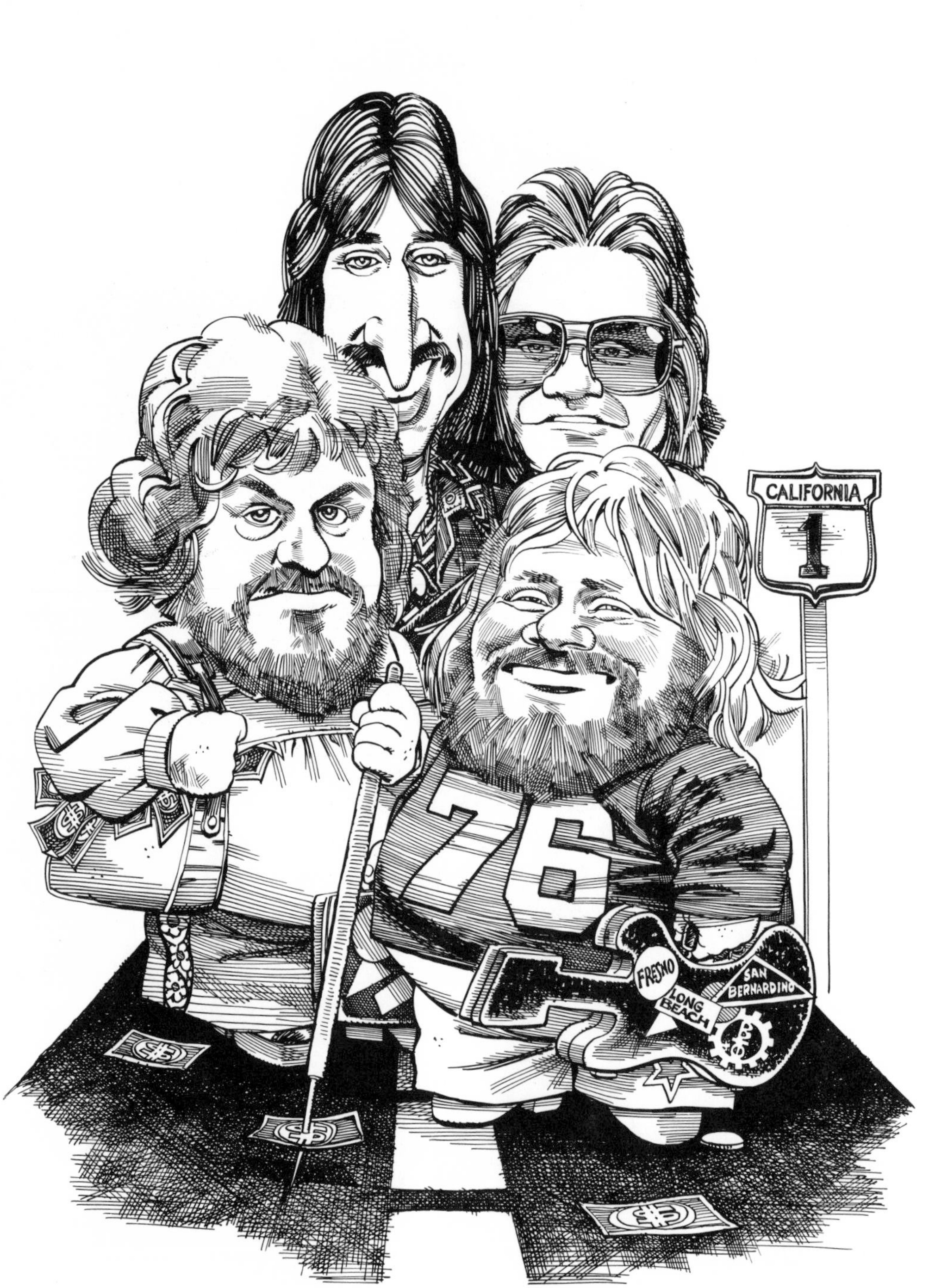
CALIFORNIA
1
76
FRESNO
LONG BEACH
SAN BERNARDINO

Bachman-Turner Overdrive

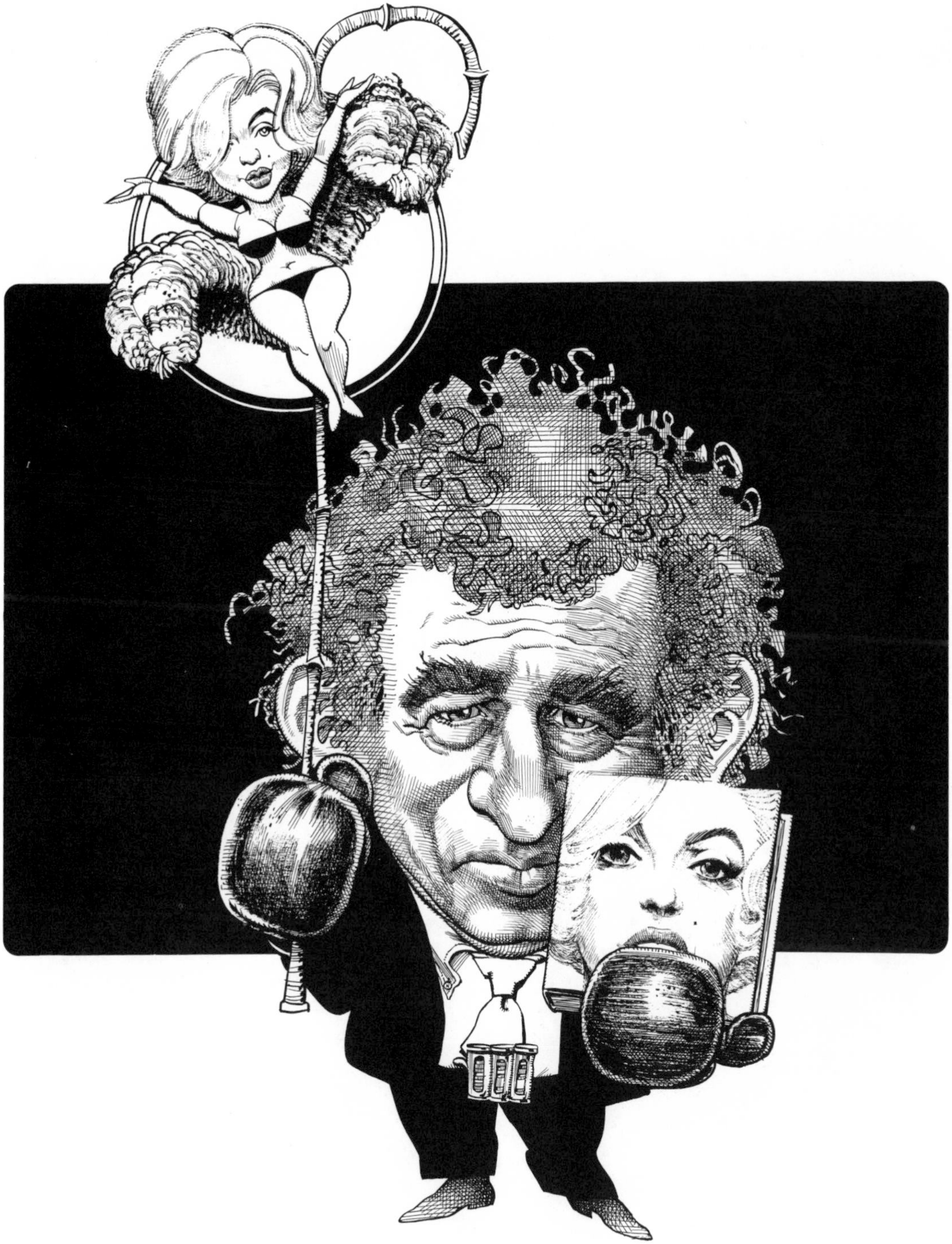

Norman Mailer and Marilyn Monroe

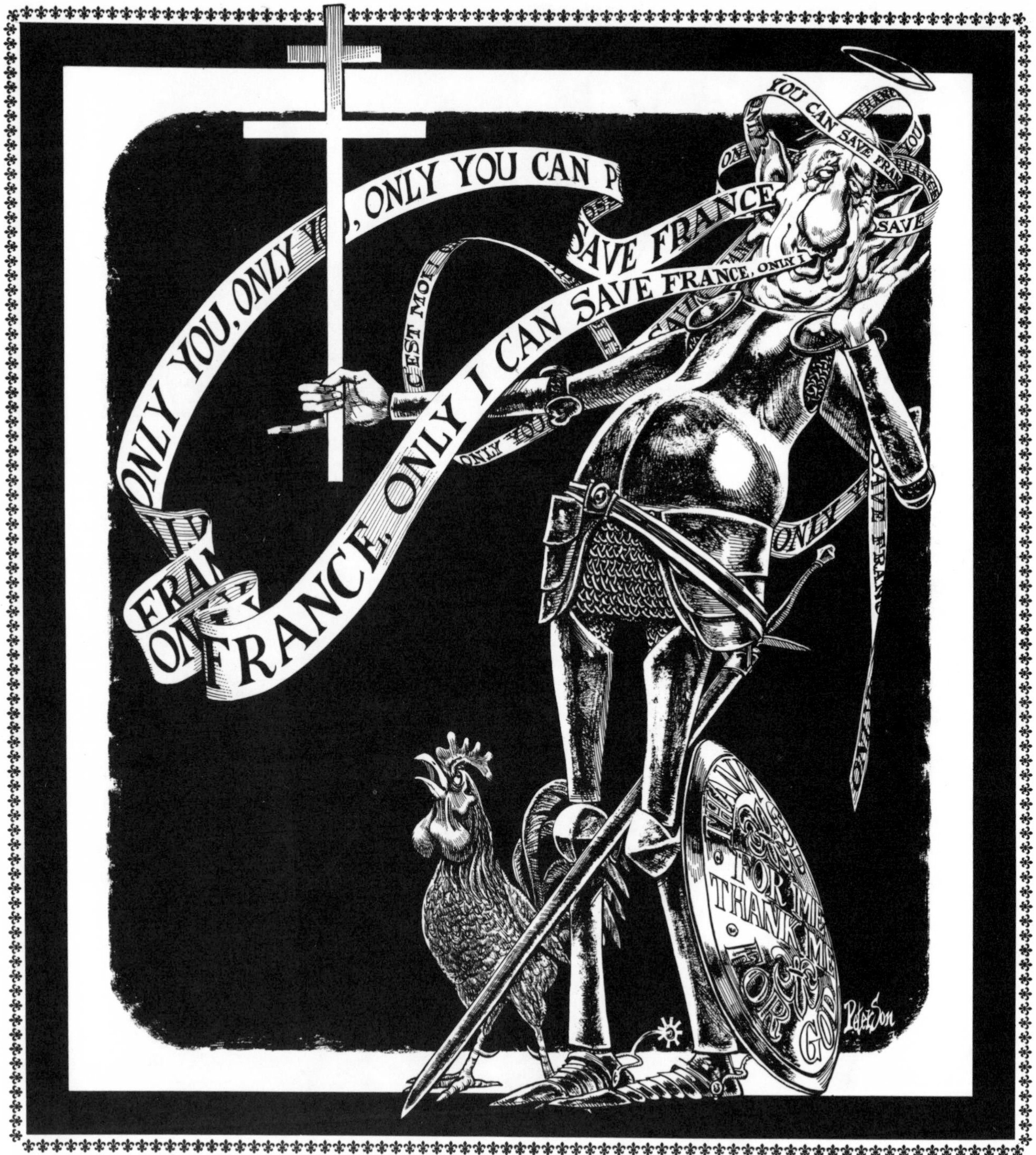
ONLY YOU, ONLY YOU, ONLY YOU CAN
SAVE FRANCE
FRANCE, ONLY I CAN SAVE FRANCE, ONLY I
C'EST MOI
YOU CAN SAVE FRANCE
ONLY YOU
FOR ME
THANK ME
GOD
Peterson

Charles de Gaulle

Claude Ryan

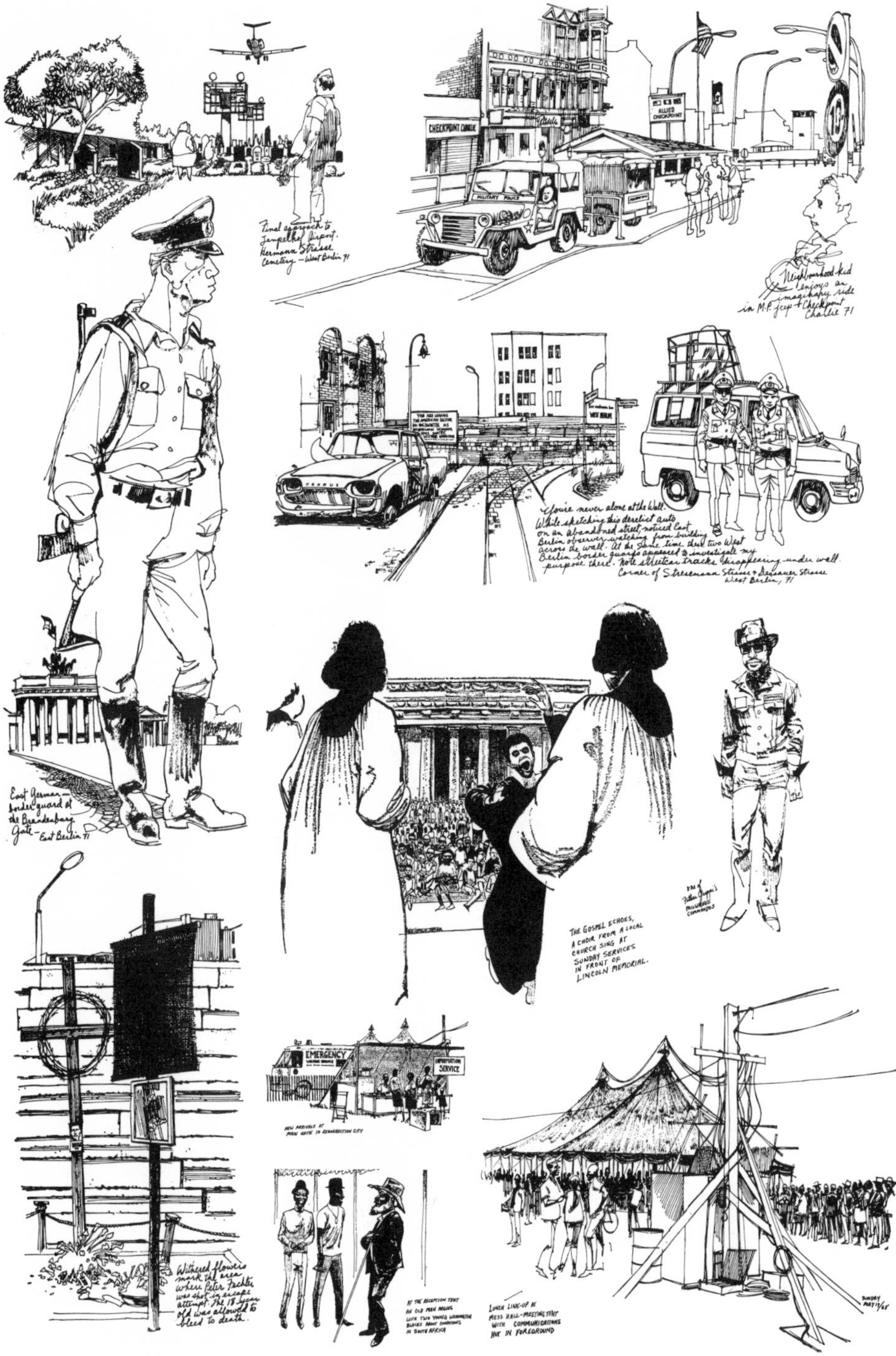
Final approach to Tempelhof Airport. Hermann Strasse Cemetery. —West Berlin 71
CHECKPOINT CHARLIE
ALLIED CHECKPOINT
MILITARY POLICE
Neighbourhood kid enjoys an imaginary ride in M.P. jeep + Checkpoint Charlie 71
WEST BERLIN
You're never alone at the Wall. While sketching this derelict auto on an abandoned street, noticed East Berlin observer watching from building across the wall. At the same time these two West Berlin border guards appeared to investigate my purpose there. Note streetcar tracks disappearing under wall.
Corner of Stresemann Strasse + Dessauer Strasse West Berlin, 71
East German—border guard at the Brandenburg Gate—East Berlin 71
THE GOSPEL ECHOES, A CHOIR FROM A LOCAL CHURCH SING AT SUNDAY SERVICES IN FRONT OF LINCOLN MEMORIAL.
EMERGENCY
SERVICE
Withered flowers mark the area where Peter Fechter was shot in escape attempt. The 18 year old was allowed to bleed to death.
AT THE RECEPTION TENT AN OLD MAN ARGUES WITH TWO YOUNG WASHINGTON BLACKS ABOUT CONDITIONS IN SOUTH AFRICA
LUNCH LINE-UP AT MESS HALL-MEETING TENT WITH COMMUNICATIONS HUT IN FOREGROUND

Berlin, 1971; The Poor People's March on Washington, 1968

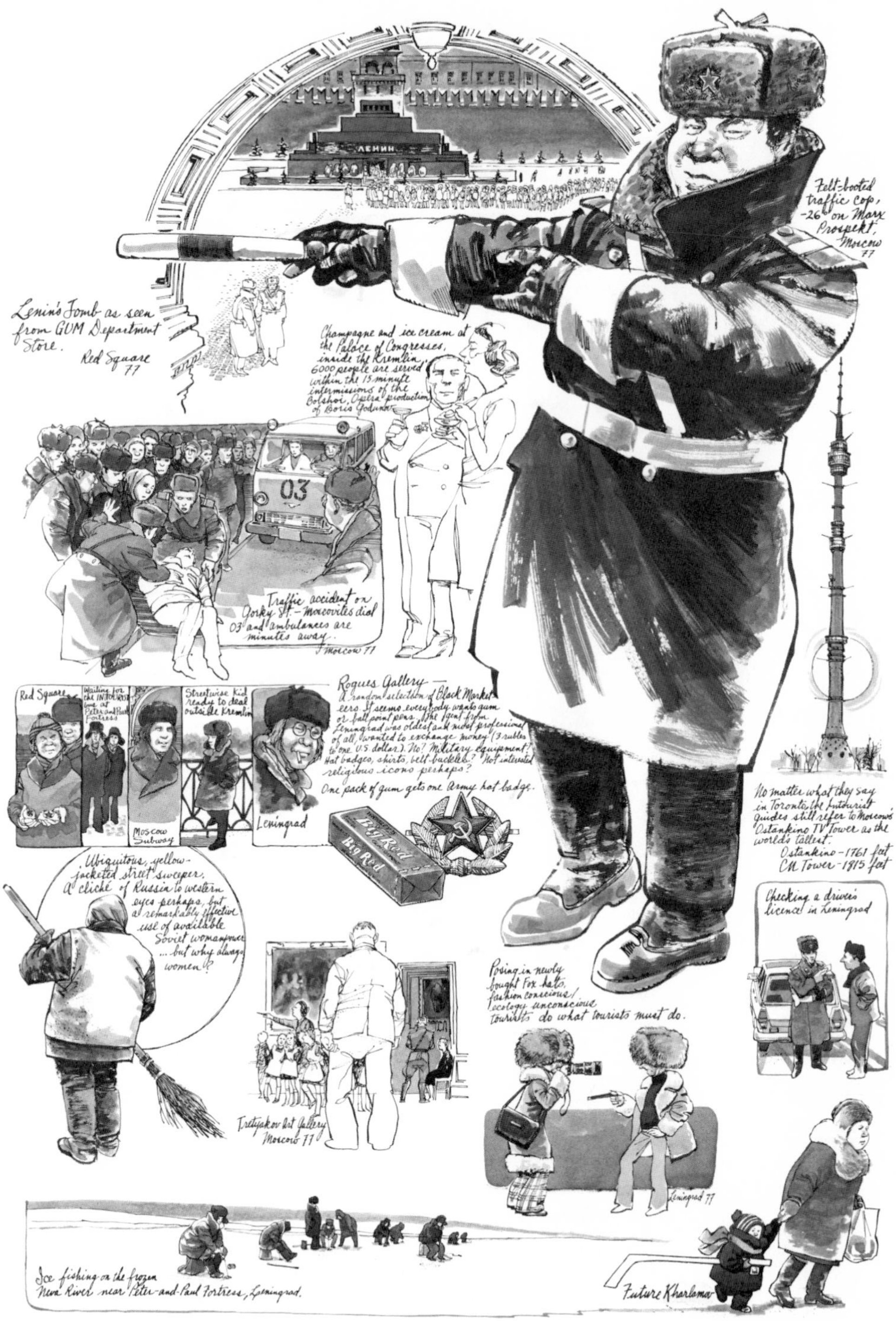
ЛЕНИН
Lenin's Tomb as seen from GUM Department Store.
Red Square 77
Felt-booted traffic cop, -26° on Marx Prospekt, Moscow 77
Champagne and ice cream at the Palace of Congresses, inside the Kremlin, 6000 people are served within the 15 minute intermissions of the Bolshoi Opera production of Boris Godunov.
03
Traffic accident on Gorky St. – Moscovites dial 03 and ambulances are minutes away.
Moscow 77
Red Square
Streetwise kid ready to deal outside Kremlin
Moscow Subway
Leningrad
Rogues Gallery —
A random selection of Black Marketeers. It seems everybody wants gum or ball point pens. The agent from Leningrad was oldest and most professional of all, wanted to exchange money (3 rubles to one U.S. dollar). No? Military equipment? Hat badges, shirts, belt-buckles? Not interested religious icons perhaps?
One pack of gum gets one Army hat badge.
Big Red
Big Red
No matter what they say in Toronto the Intourist guides still refer to Moscow's Ostankino TV Tower as the world's tallest.
Ostankino – 1761 feet
CN Tower – 1815 feet
Ubiquitous, yellow-jacketed street sweeper. A cliché of Russia to western eyes perhaps, but a remarkably effective use of available Soviet womanpower ... but why always women?
Checking a driver's licence in Leningrad
Posing in newly bought Fox hats, fashion conscious, ecology unconscious tourists do what tourists must do.
Tretyakov Art Gallery
Moscow 77
Leningrad 77
Ice fishing on the frozen Neva River near Peter-and-Paul Fortress, Leningrad.
Future Kharlamov

Moscow and Leningrad, 1977

The Unfolding of Pierre Trudeau

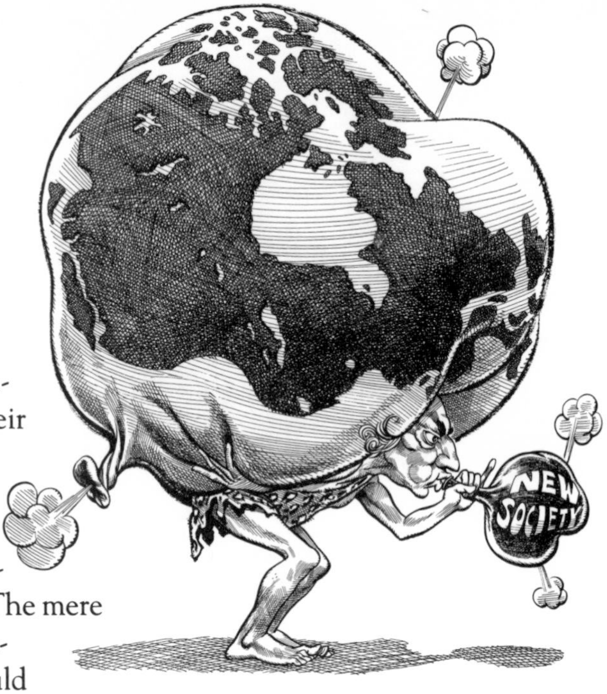
NEW SOCIETY

The most puzzling perception, alive even at home, is that Canada is regarded as a dull, plodding place. Historians, being basically dull people, have projected this image so as to protect their own market. It is their instinctive camouflage; their personalities infecting their subject. They smother the facts with ennui.

What other country has a drunk as a founder? A Mackenzie King, that kinky little cutie, who rehabilitated street whores and talked to his dog? Or a fuddleduddler who once did half gainers off his own intellect? The mere collection of men who have occupied the prime minister's chair, right down to the nervous incumbent, could populate an eccentricity ward. Larry Zolf, not Donald Creighton, is needed to do the history of the land.

It's why the country is a cartoonist's delight, why there are so many of world rank secreted away in our frontier gloom. What else do you need for a target when you have Alberta, probably the only jurisdiction in the world to advance from poverty to decadence without passing through civilization? Or the Atlantic provinces, where the major industry is nostalgia. There is puffed-up Toronto, its parochial papers and magazines goggled over the fact that denizens of Cleveland, whose range of taste is not broad, regard Toronto as Nineveh, a Samarkand-with-a-subway. (Toronto has improved greatly from its previous role as a reservoir of prim Presbyterian minds, but it is still a city-in-a-training-bra, forever aspiring to be a full woman.)

There is the dead sea of Ottawa, that city without either soul or saline-free galoshes. (A resident can be detected easily by the ring of salt halfway up his personality.) Any country with enough sense of humour to abide Ottawa as its capital will surely survive such passing aberrations as René Lévesque and Harold Ballard.

There is the Village-by-the-Edge-of-the-Rain-Forest, Vancouver, preening in its ocean, obsessed with self, the existential sandbox masquerading as a city. If you see a person hurrying in Vancouver, says Eric Nicol, it's because he's late for his nap. B.C. is one of the few provinces that has never provided a prime minister—nor regretted it. The province considers that an irrelevant contribution.

Speaking of humour, there is the Regressive Conservative party, secure in its death wish, a magnet for the losers of the nation, stubborn in its persistence in venturing to the lonely West in search of its idiosyncratic leaders: R.B. Bennett, John Bracken, John Diefenbaker, Joe If. (The Liberals, whose only principle is power, stick to the Ontario-Quebec power base.) The residents of Conservative conventions take on a familiar cast: Ontario lawyers in six-piece suits and self-satisfied smirks, genteel ladies in tweeds, pure in heart and innocent of soul—the Canadian equivalent of morose descendants of the Deep South. They wish to rise again, but there is a certain prideful glory in their humiliation.

The Tories seem almost embarrassed with their new-found power, out of office so long in this century that they don't know where the levers of power are, and touch them gingerly. Their discomfiture is reinforced by their new captain, the teen-age Eisenhower, a spindly young man who was packaged so carefully by Tory flackery during the campaign that he resembled a wind-up doll let loose each morning and rewrapped every evening. (Inside Joe Clark's voice there is a John Diefenbaker fighting to get out.)

It is a country funny enough to produce both Eugene Whelan *and* Jack Horner. The bizarre fact is that it was the defection of Horner (the worst political inspiration since Rudolph Hess parachuted into Scotland) that killed Trudeau by being piled in the voters' memory on top of his cynical reversal of policy on wage and price controls.

And it was proof that this brilliant individual wasn't really a very good politician after all. A great showman, compelling speaker, magnificent symbol—but not really a politician. This man of such a resolute and disciplined mind was done in by the outrageous switch of policy—and principle—that so violated his image and reputation.

In the end it was the Liberal party (that recruited him almost as a token intellectual) that did Trudeau in by persuading him to adopt expediency. Hilarious, wot?

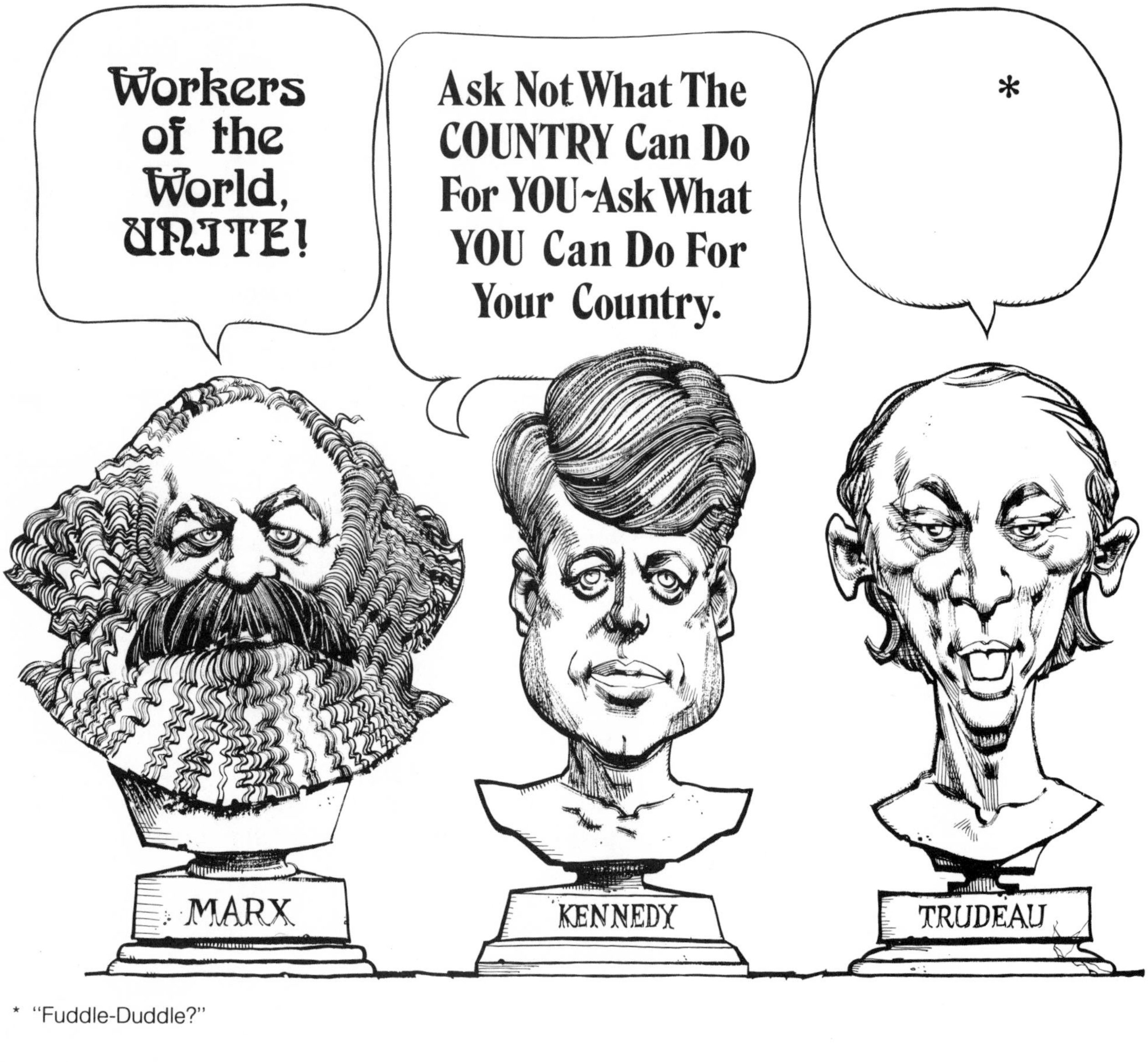
Workers of the World, UNITE!
Ask Not What The COUNTRY Can Do For YOU~Ask What YOU Can Do For Your Country.
*
MARX
KENNEDY
TRUDEAU

* "Fuddle-Duddle?"

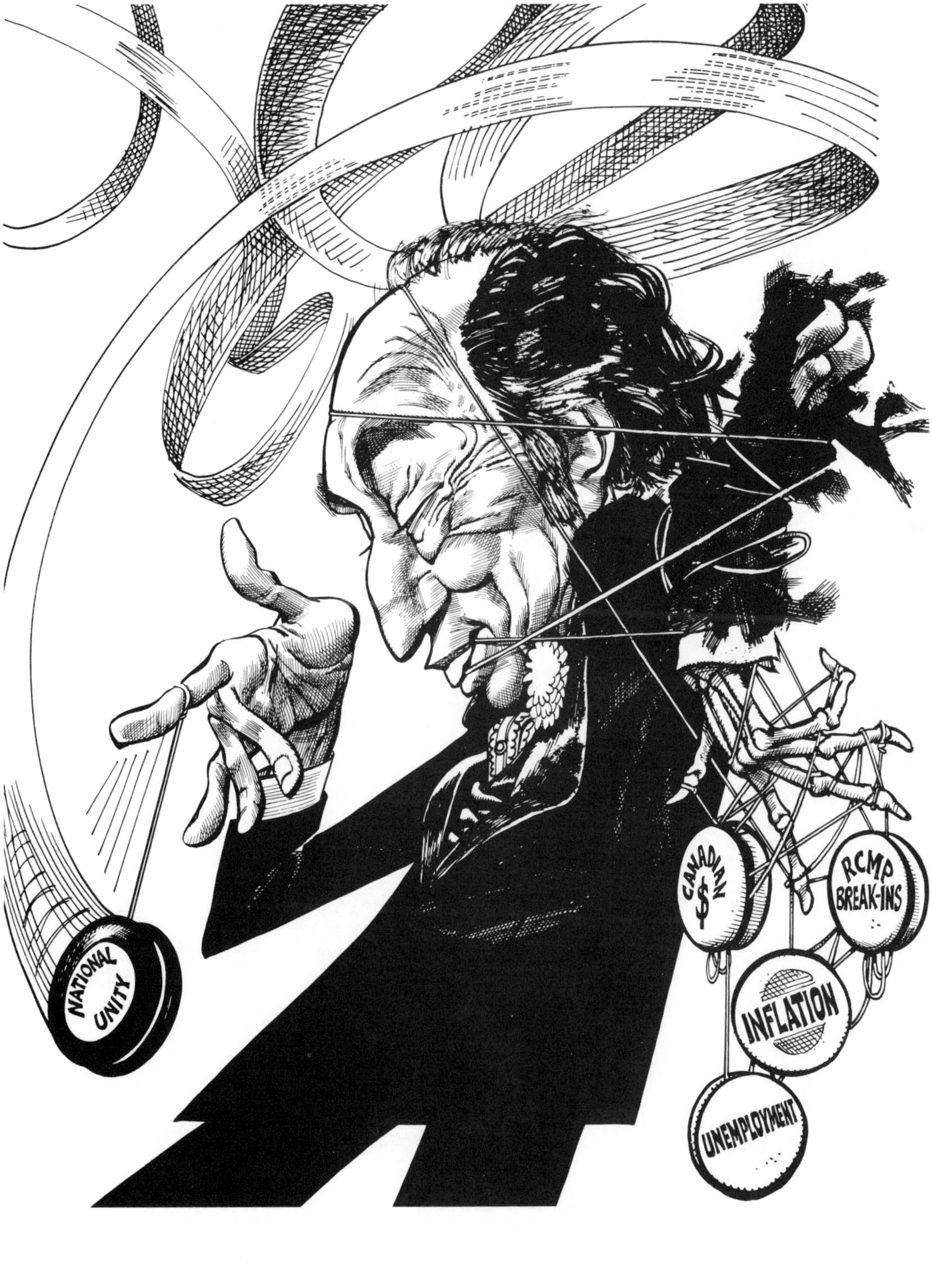
NATIONAL UNITY
CANADIAN $
RCMP BREAK-INS
INFLATION
UNEMPLOYMENT

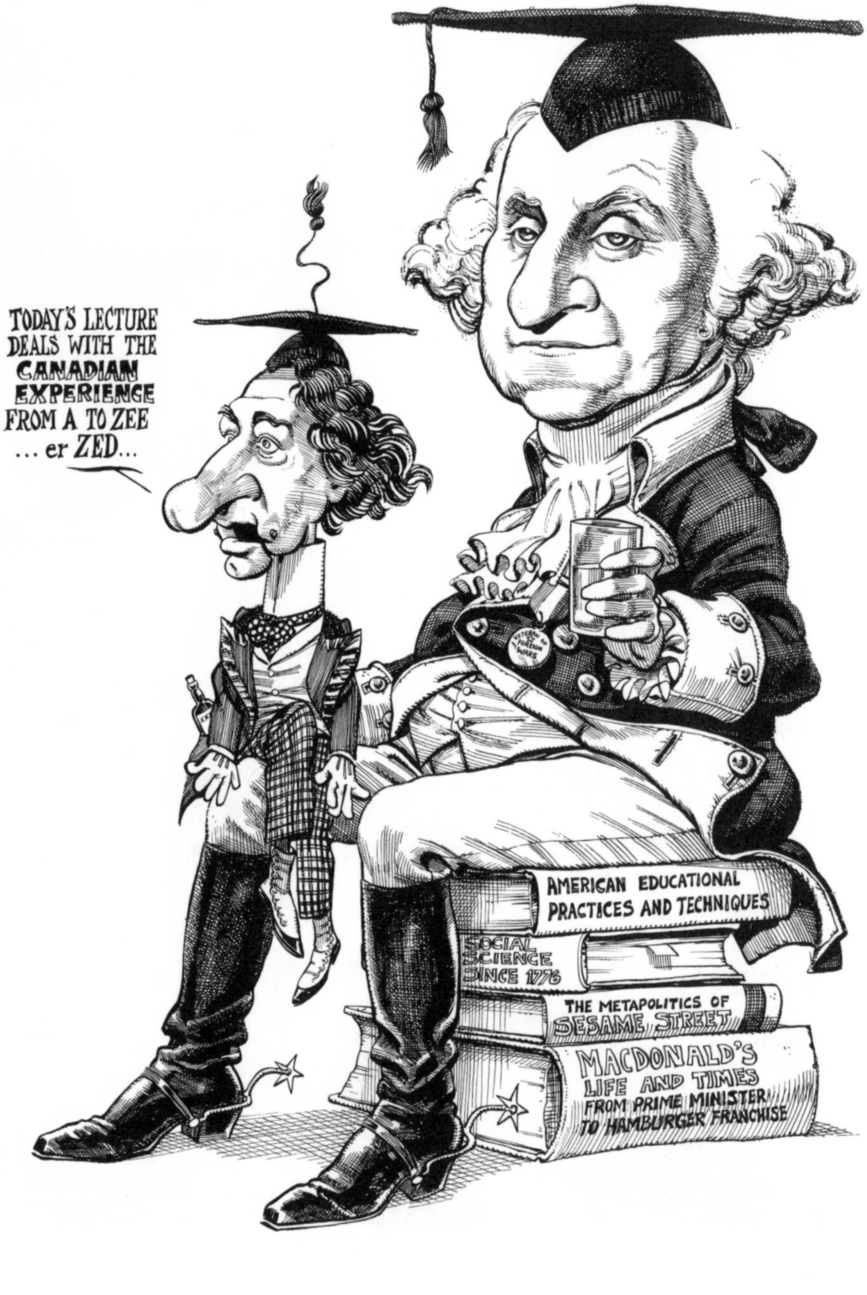
TODAY'S LECTURE DEALS WITH THE CANADIAN EXPERIENCE FROM A TO ZEE ... er ZED...
AMERICAN EDUCATIONAL PRACTICES AND TECHNIQUES
SOCIAL SCIENCE SINCE 1776
THE METAPOLITICS OF SESAME STREET
MACDONALD'S LIFE AND TIMES FROM PRIME MINISTER TO HAMBURGER FRANCHISE

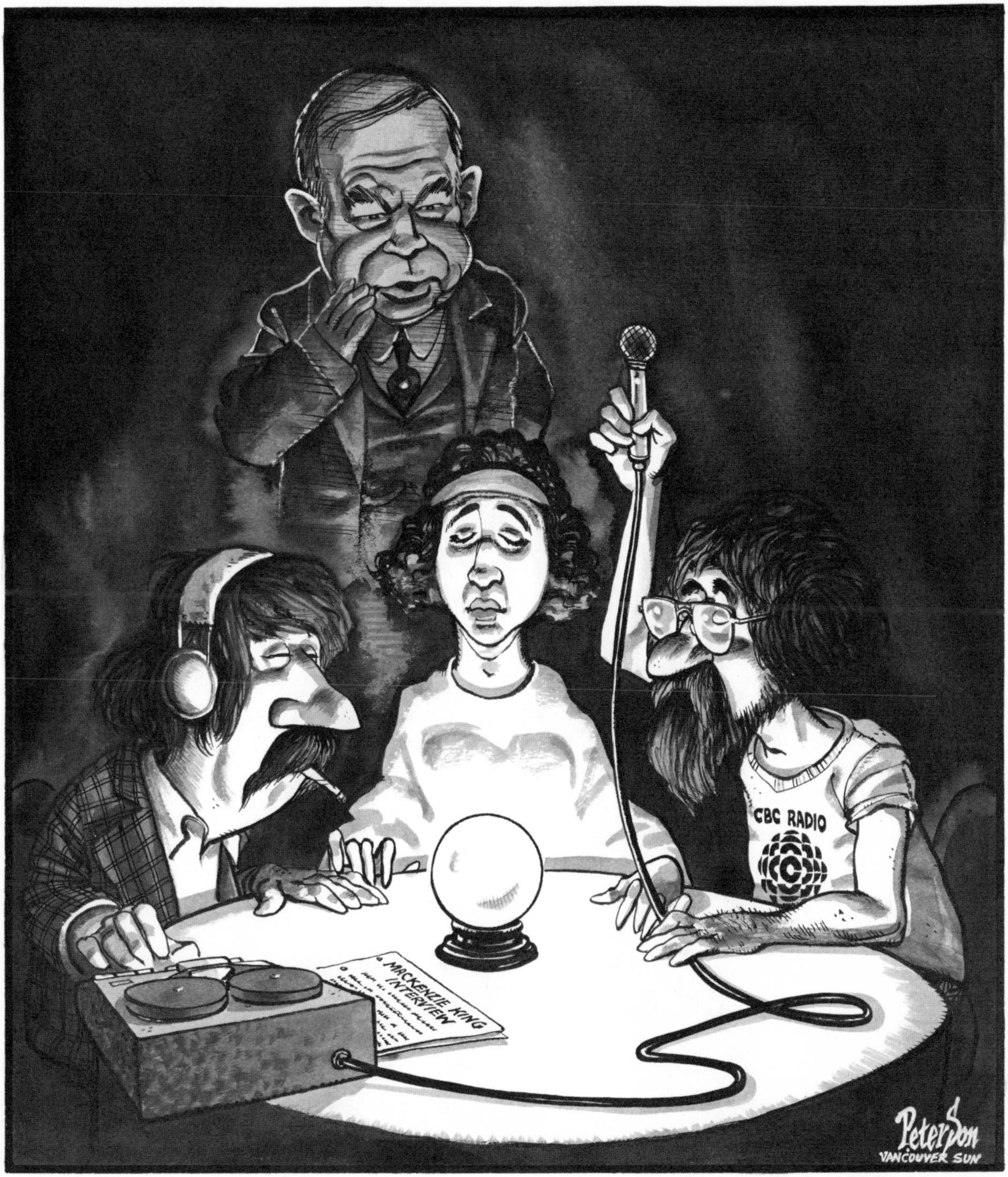
MACKENZIE KING
INTERVIEW
CBC RADIO
Peterson
VANCOUVER SUN

". . . ask them if they can get me on 90 Minutes Live . . ."

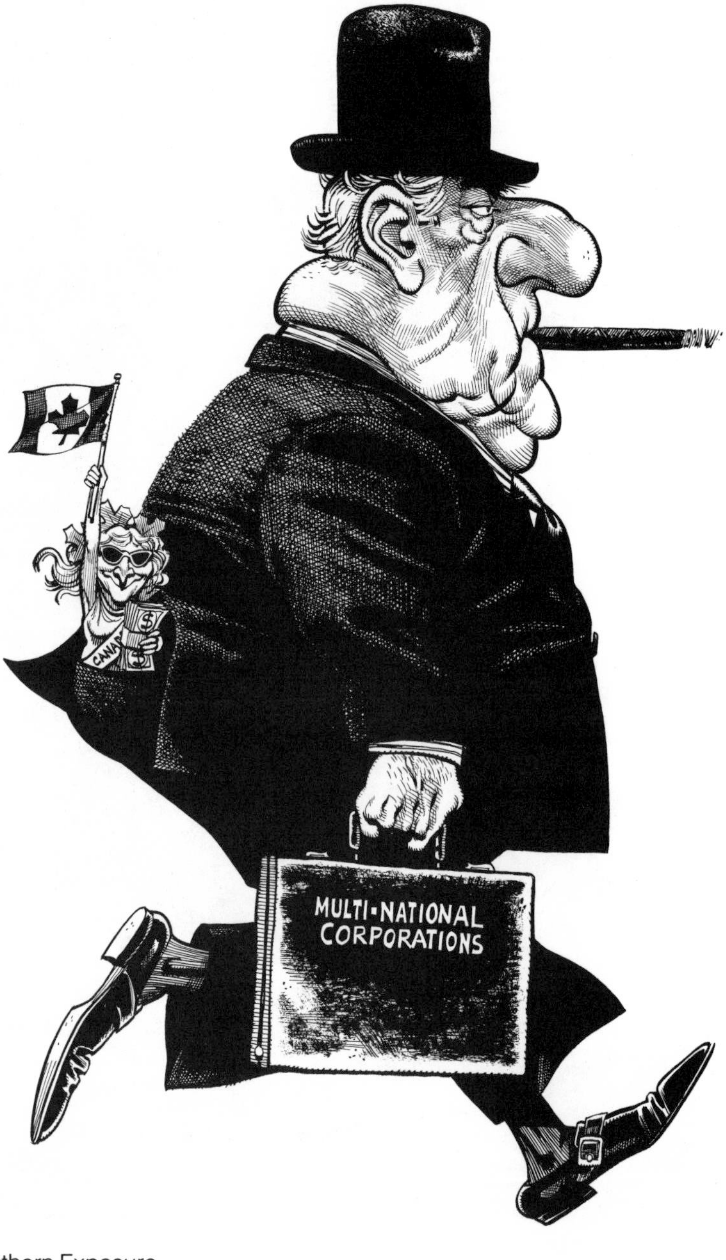
MULTI-NATIONAL CORPORATIONS

Northern Destiny . . . Southern Exposure

"Things may look bad to some students of international affairs, however we are constantly in the process of re-evaluating our perspective of Canadian-American relations . . ."
— Prime Minister Trudeau

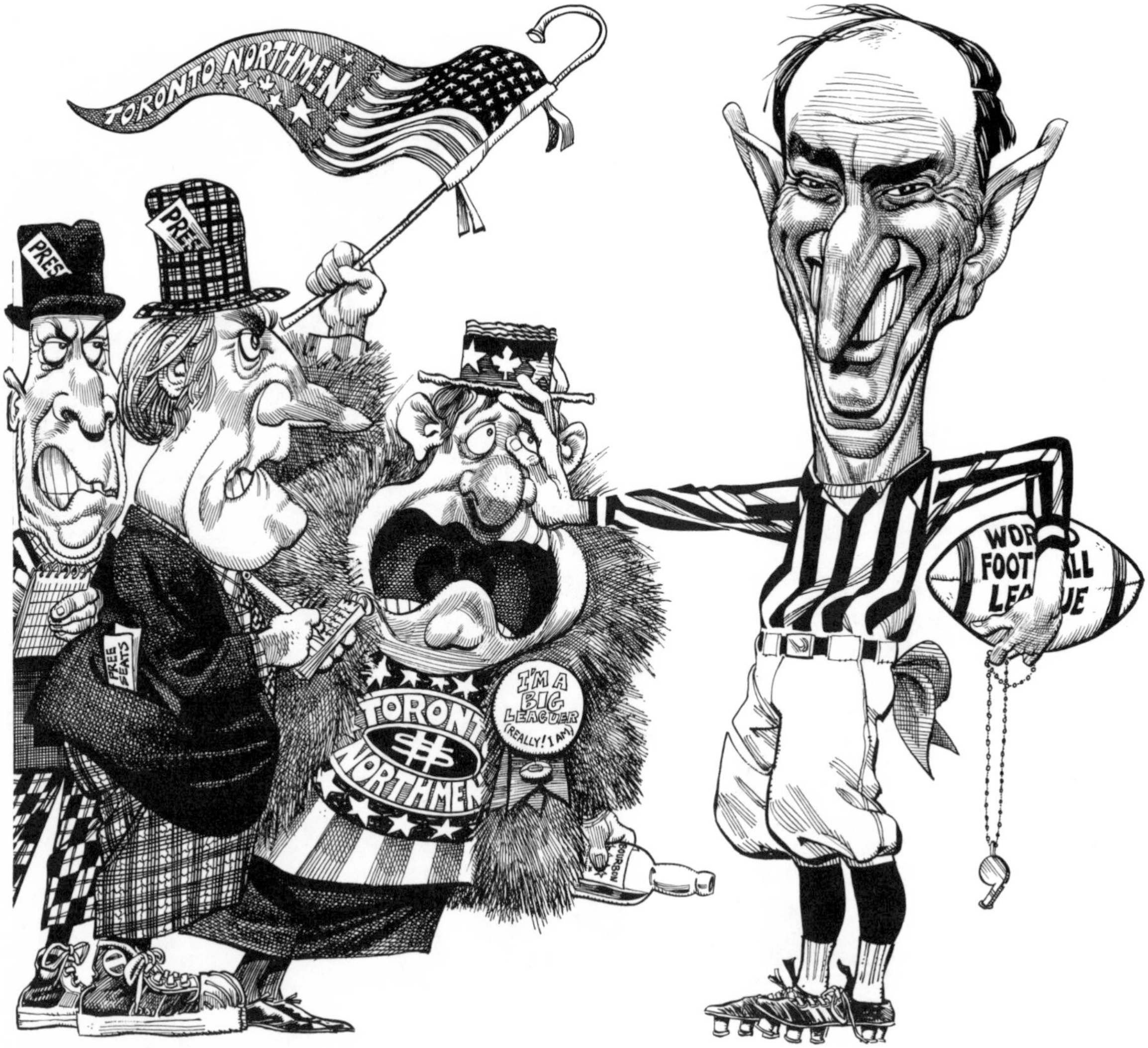
TORONTO NORTHMEN
FREE SEATS
NORTHMEN
I'M A BIG LEAGUER (REALLY! I AM)

"You realize of course that by defending Canada's tradition and heritage this way you're denying Canada's tradition and heritage of selling out its tradition and heritage!"

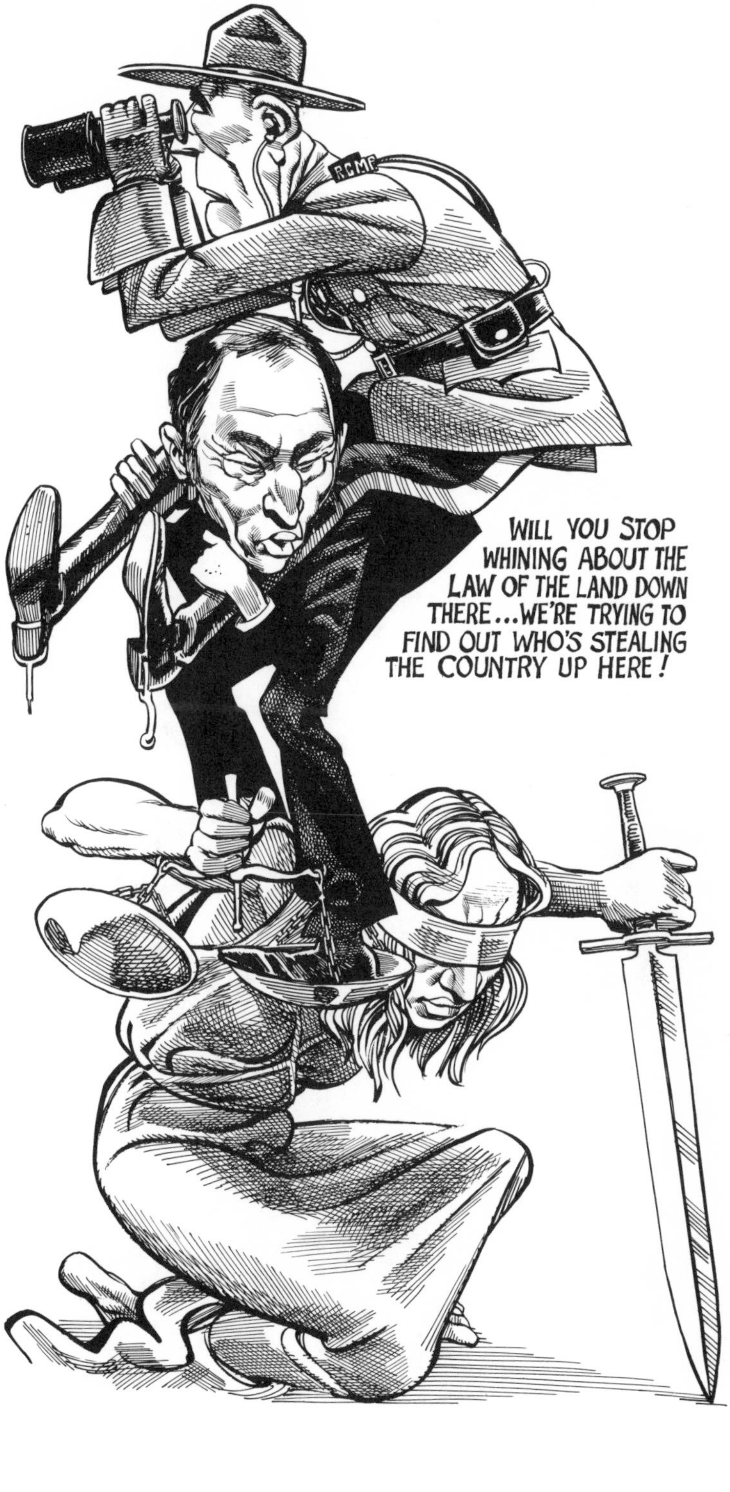
RCMP
WILL YOU STOP WHINING ABOUT THE LAW OF THE LAND DOWN THERE...WE'RE TRYING TO FIND OUT WHO'S STEALING THE COUNTRY UP HERE!

Above the Law

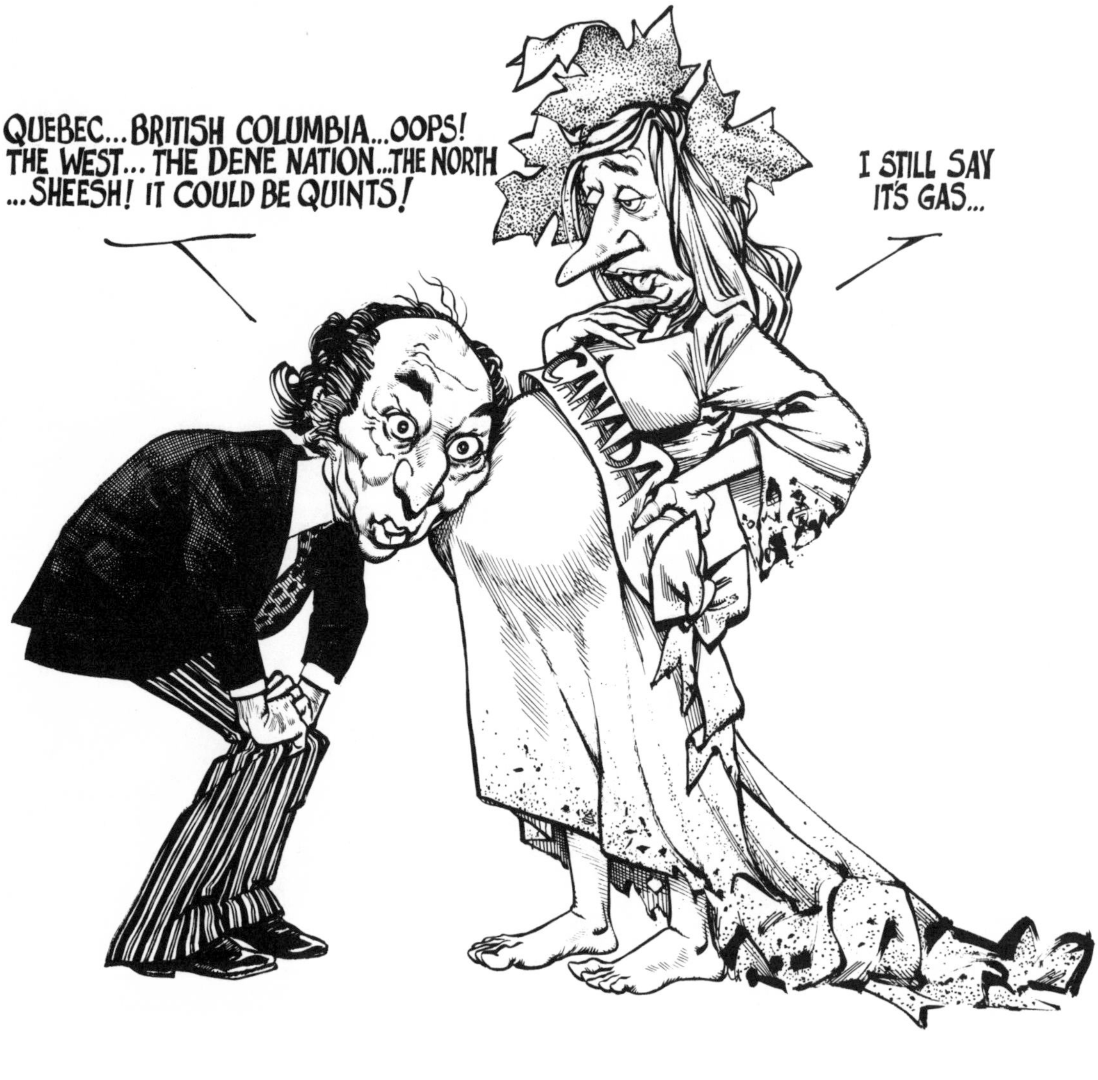
QUEBEC... BRITISH COLUMBIA...OOPS! THE WEST... THE DENE NATION...THE NORTH ...SHEESH! IT COULD BE QUINTS!
I STILL SAY IT'S GAS...
CANADA

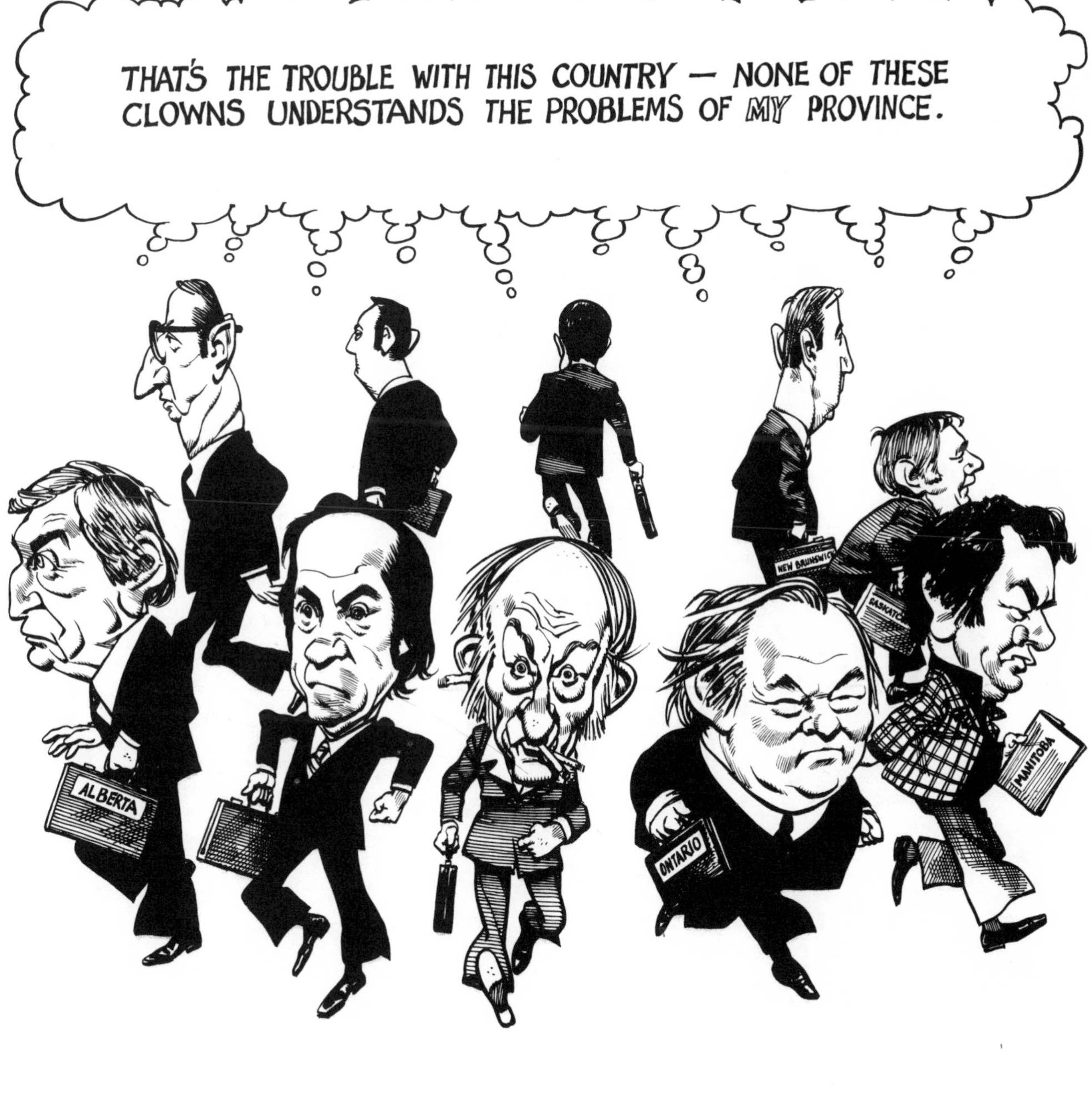
THAT'S THE TROUBLE WITH THIS COUNTRY — NONE OF THESE CLOWNS UNDERSTANDS THE PROBLEMS OF MY PROVINCE.
ALBERTA
NEW BRUNSWIC
SASKATC
ONTARIO
MANITOBA

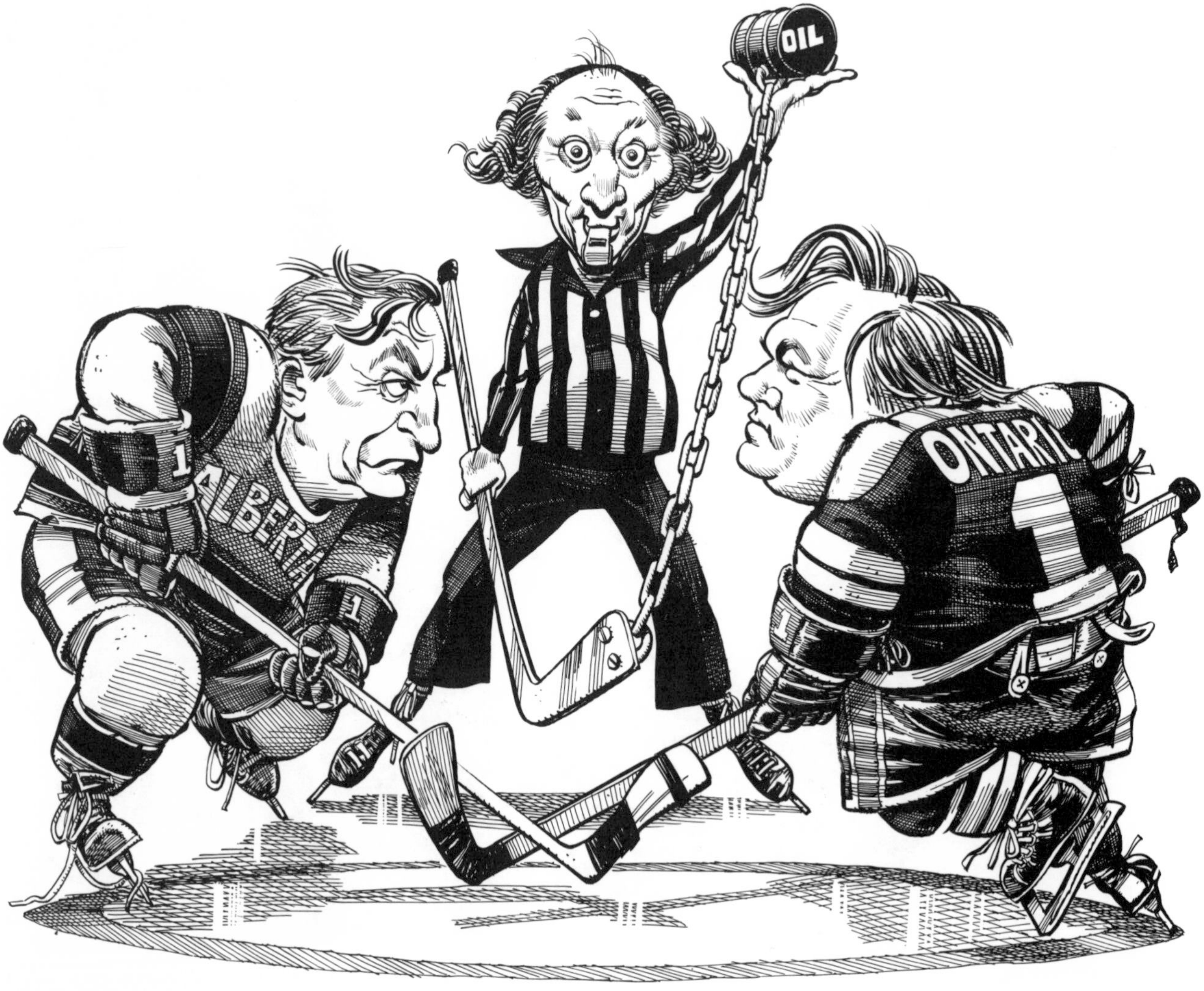
OIL
ALBERTA
1
1
ONTARIO
1

The National Sport

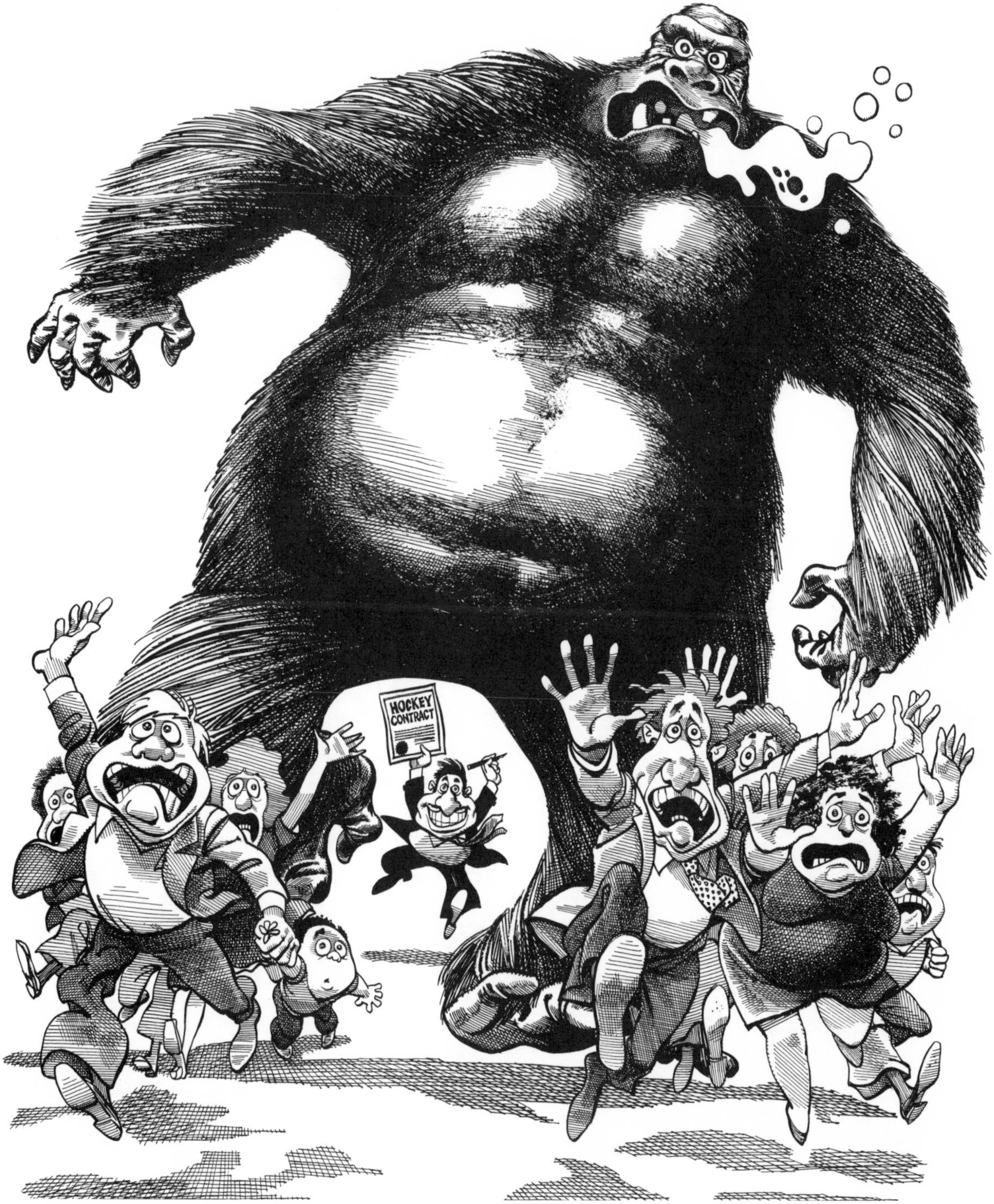
HOCKEY CONTRACT

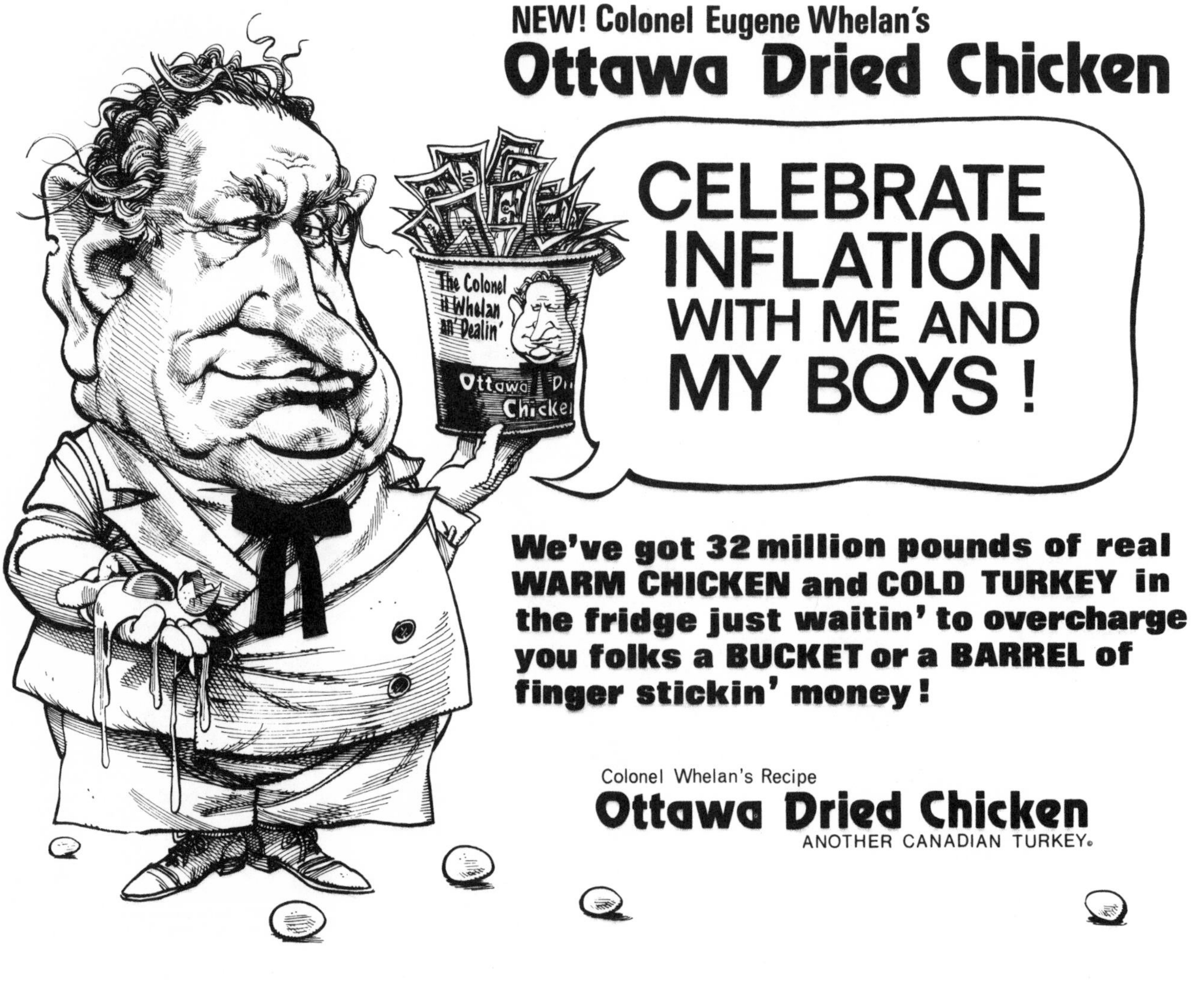
NEW! Colonel Eugene Whelan's
Ottawa Dried Chicken
The Colonel
'll Whelan
an' Dealin'
CELEBRATE INFLATION WITH ME AND MY BOYS !
We've got 32 million pounds of real WARM CHICKEN and COLD TURKEY in the fridge just waitin' to overcharge you folks a BUCKET or a BARREL of finger stickin' money !
Colonel Whelan's Recipe
Ottawa Dried Chicken
ANOTHER CANADIAN TURKEY.

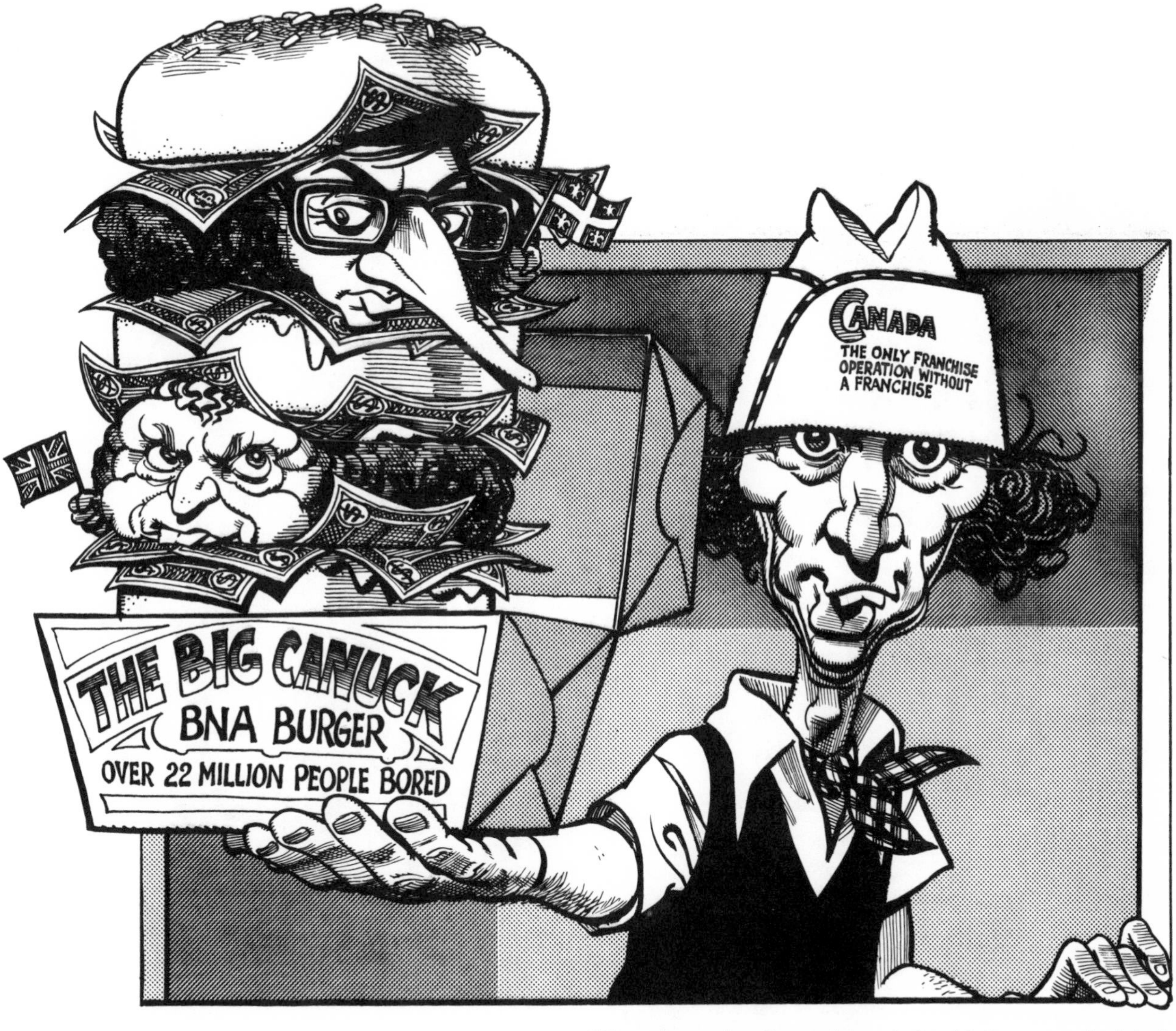
CANADA
THE ONLY FRANCHISE OPERATION WITHOUT A FRANCHISE
THE BIG CANUCK
BNA BURGER
OVER 22 MILLION PEOPLE BORED

"Two always-beefing patsies, federal lettuce, provincial attitudes, bilingual sauce on a constitutional bind!"

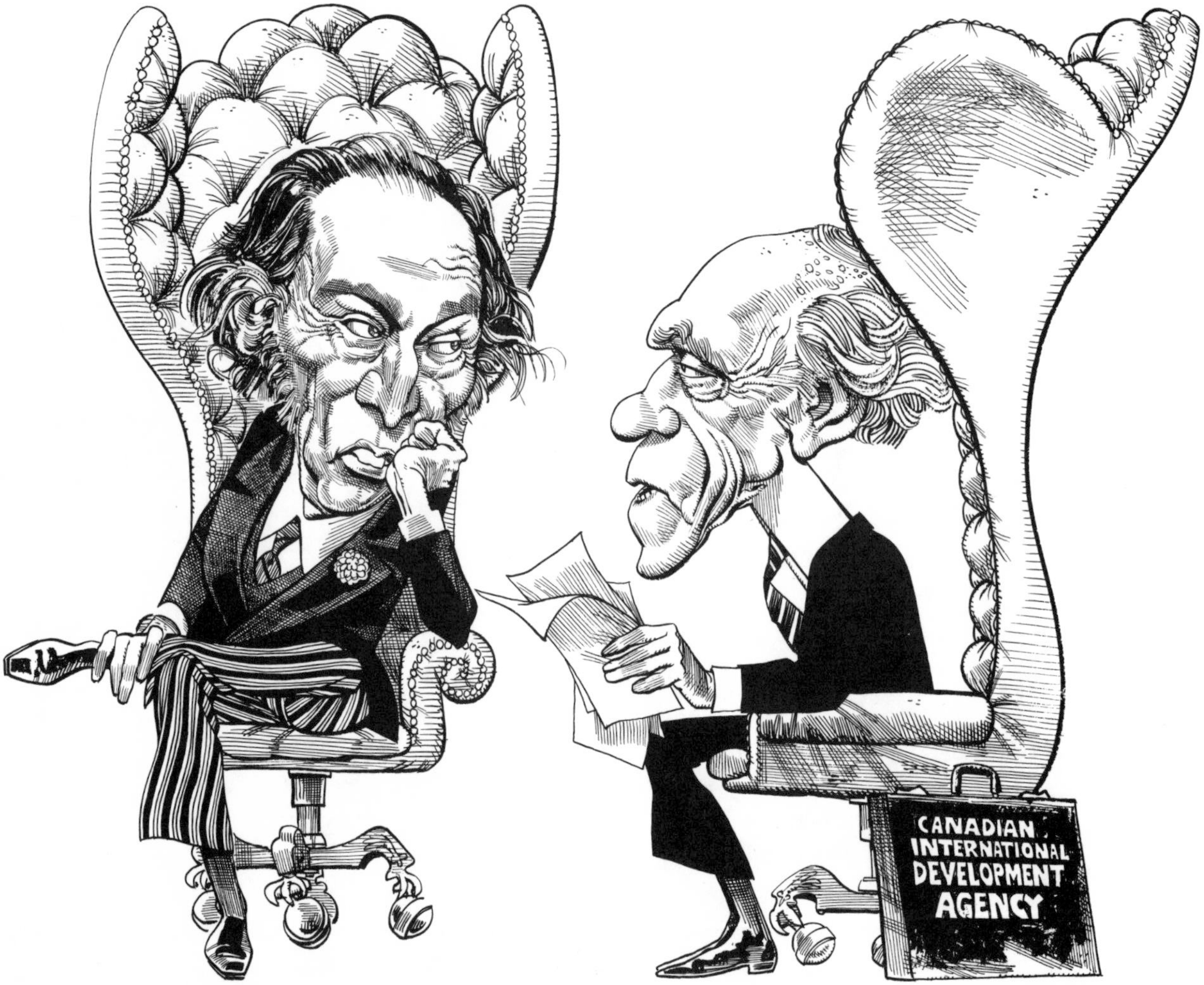
CANADIAN
INTERNATIONAL
DEVELOPMENT
AGENCY

". . . no problem with the grants to the African freedom fighters, Pierre, however we've had this request for a travelling grant from someone called Lévesque in Quebec . . ."

". . . and when did you first suspect that there were separatists in Radio Canada, André?"

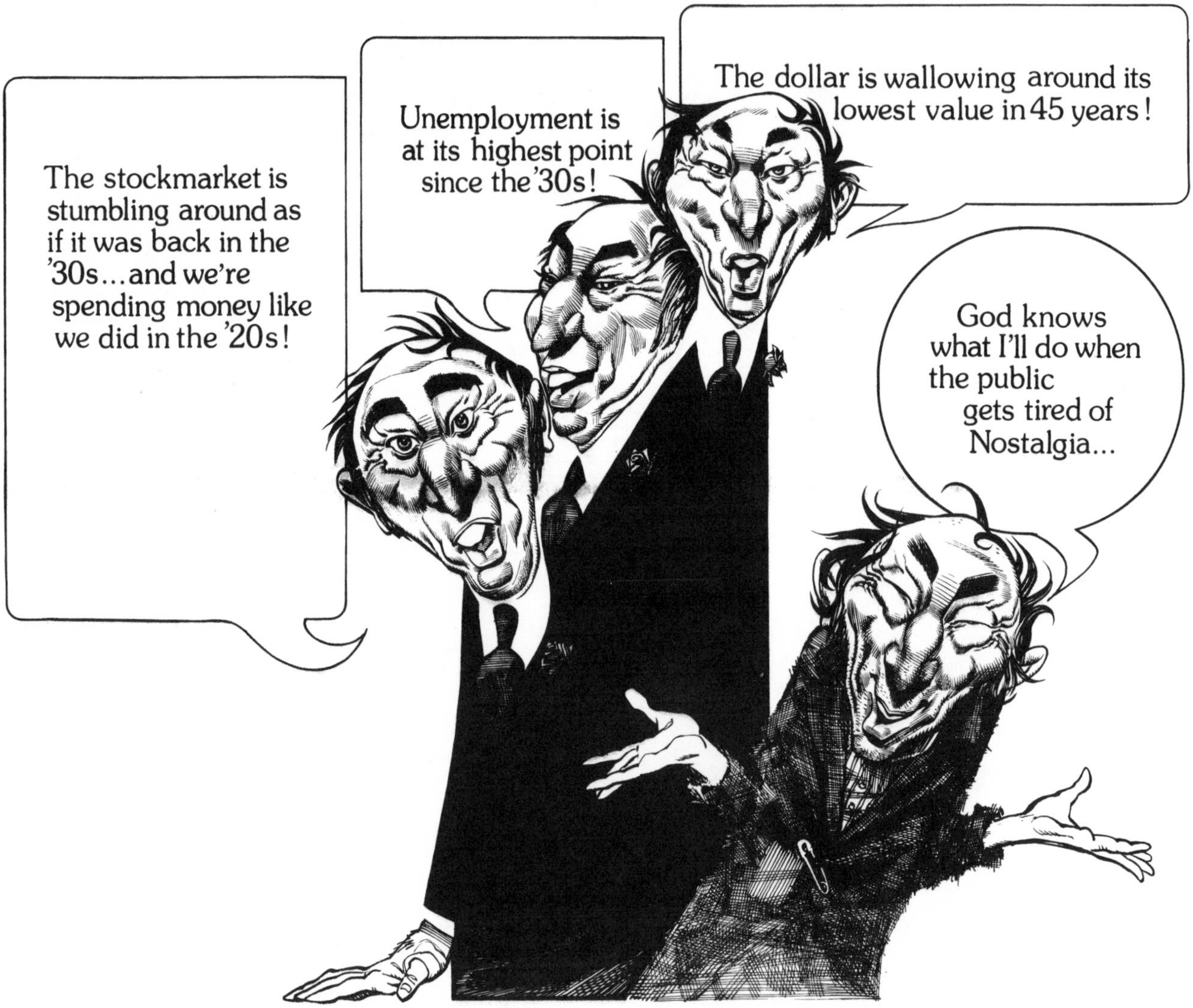
The stockmarket is stumbling around as if it was back in the '30s...and we're spending money like we did in the '20s!
Unemployment is at its highest point since the '30s!
The dollar is wallowing around its lowest value in 45 years!
God knows what I'll do when the public gets tired of Nostalgia...

High unemployment, staggering inflation, a weak pound, general lack of investor and consumer confidence, and Scotland wants to jump ship... and what is the situation on your side?

High unemployment, staggering inflation, a weak dollar, general lack of investor and consumer confidence, Quebec wants to jump ship and 'Joe Who?' is rising in the polls...

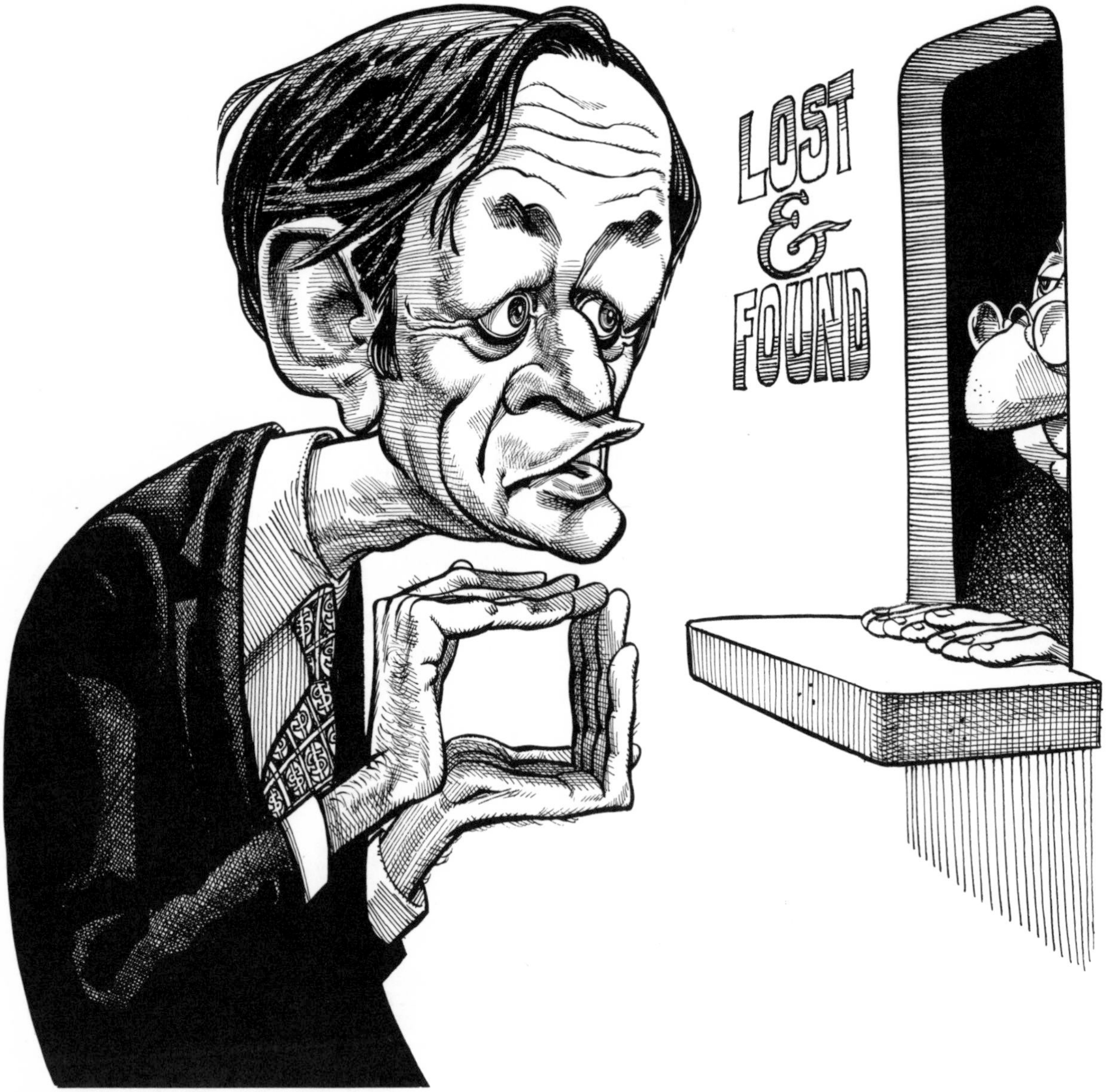
LOST & FOUND

". . . green, bilingual, about six inches by two and three-quarters, a portrait of the Queen on one side, a rather meaningless numeral 'one' in each corner . . ."

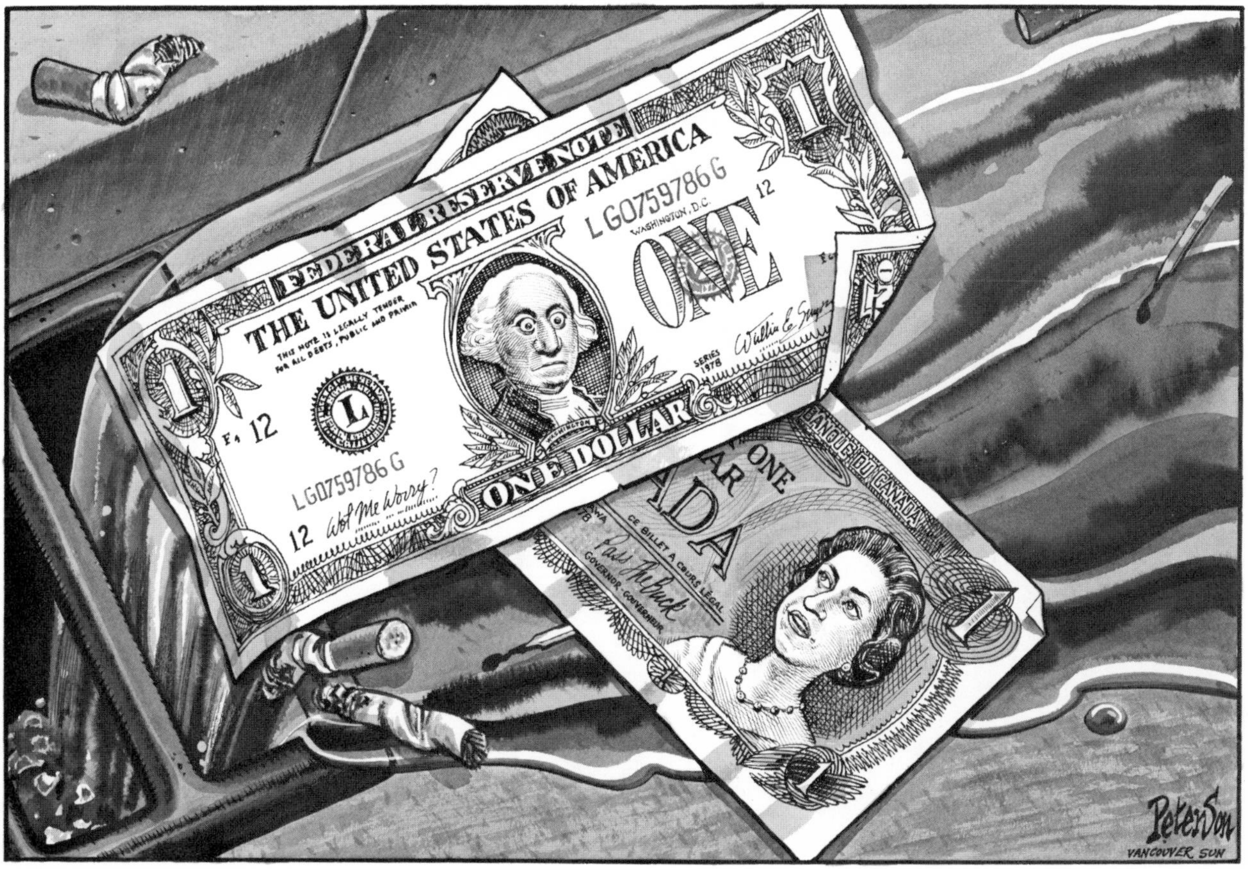
FEDERAL RESERVE NOTE
THE UNITED STATES OF AMERICA
L G0759786 G
ONE
ONE DOLLAR
Wot Me Worry?
BANQUE DU CANADA
Pass The Buck
Peterson
VANCOUVER SUN

"George, we've got to stop meeting like this . . ."

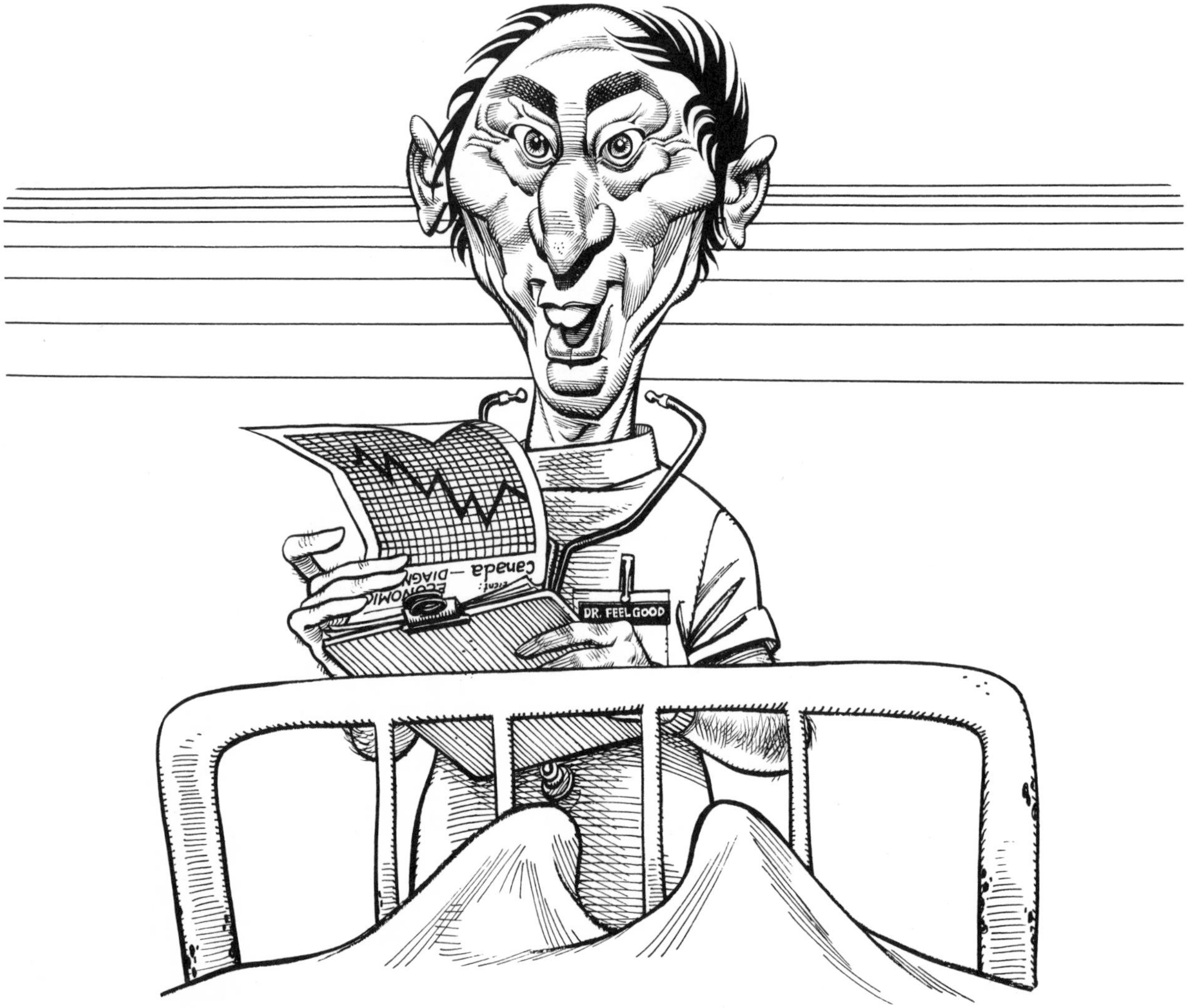
DR. FEELGOOD

"Let me put it this way: you're looking rather sick for a healthy economy . . . on the other hand, you're looking damn healthy for a sick economy."

APPLES
$1.00

DOLLARS
83.57¢

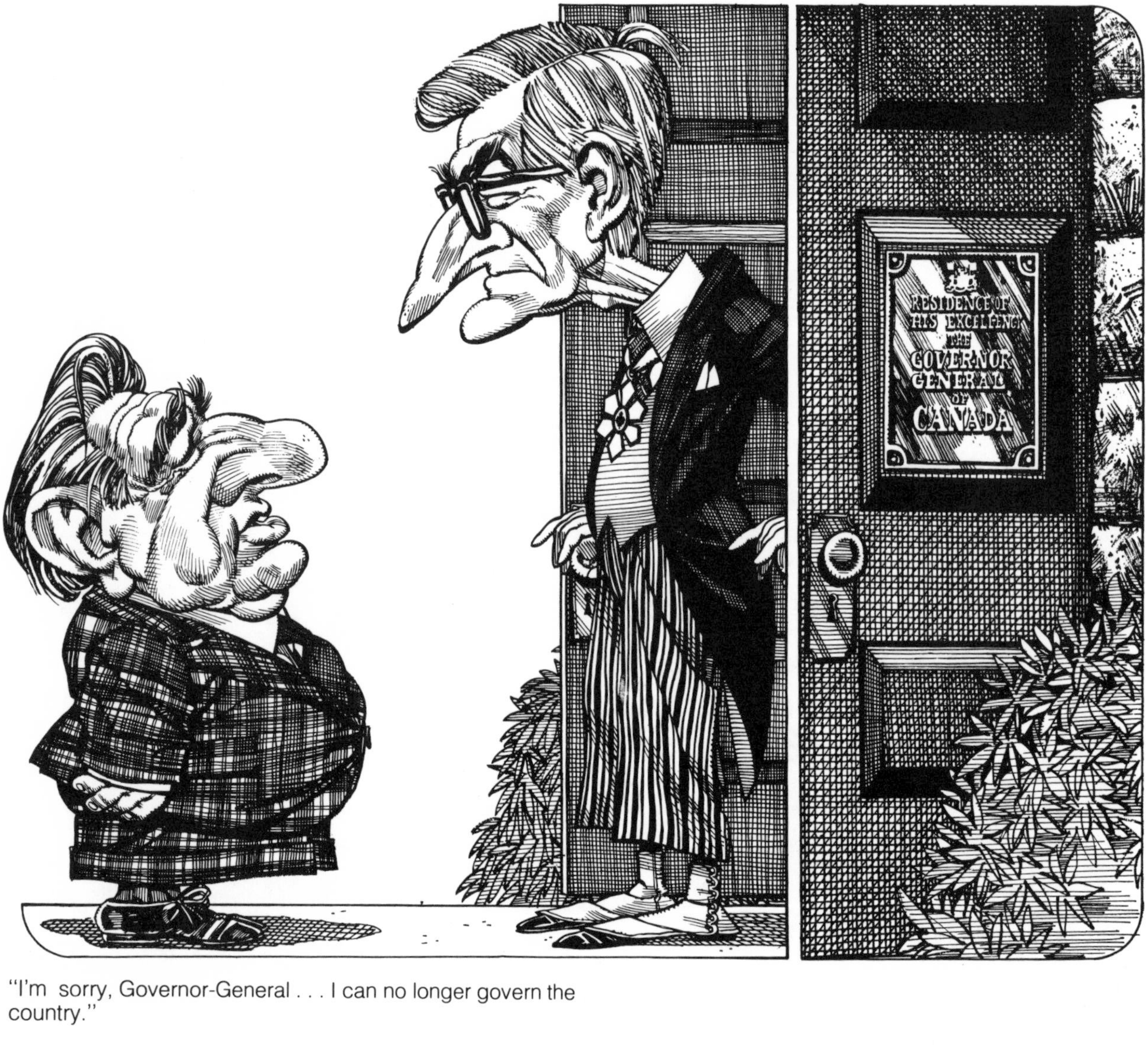
RESIDENCE OF
HIS EXCELLENCY
THE
GOVERNOR
GENERAL
OF
CANADA

"I'm sorry, Governor-General . . . I can no longer govern the country."

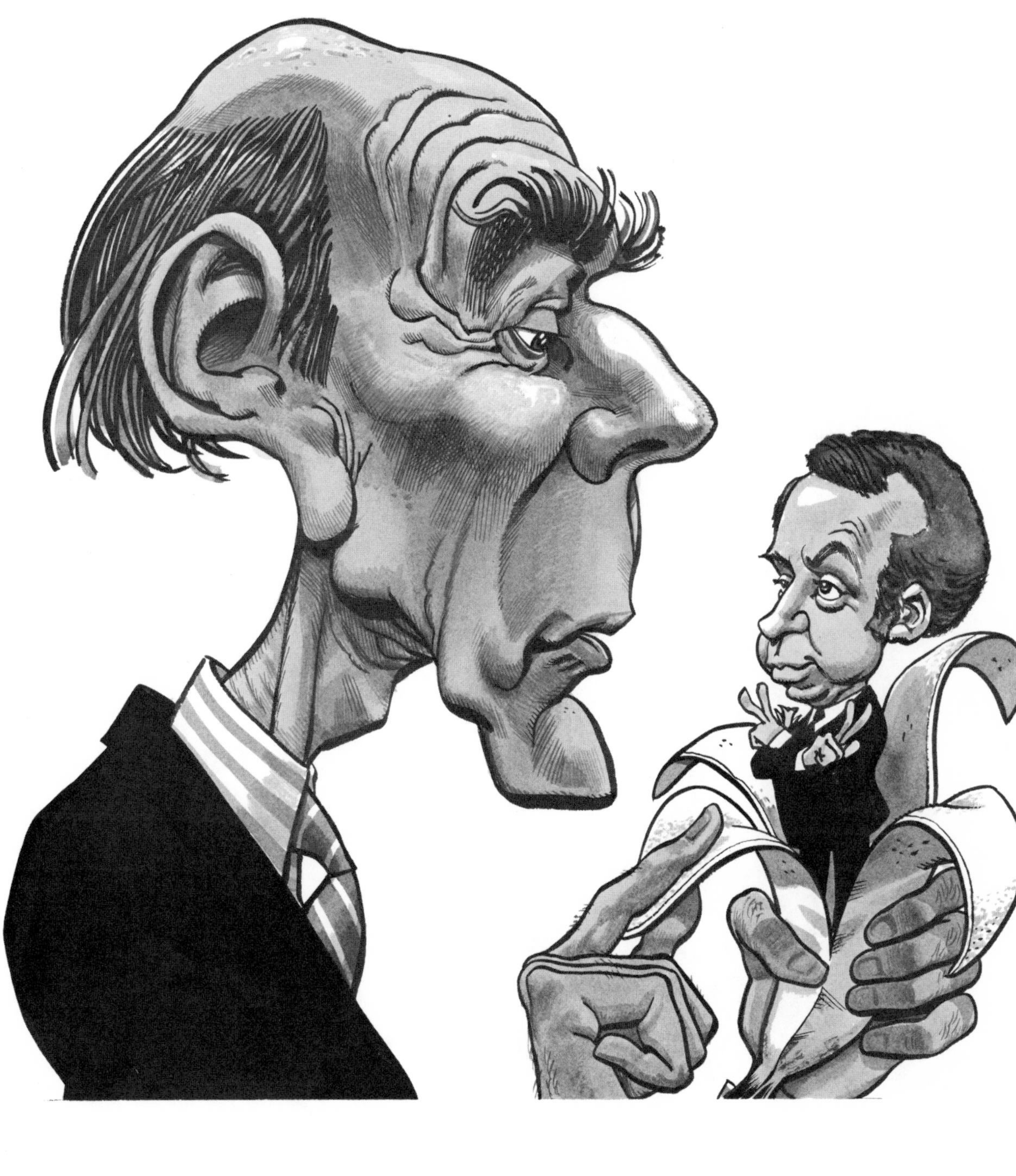

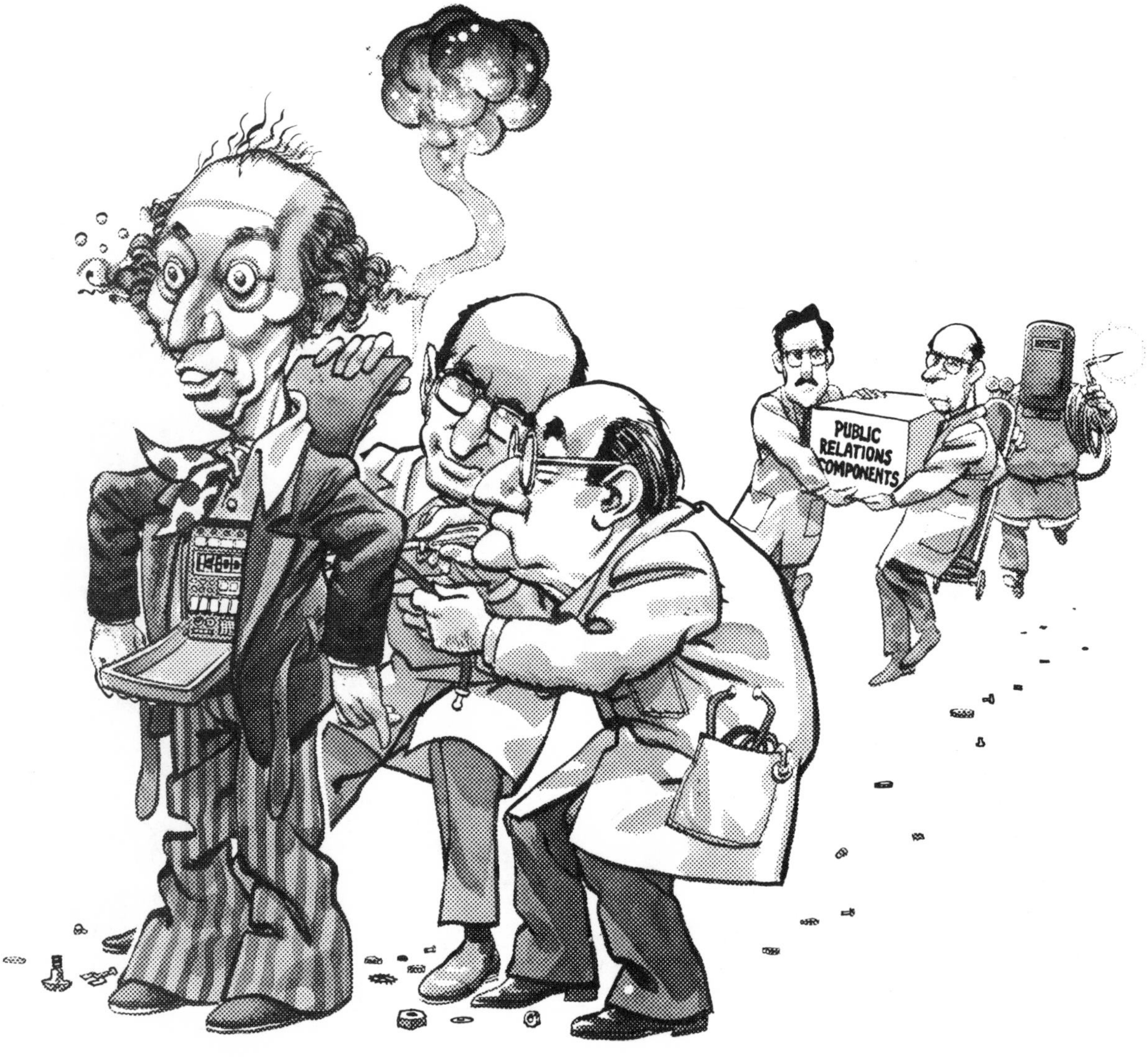
PUBLIC
RELATIONS
COMPONENTS

The Bionic Man

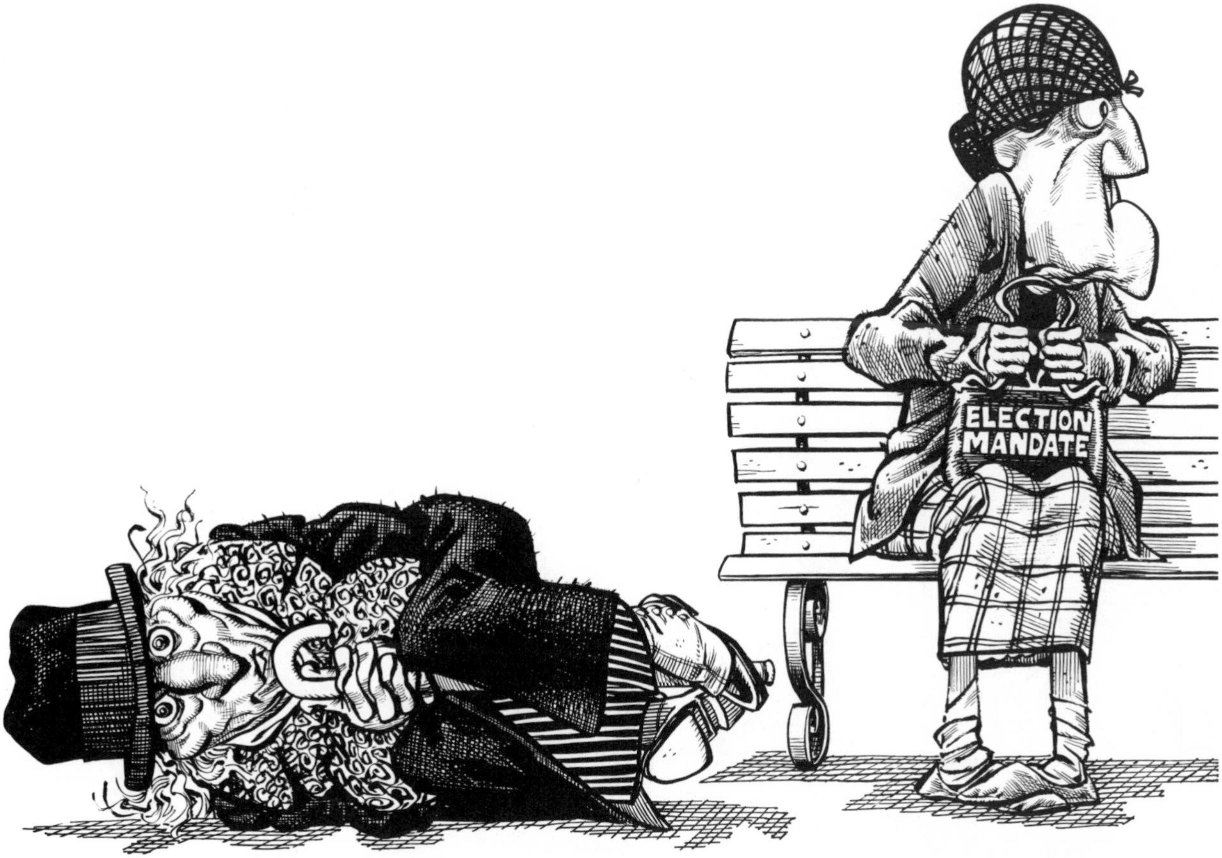
ELECTION
MANDATE

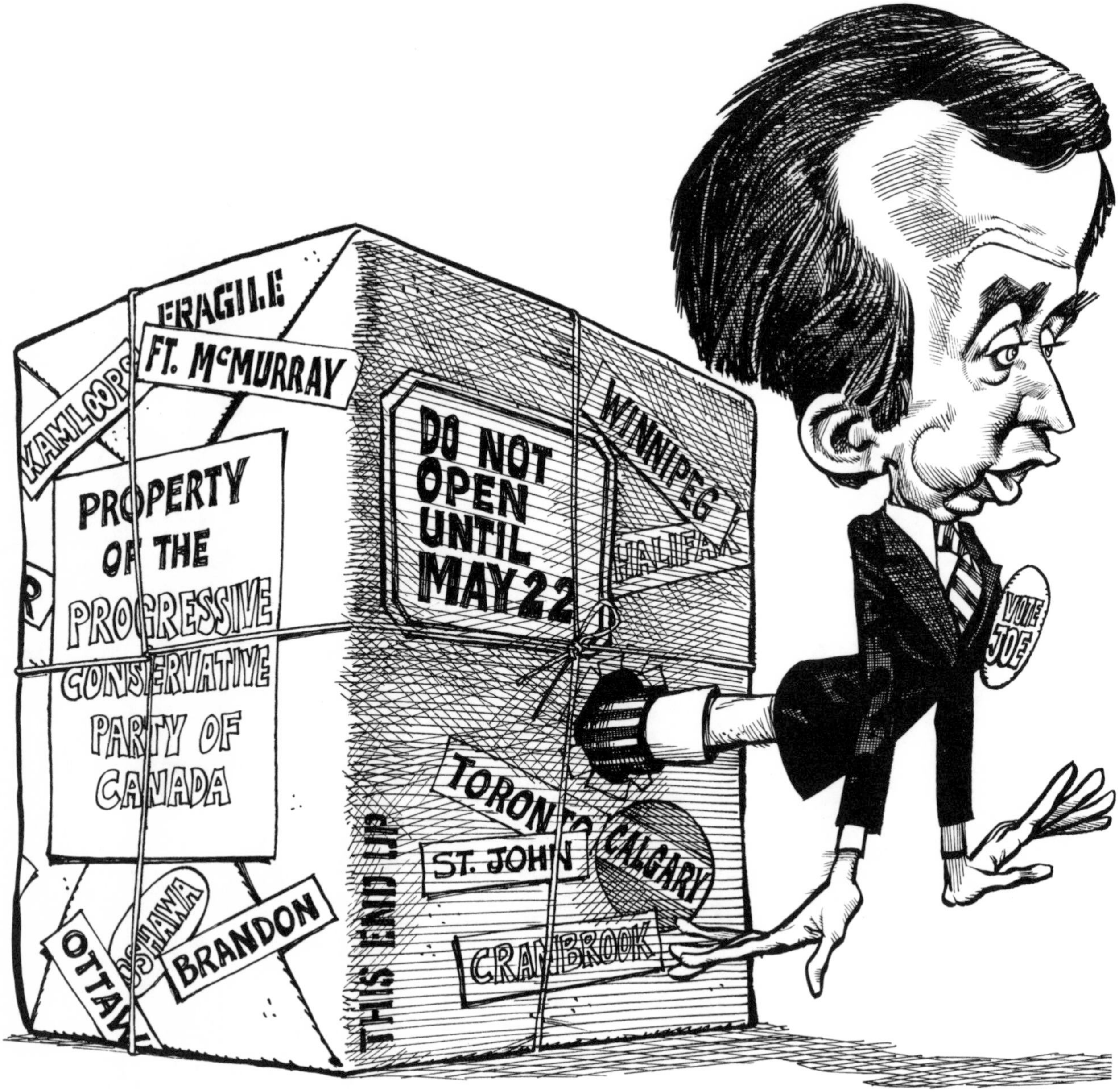
FRAGILE
FT. McMURRAY
KAMLOOPS
PROPERTY OF THE PROGRESSIVE CONSERVATIVE PARTY OF CANADA
DO NOT OPEN UNTIL MAY 22
WINNIPEG
HALIFAX
TORON
ST. JOHN
CALGARY
CRANBROOK
THIS END UP
OSHAWA
BRANDON
OTTAW
VOTE JOE

"Well, Joe, on the international level we've defused the Jerusalem embassy problem and we looked good at the Tokyo summit . . . now if we can just keep you away from Skylab's flight path . . ."

59

René Chez Nous

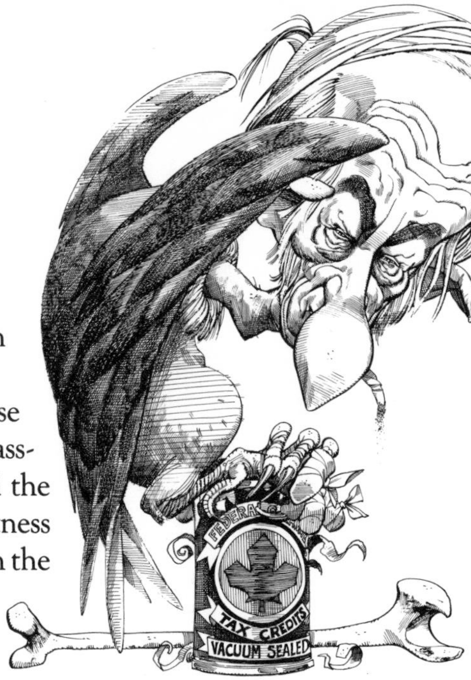
TAX CREDITS
VACUUM SEALED

This improbable country, for some reason, specializes in evangelical movements—stirrings of the soul.

There was, originally, the quiet resignation of those tired of eating blowdirt and listening to the rattle of the grasshopper in Saskatchewan in the Depression. They formed the Co-operative Commonwealth Federation (in their earnestness they could not recognize the awkwardness of the label) with the Regina Manifesto and founded Canadian socialism.

Later, Alberta, in its free-enterprise perversity, combined the teachings of the Bible with the quirkiness of the mathematical table and established an economic mumbo jumbo entitled Social Credit. Eventually, like foot fungus, it crossed the Rockies and combined—as one historian put it—with "a drab collection of monetary fetishists, British Israelites, naturopaths, chiropractors, preachers, pleaders and anti-Semites" led by a former major with the Ninth Gurkha Rifles of the Indian Army. (These are the political ancestors of Peter Lougheed and Mini Wac Bennett.)

The current example of this passionate streak in the Canadian psyche is the Parti Quebecois, René Lévesque's amalgam of social reform, Gallic flair and linguistic purity. The PQ is not so much a political party as it is a movement of true believers, serene in their knowledge (like early CCF/NDP types and Social Credit fanatics) that only to them is the divinity revealed. Their passion is admirable; their zeal to be esteemed; their contempt for all nonbelievers is of a vastly condescending nature.

The PQ's early lofty belief that it held the sole patent on truth and righteousness rested, essentially, in the elite nature of the brainpower of its upper echelons. Most crucially, it was an elite that had been trained and conditioned abroad—it looked outward to the world and had little experience (or interest) in Canada itself.

René Lévesque is possibly the most worldly of all Canadian politicians. He joined the U.S. Army as a war correspondent (jettisoning a legal career because law school, as it did Joe Clark, bored him). He survived the London blitz with Edward R. Murrow, crossed the Rhine with Gen. George Patton, was one of the first entrants to the Dachau death camp, saw Mussolini strung up by the heels, interviewed Goering, with Lester Pearson met Khruschev in Moscow, was Canada's outstanding war correspondent in Korea, and roamed the world for his sensational Quebec television program. His analogies on independence are always drawn on global examples.

His lieutenants look outward, not inward. Education Minister Jacques-Yvan Morin studied at Harvard and Cambridge and served on the International Court at the Hague. Finance Minister Jacques Parizeau is a product of the London School of Economics, and of Paris. Claude Morin went to Columbia, Denis Lazure to the University of Pennsylvania. Camille Laurin, the shrink to a nation, was educated in Boston and the International University in Geneva. Bernard Landry was polished in France and Germany. Jacques Couture was a missionary in Taiwan. Louis O'Neill studied theology in Rome.

Against this we have the Royal Bank's Earle J. McLaughlin, 30 years in Montreal without his tongue having attempted French, the descendant of Cecil Rhodes in the counting house. The Westmount Rhodesians, using the Maritime Bar of the Ritz-Carlton Hotel as their Alamo. A minority that acted too long as a majority, bringing on, as always, the revolution. The PQ evangelists, led by Laurin, overreact and attempt to impose their theology. The Québecois, who vote their wallet, are turning the evangelists into politicians, now more concerned with re-election than with a suicide mission into a fuzzy referendum.

René Lévesque and His Missionaries—a surefire skiffle group if I ever heard one—are learning the sad truths of the evangelists who preceded them. The fire-breathing radicals out of Regina, Fabian dreams of brotherhood watering their eyes, eventually hopped into bed with a clutch of materialistic and dirty-fingered union workers from detested Ontario and now cannot even win the votes of wives of NDP unionists in the urban centres. The goofy disciples of Major Douglas's A+B Theorem have now disappeared into a group-and-grope with Grits and Tories in a B.C. smorgasbord coalition designed to fight off the castrated socialists. Little is what it seems. The wine in Quebec is being watered, too.

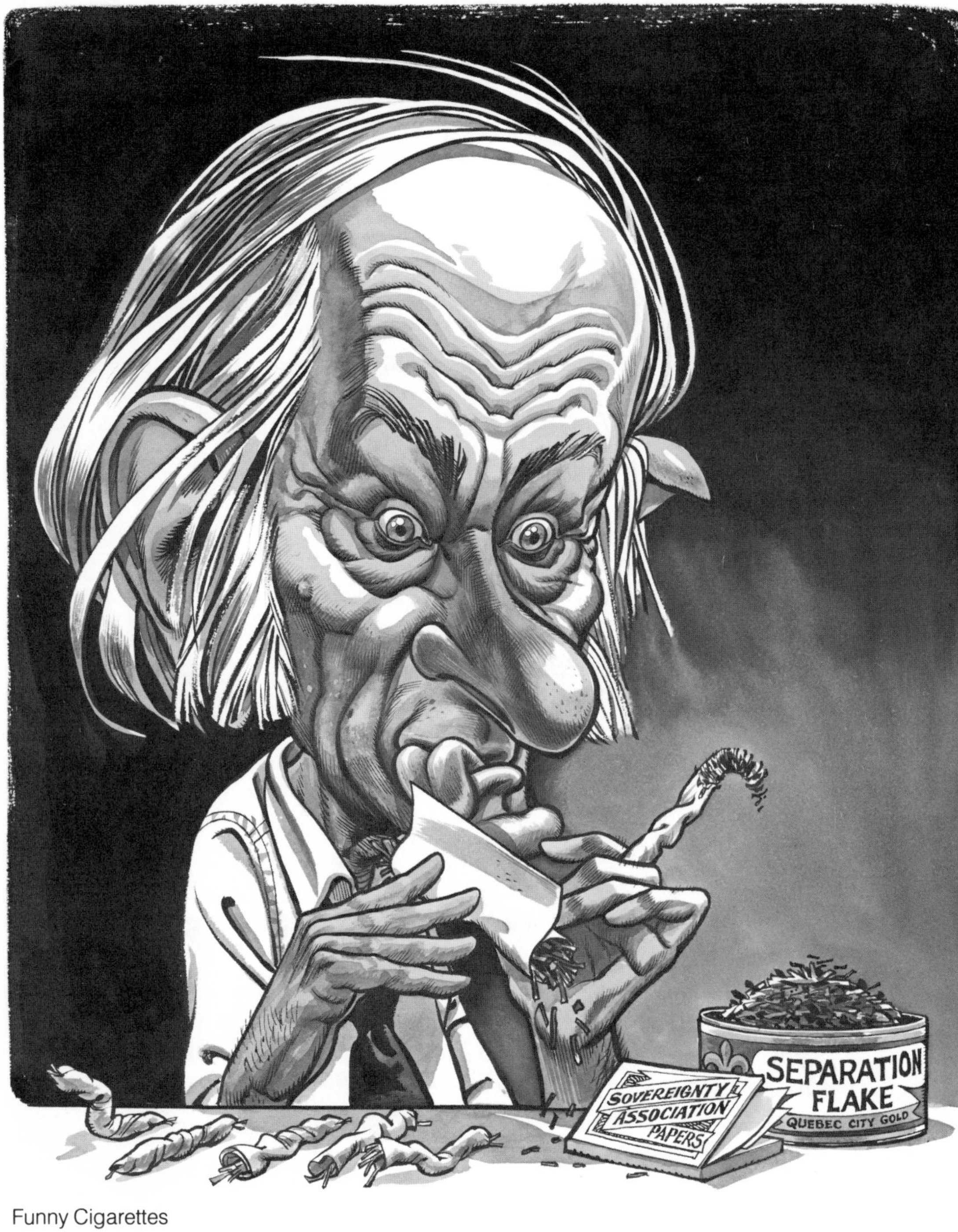
SOVEREIGNTY
ASSOCIATION
PAPERS
SEPARATION
FLAKE
QUEBEC CITY GOLD

Funny Cigarettes

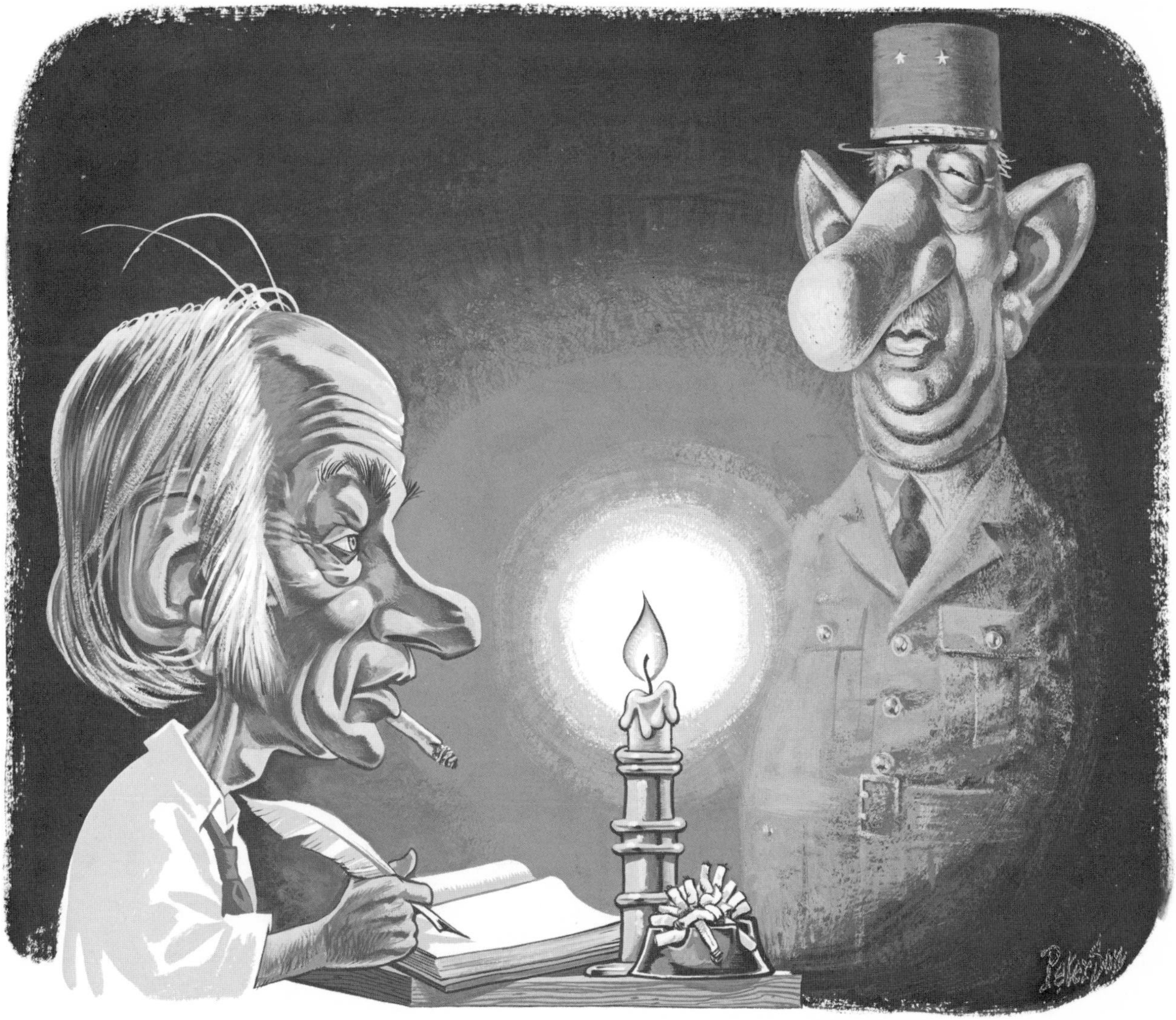

"I don't care what Mackenzie King says, Charles, by the time they get to read MY diaries we'll have won the referendum."

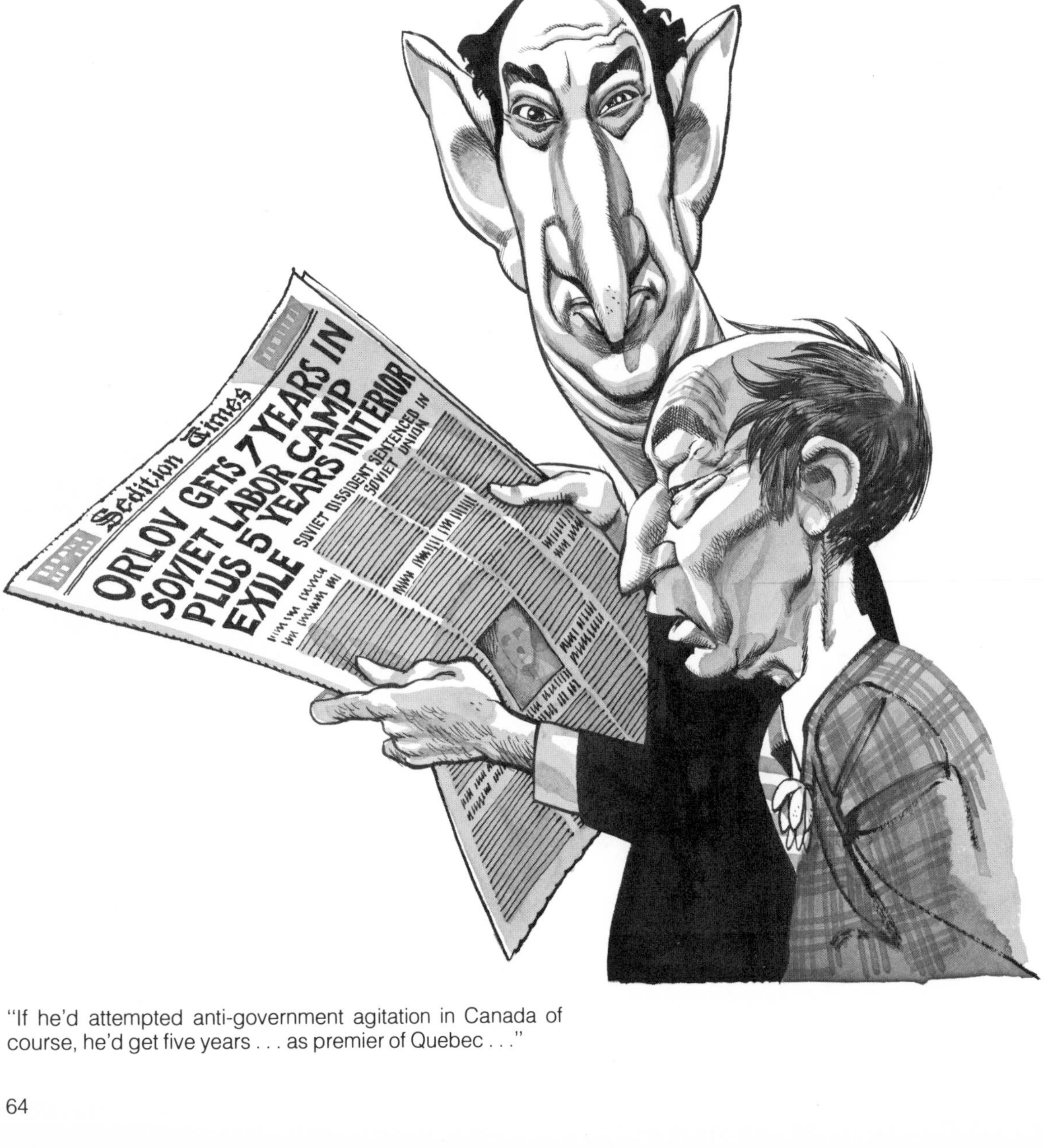
Sedition Times
ORLOV GETS 7 YEARS IN SOVIET LABOR CAMP PLUS 5 YEARS INTERIOR EXILE
SOVIET DISSIDENT SENTENCED IN SOVIET UNION

"If he'd attempted anti-government agitation in Canada of course, he'd get five years . . . as premier of Quebec . . ."

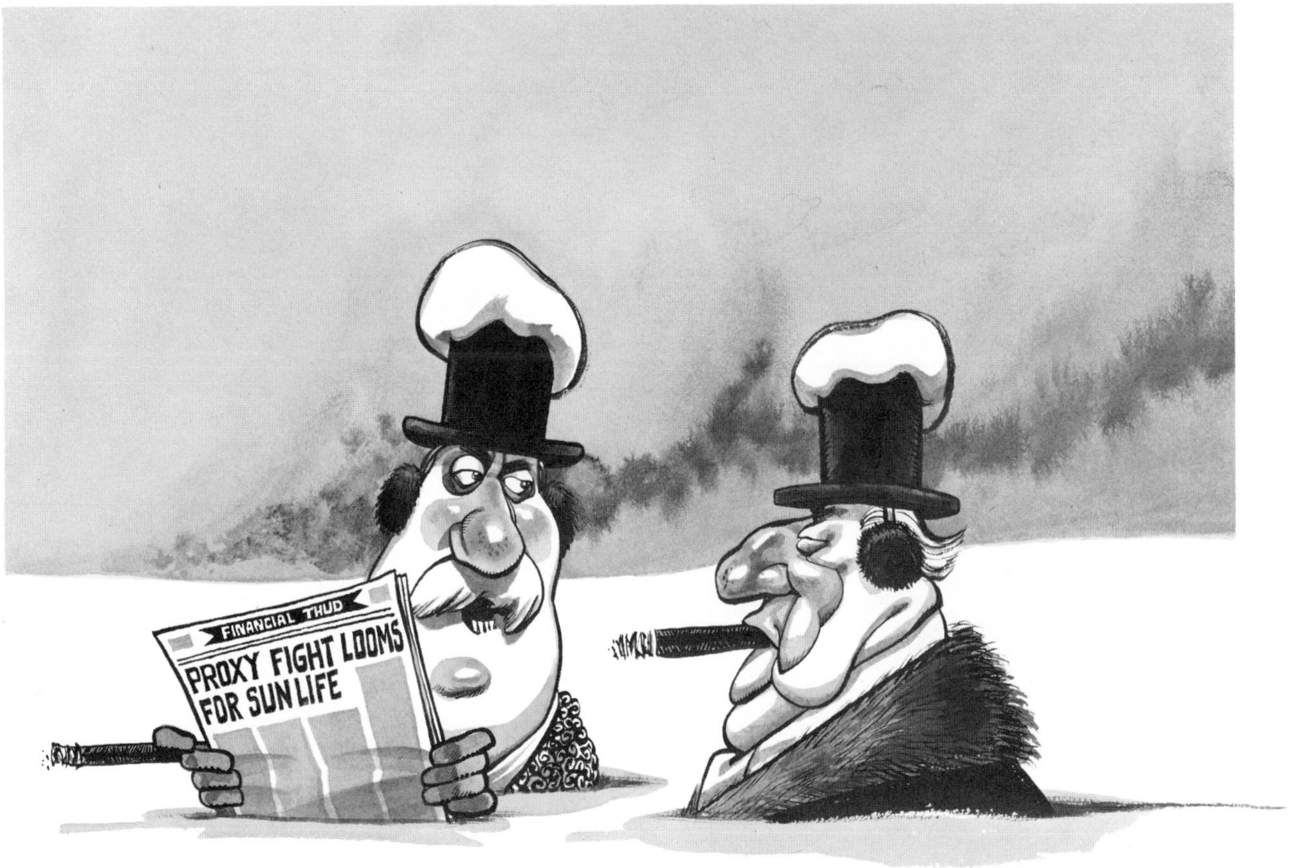
FINANCIAL THUD
PROXY FIGHT LOOMS FOR SUN LIFE

"It's reprehensible that Sun Life should even think of moving to Toronto — everyone knows the financial centre of Canada nowadays is Alberta."

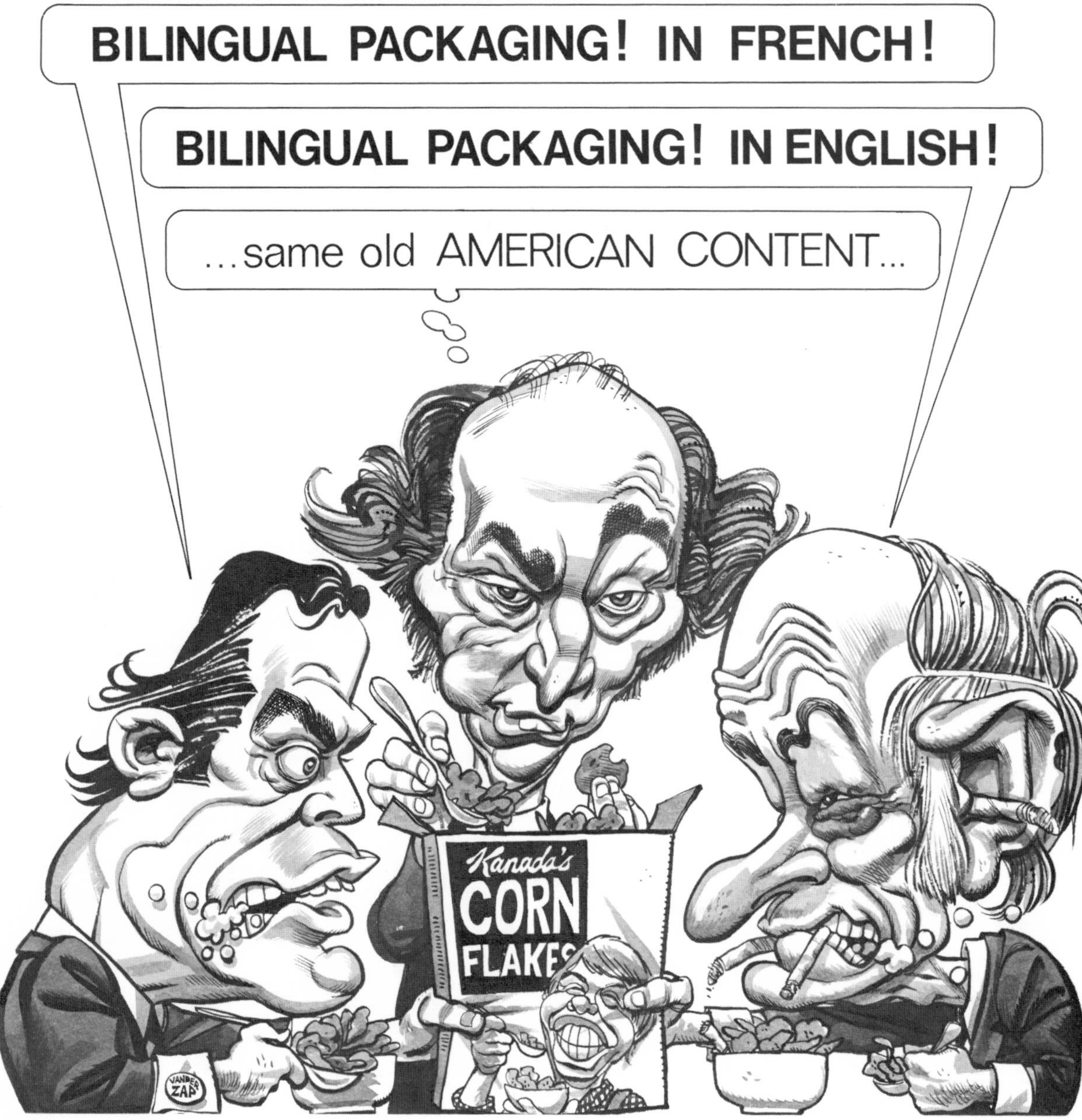
BILINGUAL PACKAGING! IN FRENCH!
BILINGUAL PACKAGING! IN ENGLISH!
...same old AMERICAN CONTENT...
Kanada's
CORN

Snap, Crackle and Pap

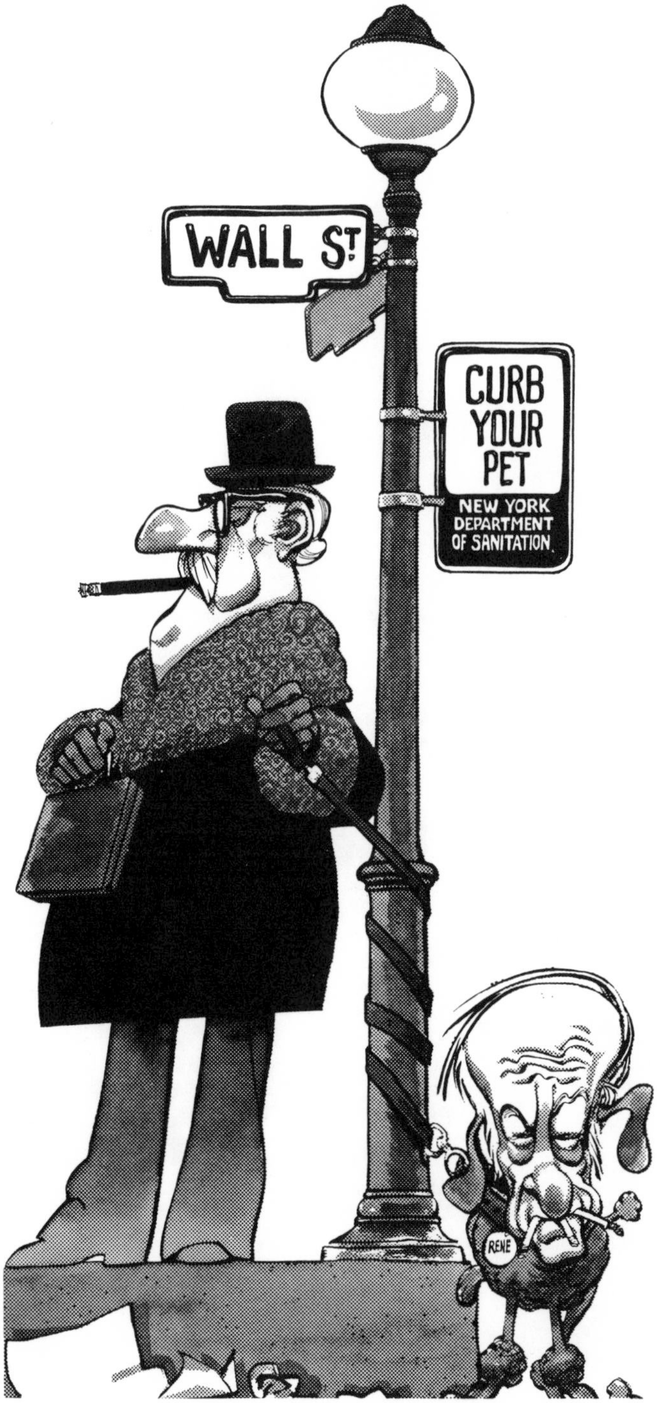
WALL St
CURB YOUR PET
NEW YORK DEPARTMENT OF SANITATION
RENE

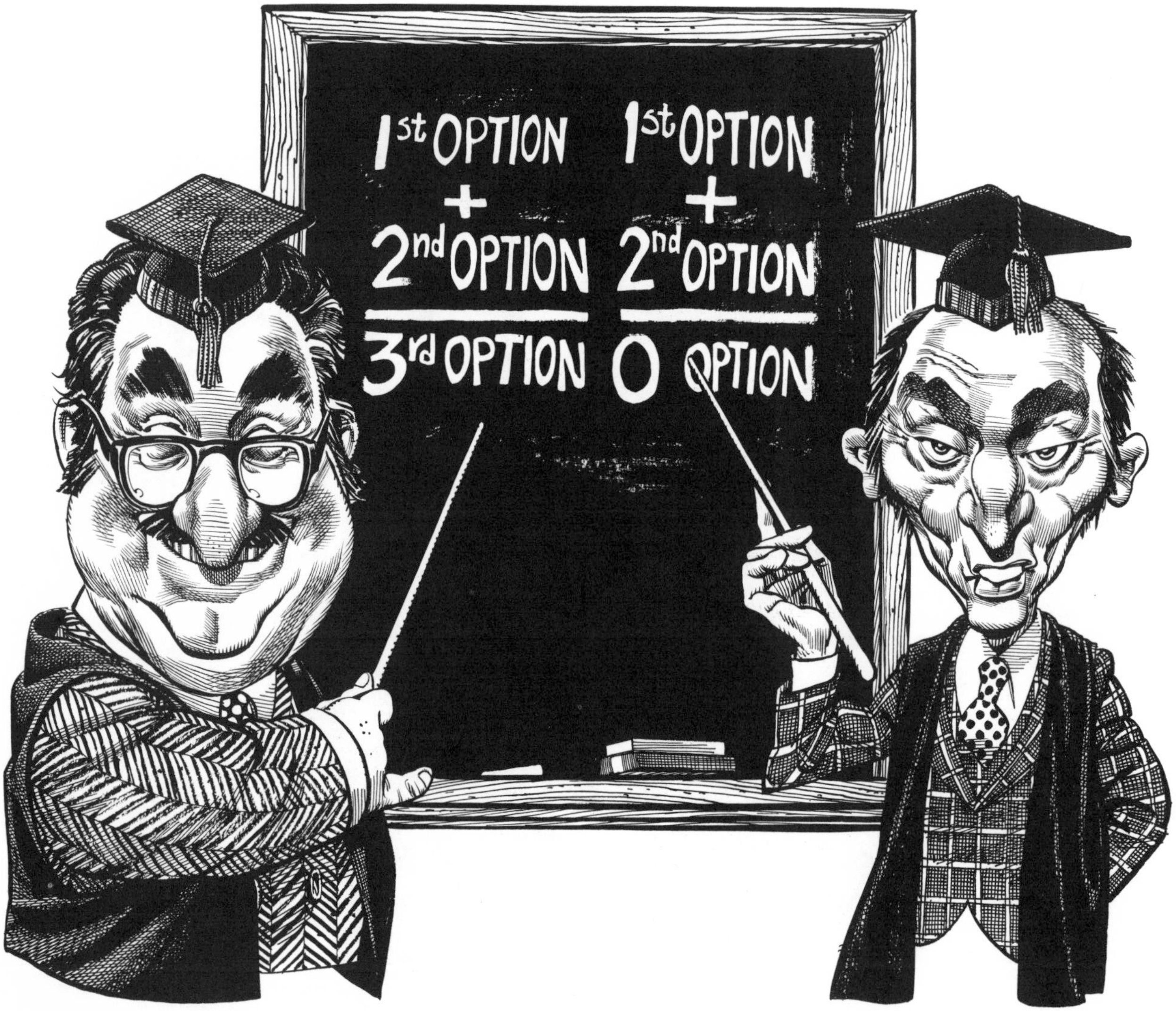
1st OPTION + 2nd OPTION
3rd OPTION
1st OPTION + 2nd OPTION
0 OPTION

Semantic Conversion

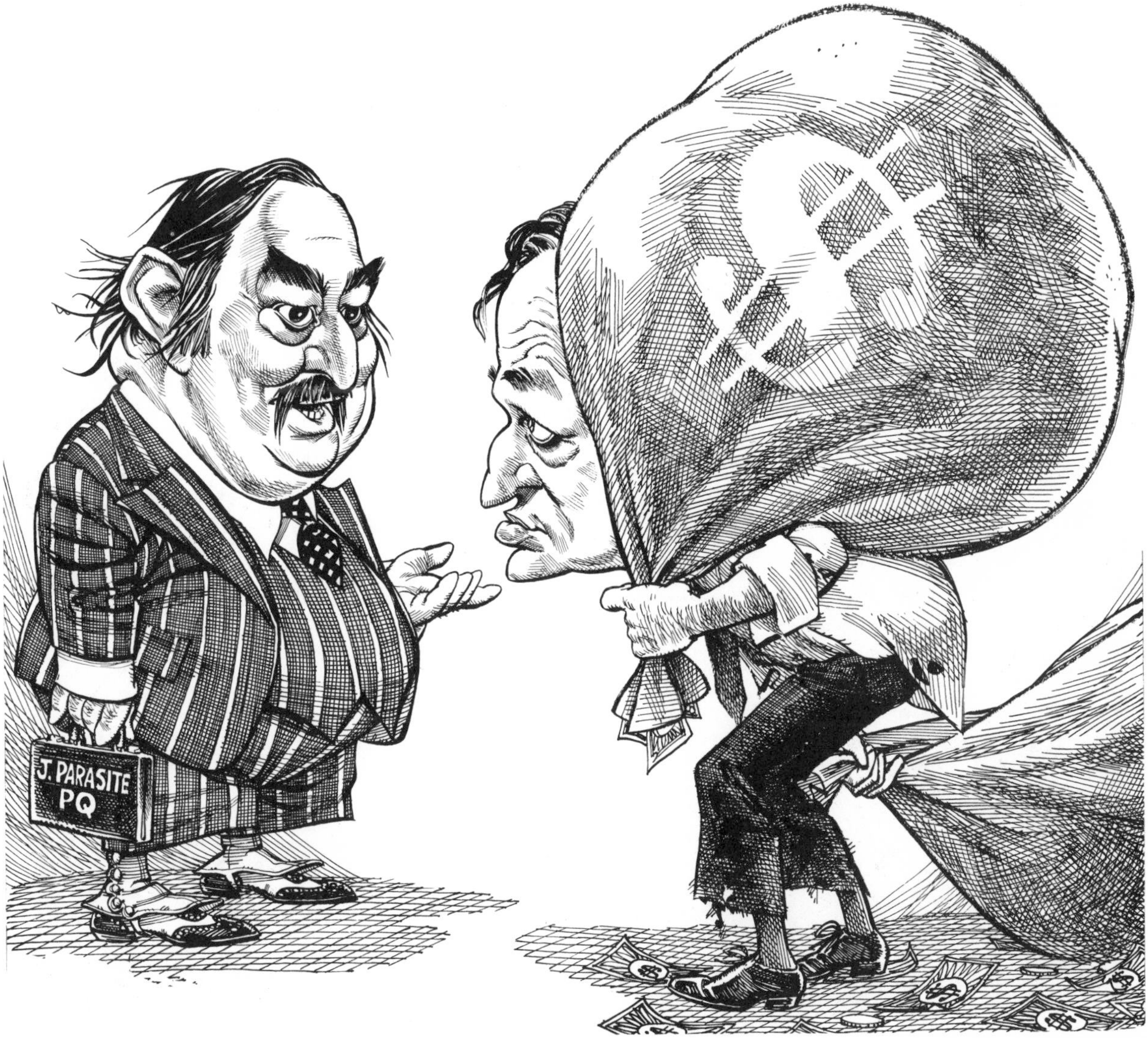
J. PARASITE
PQ

"In the interest of sovereignty-association we will now associate with your sovereigns, guineas, crowns, dollars, quarters and dimes . . ."

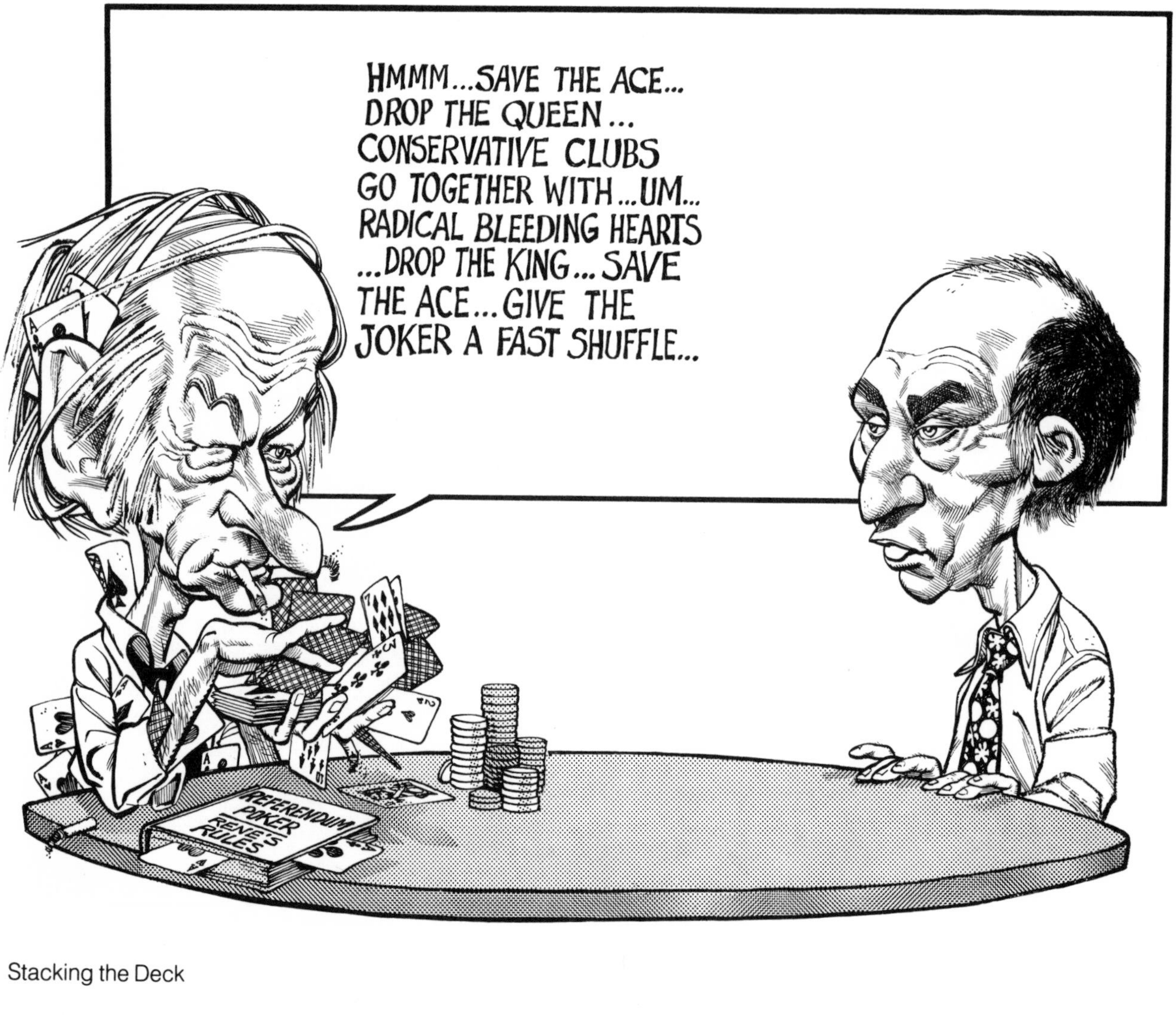
HMMM...SAVE THE ACE... DROP THE QUEEN... CONSERVATIVE CLUBS GO TOGETHER WITH...UM... RADICAL BLEEDING HEARTS ...DROP THE KING... SAVE THE ACE... GIVE THE JOKER A FAST SHUFFLE...
REFERENDUM POKER
RENE'S RULES

Stacking the Deck

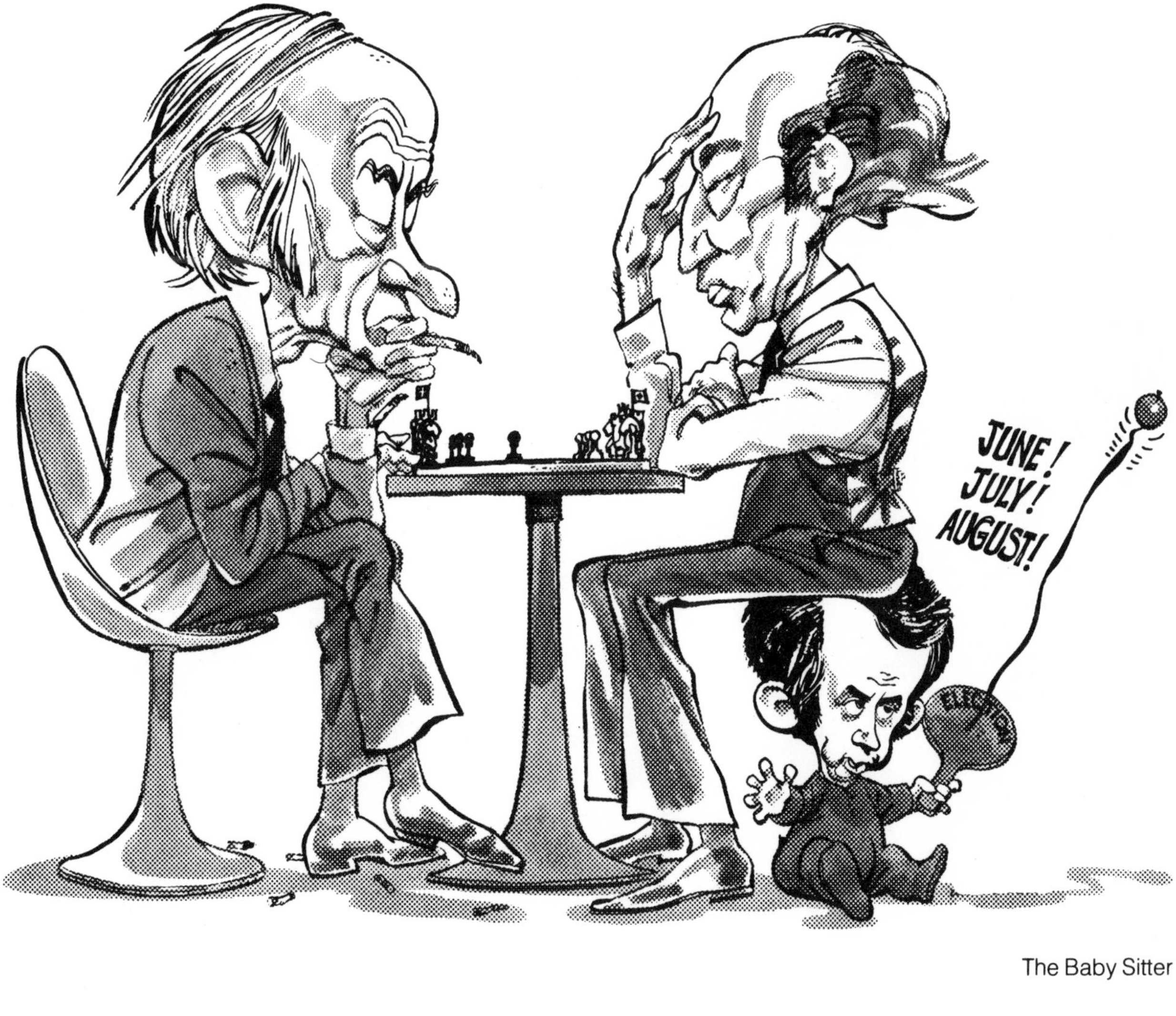
JUNE!
JULY!
AUGUST!

The Baby Sitter

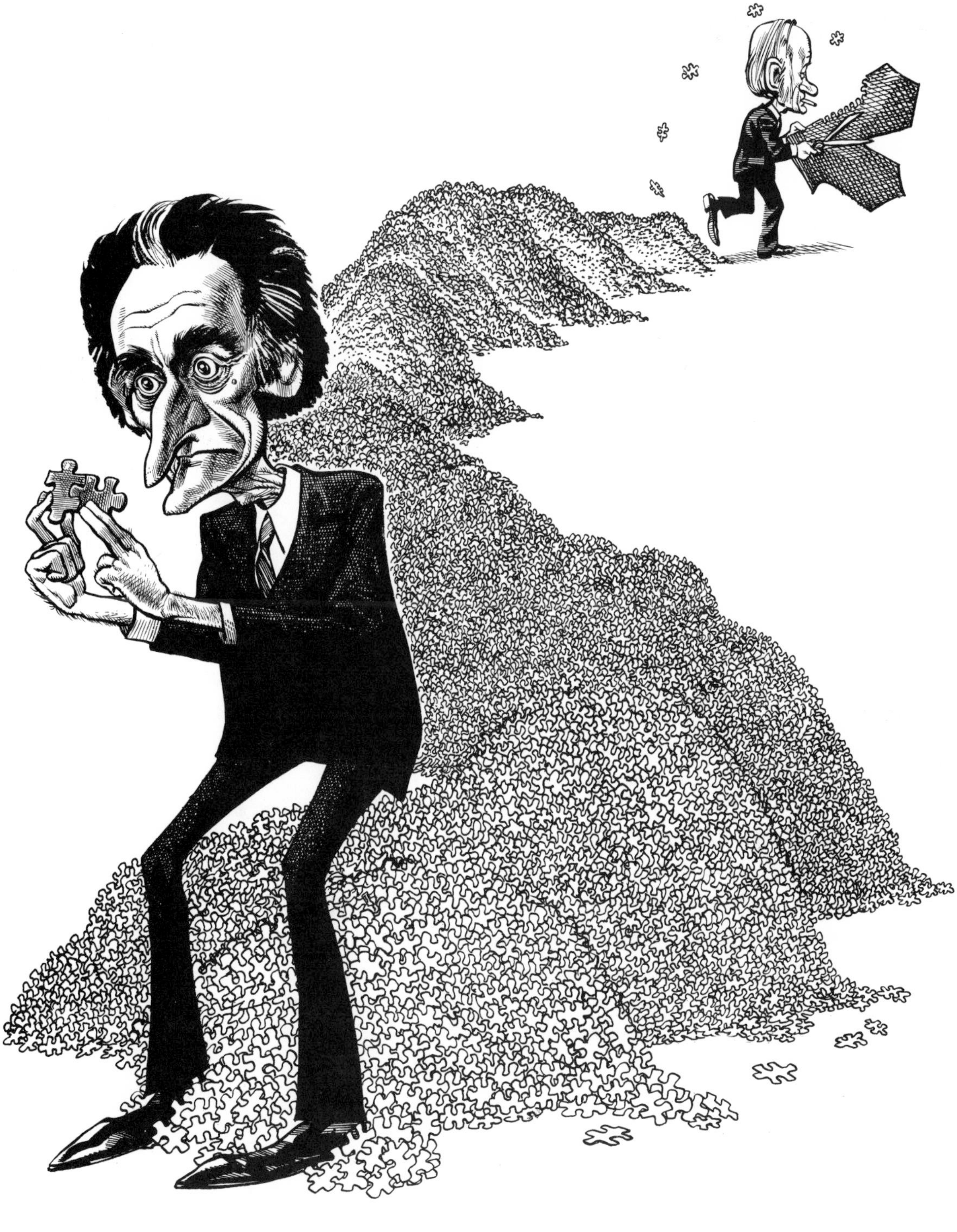

In the Land of the Lotus

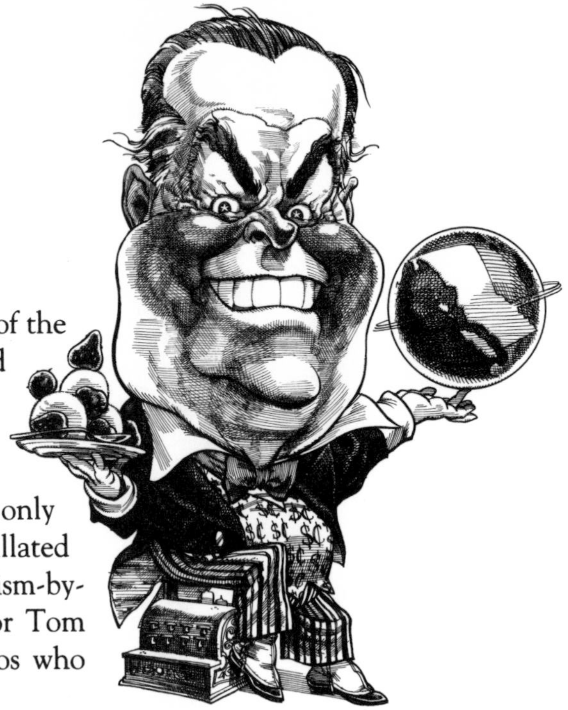

It was the dignified Angus MacInnis, one of the founders of the CCF, who perceived the truth. In the Maritimes, he said politics was a disease; in Quebec, a religion; in Ontario, a business; on the Prairies, a protest; and in B.C., entertainment.

British California, alias Bennett Columbia, is the only jurisdiction in Canada where the voters insist on being titillated before they will submit to being informed. Only Narcissism-by-the-Pacific could produce Phlying Phil Gaglardi, Mayor Tom Terrific, Wacky Bennett and the other political weirdos who periodically surface on the waves of national headlines.

The province, it must be understood, is populated by refugees from the hated "East." Frank Lloyd Wright said that if the United States were a table and you tipped it up so that all the junk fell to one end, that would be California. B.C. is the Canadian equivalent. Yet most British Columbians regard the rest of Canada with an air of amused pity. Anyone, they feel, who would live in a climate like *that* deserves whatever fate metes out.

To this mix comes a whiff of the anti-banker agrarian protest movement of the Prairies. Combine dirt-stained socialists and goofy monetary reformers with the basic robber-baron character of the coastal resource rapists and you have the land of the political spectacular: all the fundamental philosophies imported from beyond the mountains but married to the demand for vaudeville.

The pantomime has its honest roots. A century ago, an itinerant from the California goldfields by name of William Smith hove to. Deciding that his moniker was too commonplace for this locale of liars, he changed it to Amor de Cosmos, became B.C.'s second premier and once made a legislative speech lasting 20 hours. The theme was born.

A natural heir to the tradition is Social Credit cabinet minister Bill Vander Zalm, who on being accused of catering to the lunatic fringe, allowed that there were a lot of them out there and *somebody* had to represent them. (This is reminiscent of the Nixon battle to place a pedestrian Republican hack, Judge Carswell, on the U.S. Supreme Court. When it was pointed out by legal minds that Carswell, among other things, was dumb, Senator Roman Hrushka, an outraged Republican from the Midwest, cried that there were a lot of dumb people in the republic and surely they deserved their own man on the Court.)

It is Vander Zalm who thought it hilarious to compose a song calling René Lévesque a "frog" and who, on the night of the Parti Québécois election, expressed relief that his corn flake box would no longer be clouded by that other language. As the darling of the beer parlours and truck stops, he is the natural successor to the Reverend Gaglardi, the evangelical speed freak who, while carrying on the work of the Lord and upholding the law as highways minister, was convicted of speeding and careless driving offences, had his licence suspended, was fined $1,000 for contempt of court and once was caught by an irate motorist after he ran over a dog in the middle of plush Shaughnessy Heights and was speeding away. Gaglardi, like Vander Zalm, started his own War on Poverty. He threw rocks at beggars.

But when you think of it, wasn't Churchill the greatest showman of them all? FDR was a master manipulator, JFK a shrewd user of PR. British Columbia politicians have merely taken this simple truth and pushed it to the extreme, ever willing to do the verbal version of dropping their pants in public.

Another overlooked distinction is that B.C. is undoubtedly the most prosperous populace in the world ever to vote voluntarily for socialism. The advent, in 1972, of sanctimonious socialism naturally did nothing to dilute the level of buffoonery. The premier turned out to be short, fat, profane Dave Barrett—a socialist Lou Costello. He combined the timing of John Diefenbaker with the vocabulary of Lenny Bruce. Within a year he had to sack a minister who was caught *in flagrante delicto* in a car within 50 yards of the premier's window. And a sleepless Social Credit lady MLA had to request of the Empress Hotel's management that her room be switched because of the steady tattoo of passion exerted on the headboard of the adjoining room during the nightly adventures of one particularly randy NDP minister.

B.C. is not so dumb. It needs politicians who can match the scenery. Why accept anything less?

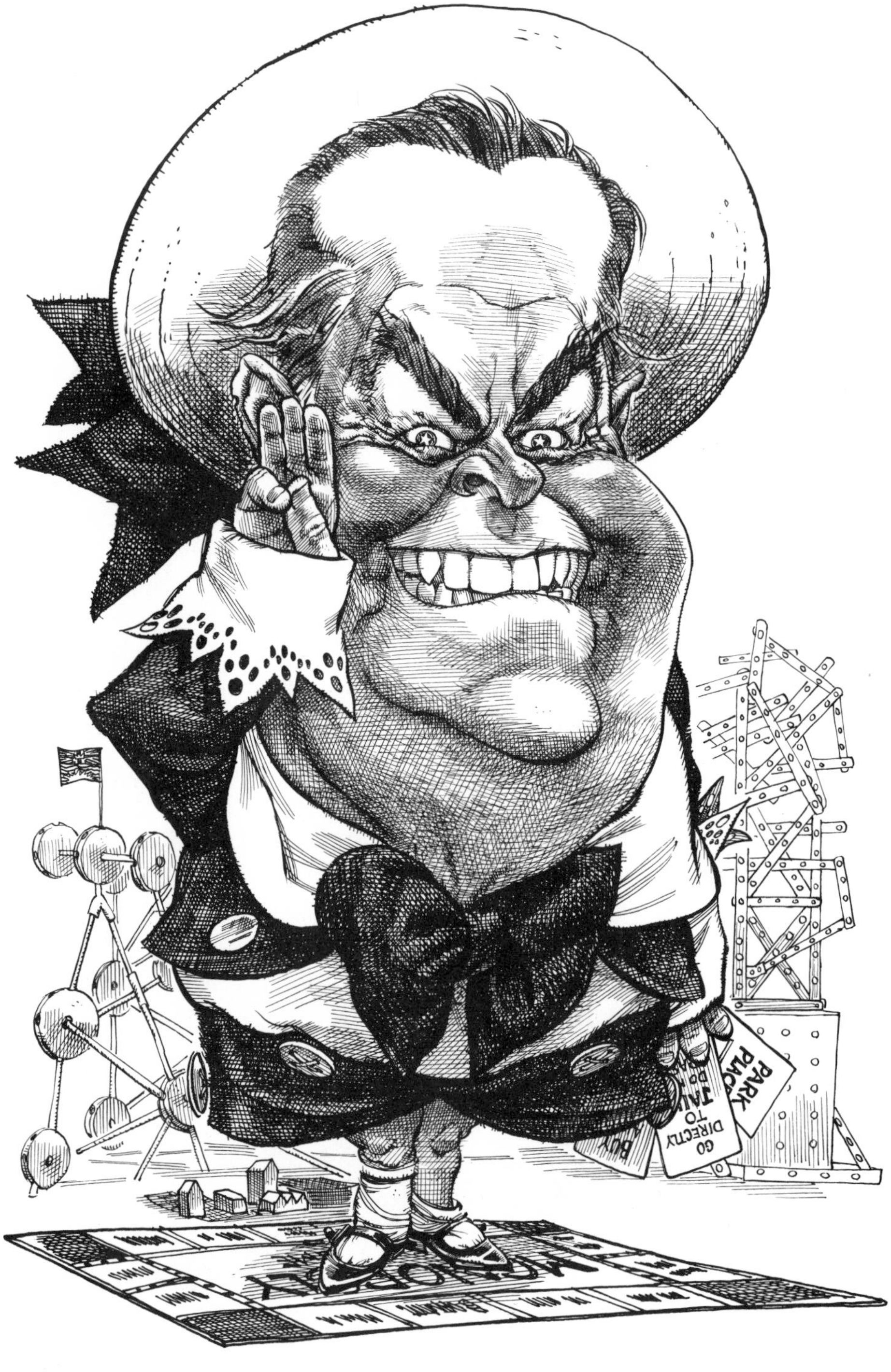
PARK
GO DIRECTLY TO

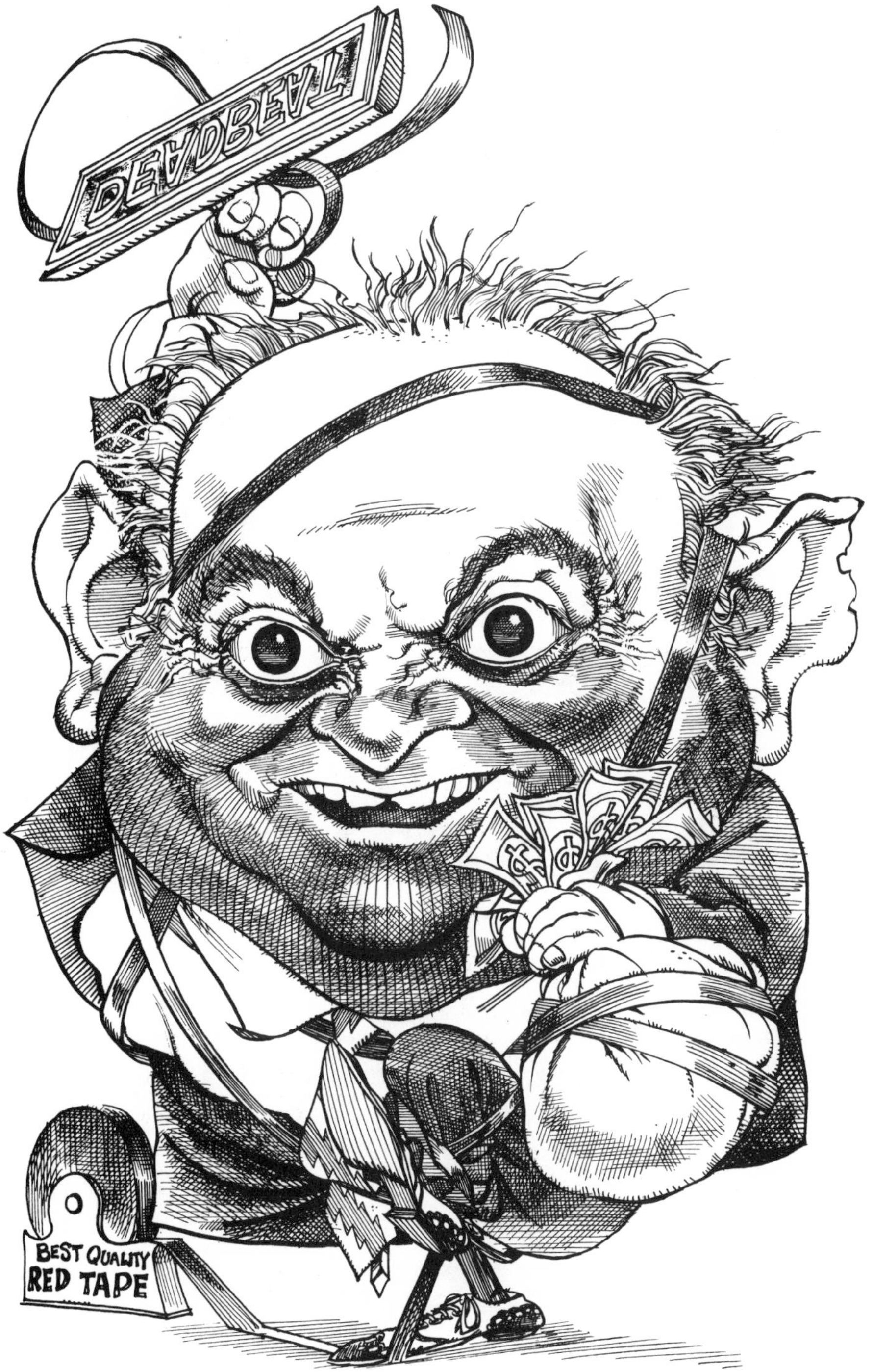
DEADBEAT
BEST QUALITY
RED TAPE

WANTED

**W.A.C.
'BUTCH' BENNETT**   **THE
SONG'N'DANCE KID**

TO ACCOUNT FOR THE
DISAPPEARANCE

OF

$98.3 MILLION

OF

PROVINCIAL FUNDS

LAST SEEN ABOARD THE

B.C. RAILWAY !

SOMEWHERE NORTH OF

VICTORIA

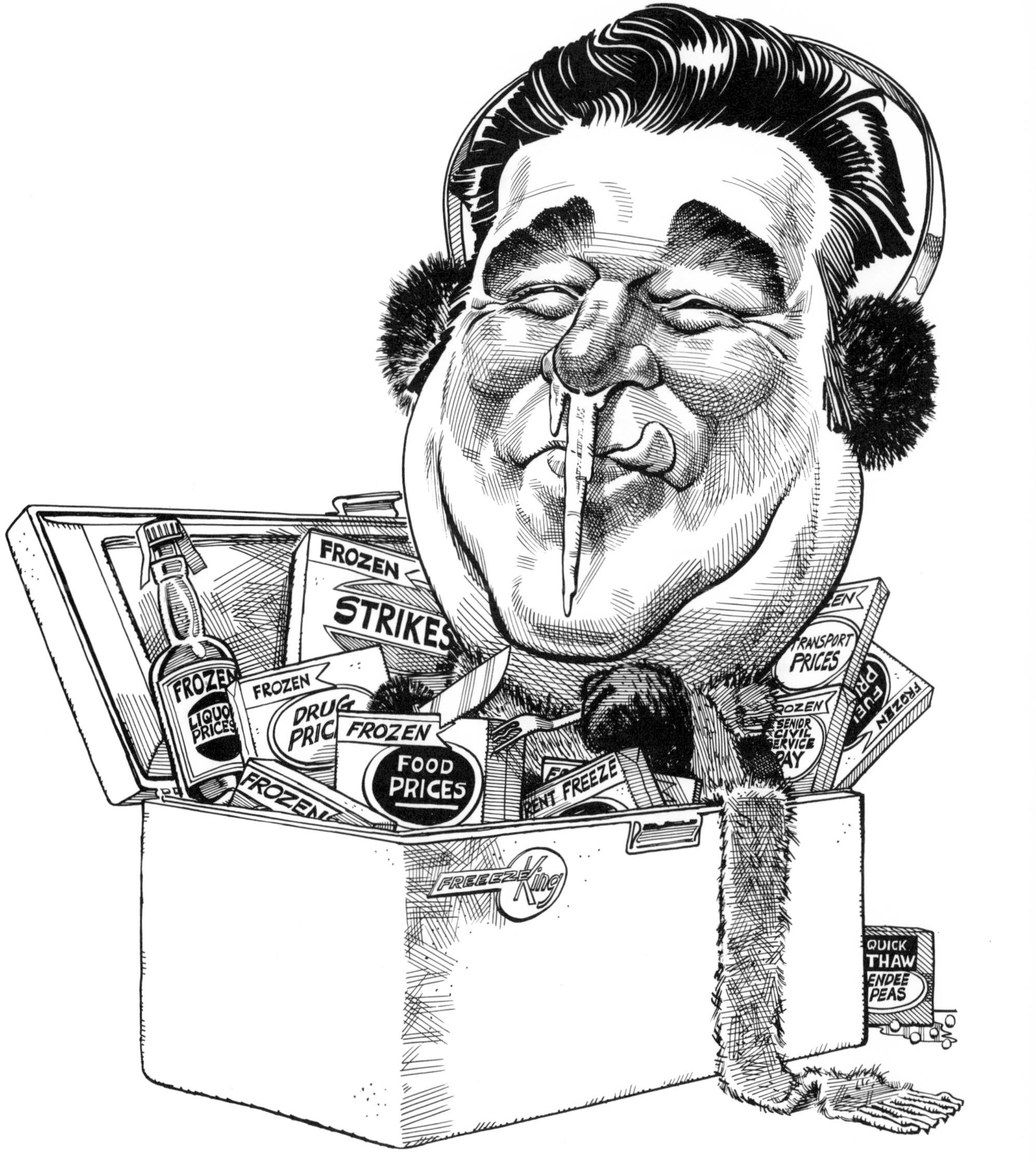
FROZEN
STRIKES
FROZEN
LIQUO
PRICES
FROZEN
DRUG
PRIC
FROZEN
FOOD
PRICES
FROZEN
RENT FREEZE
TRANSPORT
PRICES
FROZEN
SENIOR
CIVIL
SERVICE
PAY
FROZEN
FREEEZE King
QUICK
THAW
ENDEE
PEAS

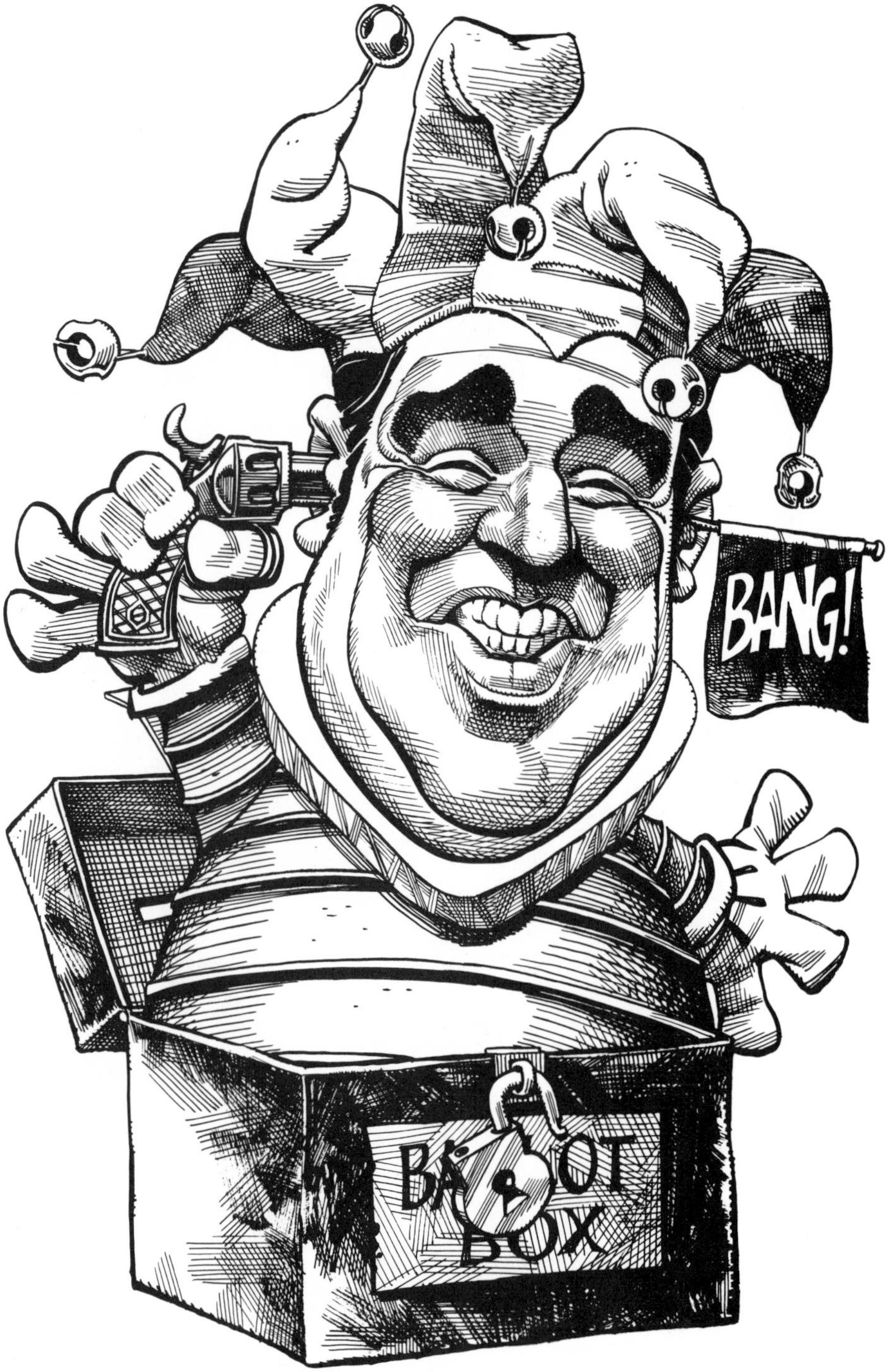
BANG!
BOX

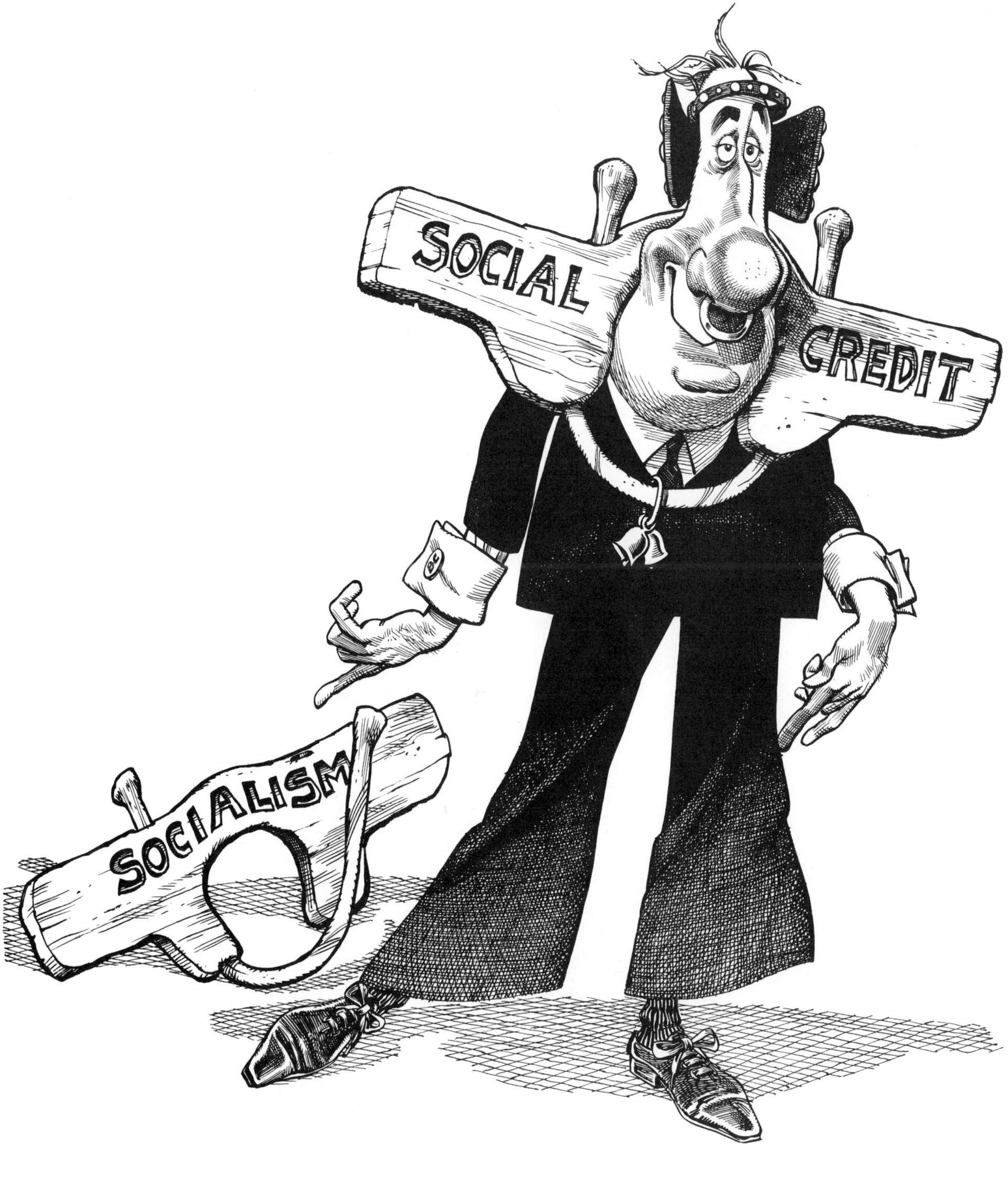
SOCIAL
CREDIT
SOCIALISM

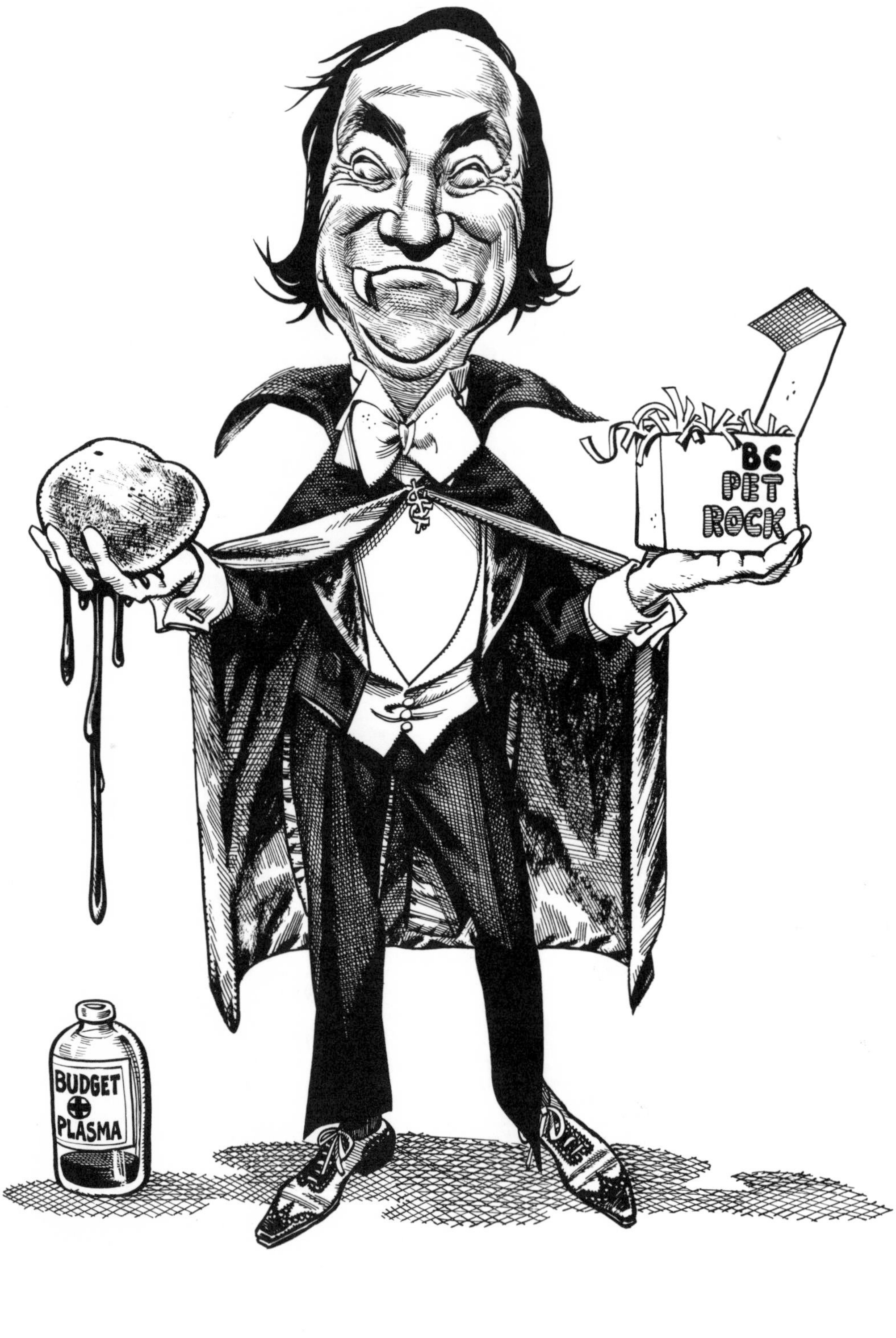
BC
PET
ROCK
BUDGET
PLASMA

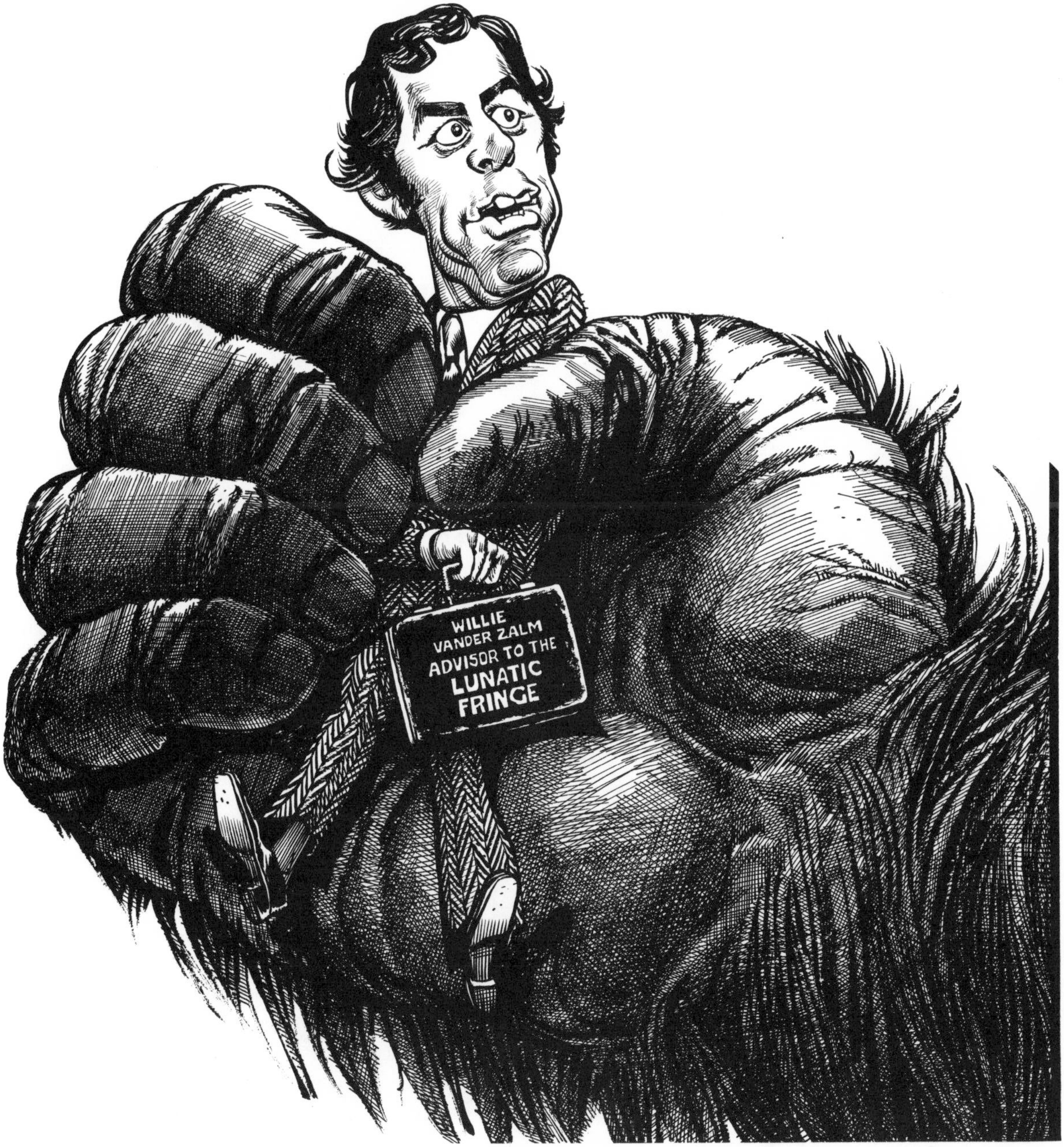
WILLIE
VANDER ZALM
ADVISOR TO THE
LUNATIC
FRINGE

"OK! OK! But remember, when we get to the roof of the legislature, *I* do the talking!"

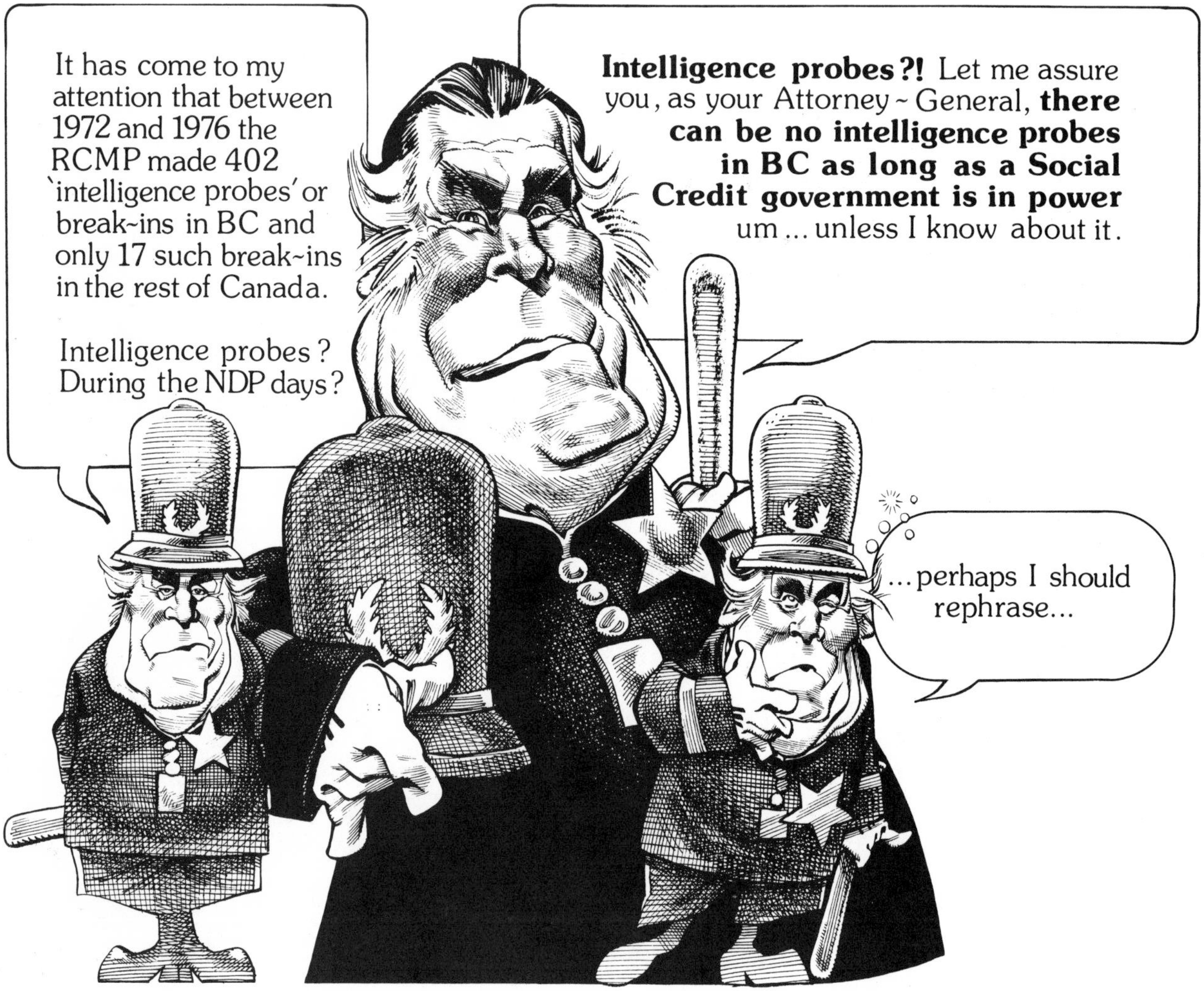
It has come to my attention that between 1972 and 1976 the RCMP made 402 'intelligence probes' or break~ins in BC and only 17 such break~ins in the rest of Canada.
Intelligence probes? During the NDP days?
Intelligence probes?! Let me assure you, as your Attorney ~ General, **there can be no intelligence probes in BC as long as a Social Credit government is in power** um ... unless I know about it.
...perhaps I should rephrase...

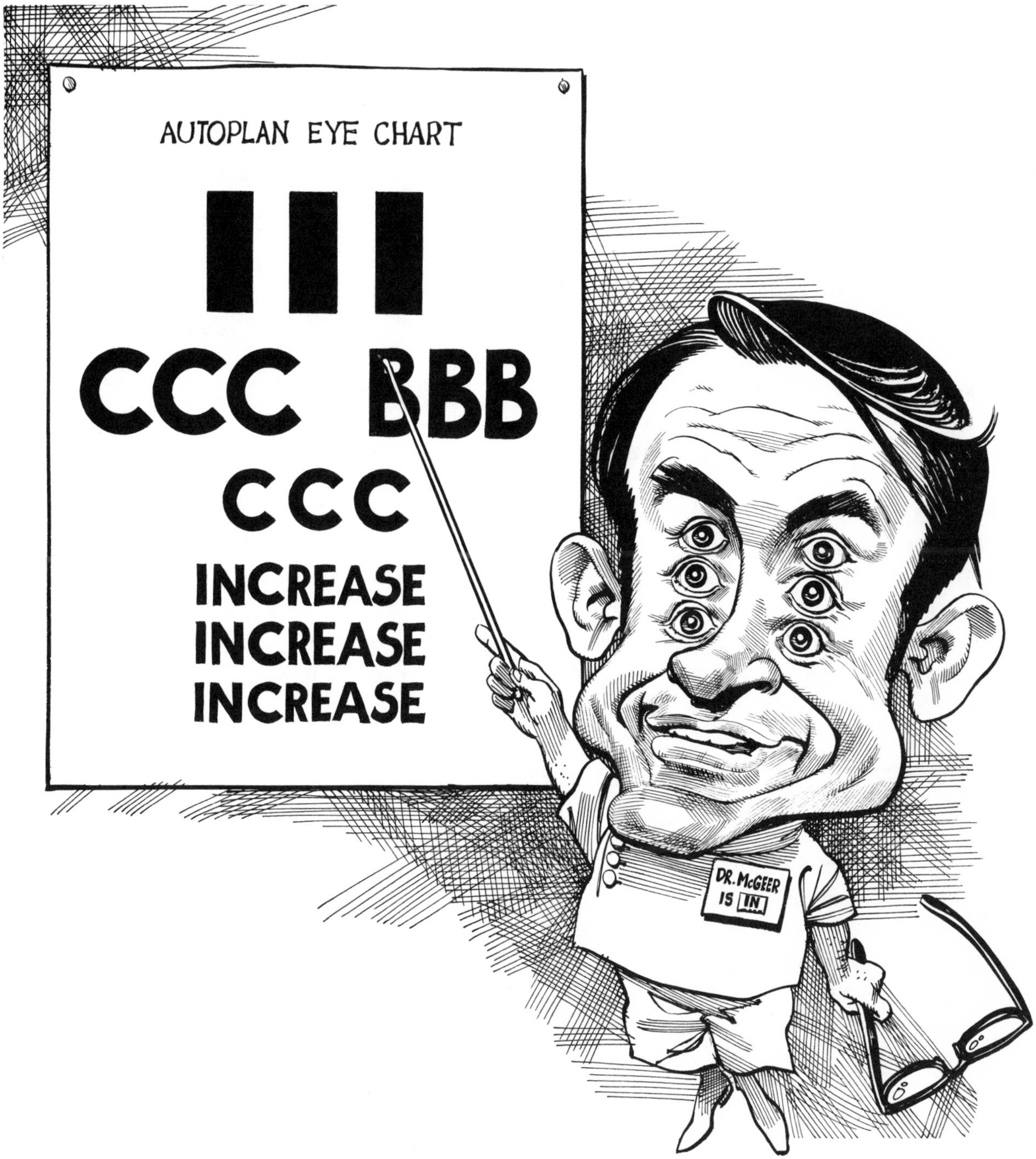
AUTOPLAN EYE CHART
III
CCC BBB
CCC
INCREASE
INCREASE
INCREASE
DR. McGEER IS IN

All the World's a Stage

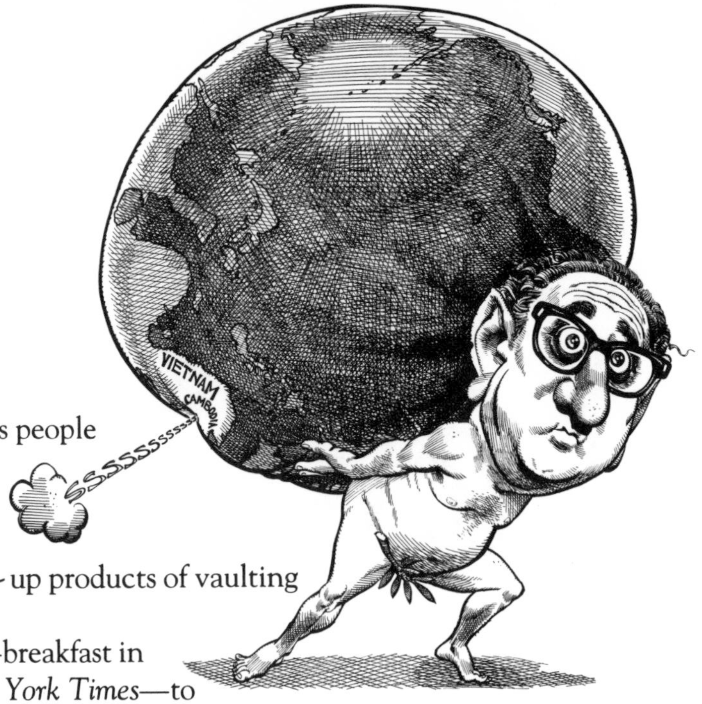
VIETNAM
CAMBODIA

Power is the greatest aphrodisiac of all.
— Henry Kissinger

Roy Peterson loves power. I should say he loves people who love power. If they combine power with pomposity, so much the better. Henry the K and Hoover and the Hearst apparition, Brezhnev, Pompidou, de Gaulle, all the puffed-up products of vaulting ambition.

We are lazy. We all want a Superman—breakfast in Washington, lunch in Cairo, ego in the *New York Times*—to make the 6 o'clock news not only palatable but also understandable and soluble. That was Kissinger in his brief career, rocketing across the headlines and newscasts on the way to his best-selling royalties. The disservice was in giving the impression that one man could actually solve the problems. Will history really regard the mercurial Henry as the major figure that our excited headlines told us he must be?—the inventor of diplomacy by jet engine, Metternich out of Boeing. Don't ask High-Speed Henry; he's too busy back at Harvard typing out his notes.

The dutiful Gerry Ford and Jimmy Carter—our latest two examples of the triumph of ambition over intellect—needed such an agile mind married to a strong stomach, the both impervious to jet lag. Henry was the academic flasher, his trench coat a peace-teaser to the Middle East while his dull bosses wrestled with problems more to their ken: wheat support programs and gasoline line-ups. Peterson early on detected in Carter what has only recently become so apparent: his essential confusion. Puzzlement is written on his wrinkled face. He is, in truth, a slick bumpkin, who achieved power simply by running harder and longer than anyone else. He is the Candidate from Attrition, his major achievement being his success in stealthily snatching power before anyone had a chance to figure him out.

Here is the shrewd user of power, J. Edgar Hoover, the sleaze on high, who realized that smut was power, that information (especially information that could be used for official blackmail) was power. With his tail of video tape and his mind obsessed with salacious secrets, he well qualifies for consideration by Peterson, a high honour awarded to not just everyone. (It was Lyndon Johnson, that master manipulator, who testified to J. Edgar's fearsome power. When LBJ was asked why he had not sacked Hoover as promised, he explained: "I decided that it was safer to have him inside the tent pissing out than outside the tent pissing in.")

Peterson loves Leonid Brezhnev's face. There is an entire acre of casehardened flesh to roam in, seams of contempt and arroyos of cruelty, eyebrows like Normandy hedges and ears that take on a life of their own, jowls that meld into shoulders without waiting for a neck, those pig-like eyes gauzed with inscrutability. One can almost sense the artist's glee at approaching the subject. Power corrupts the Soviet president and power delights Peterson's pen.

There is the sanctimonious Indira Gandhi, piously nuclear, and the humourless Hearst girl, the sociological transvestite, providing the ultimate triumph of the counterculture by injecting it with the ambience of the debutante. How ironic that her merciless grandfather, who perfected fiction-as-journalism and invented wars, watches from the grave as the family name is brought to ultimate disgrace via a plot that even his most imaginative hired hacks could not have concocted. Power has its own rewards.

Pompidou of France, persisting in a nuclear test on Mururoa in the South Pacific, is a true test of the Peterson passion. It was Pompidou as Le Sommelier Grotesque that won first prize for Peterson in the 1973 International Salon of Cartoons. His reincarnation of the prime minister, a year later, as Madame de Pompidou, with bomb tips as nipples, is equally brutal (i.e., truthful).

Charles de Gaulle, surely, must have been the cartoonists' dream. All the required ingredients are there—power, pomposity, arrogance, not an ounce of humour—a walking balloon waiting for darts. One cannot imagine de Gaulle requesting an original to hang in his study. He was, after all—applying the Kissinger definition—an absolute bundle of sexual vibrations. He was his own best portrait.

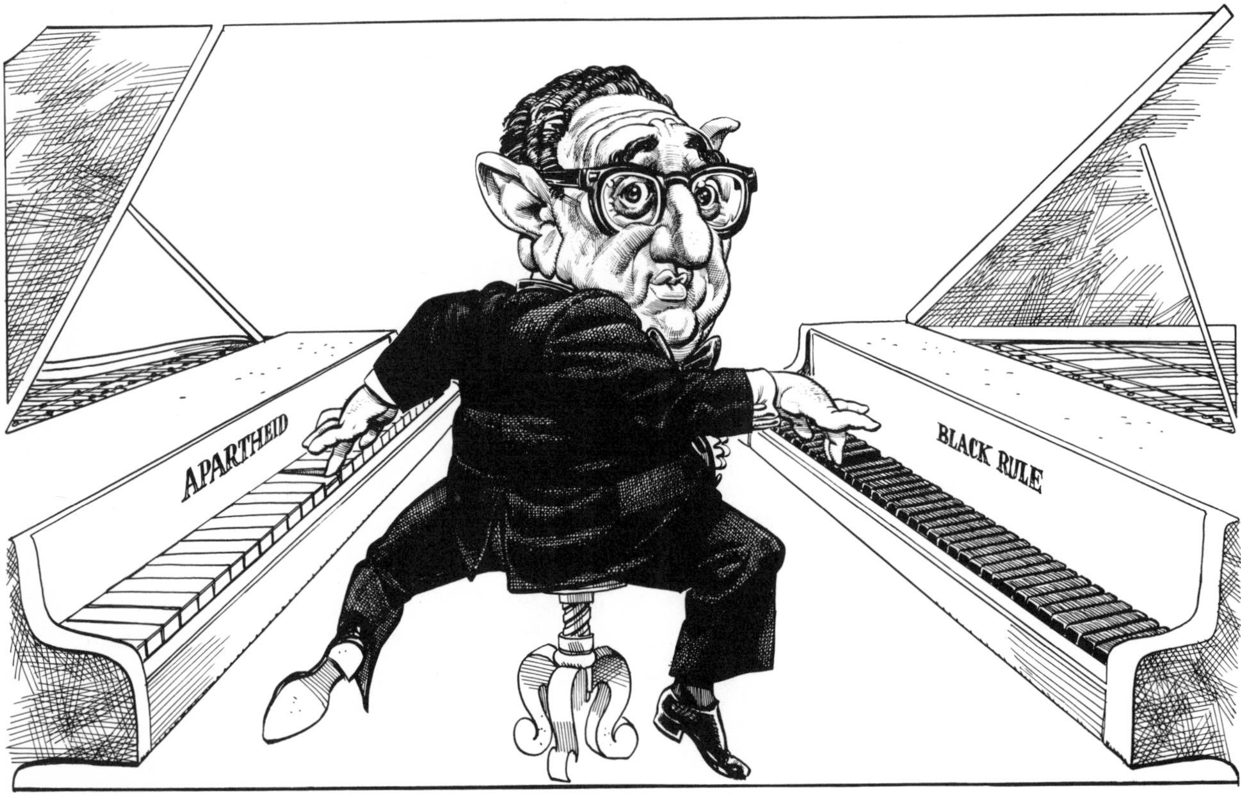
APARTHEID
BLACK RULE

Harmony Henry

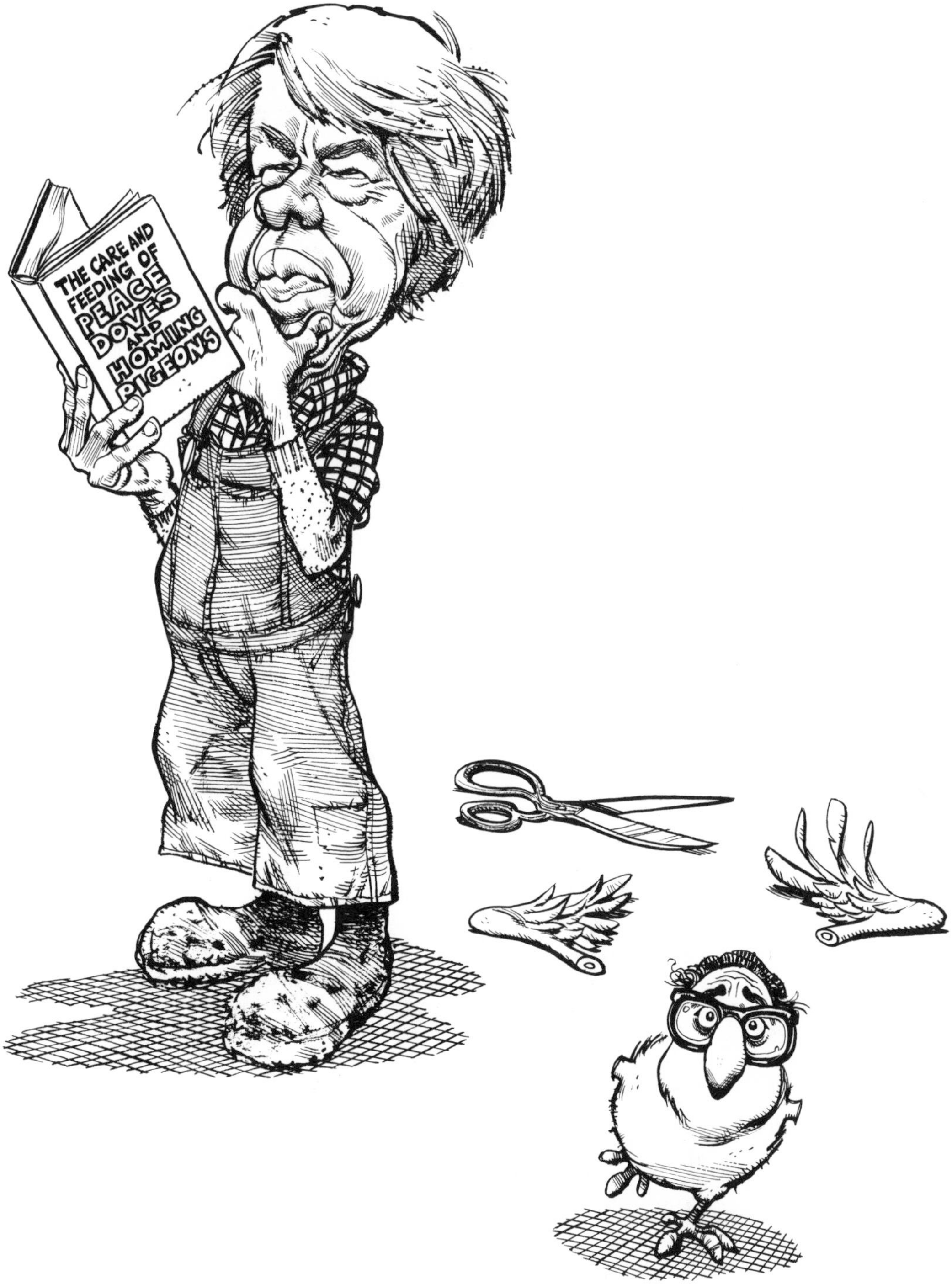
THE CARE AND FEEDING OF
PEACE
DOVES
AND
HOMING
PIGEONS

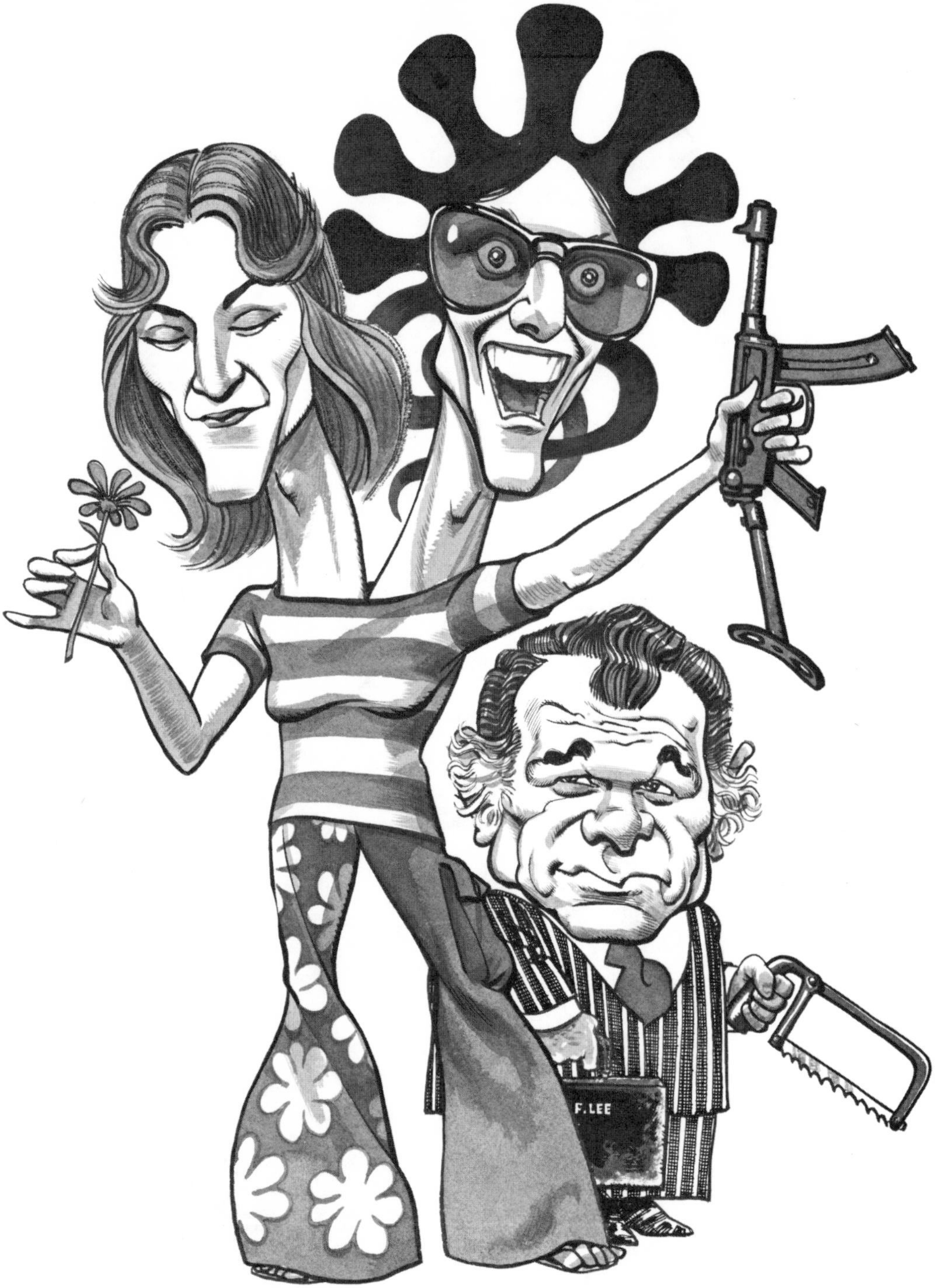
F.LEE

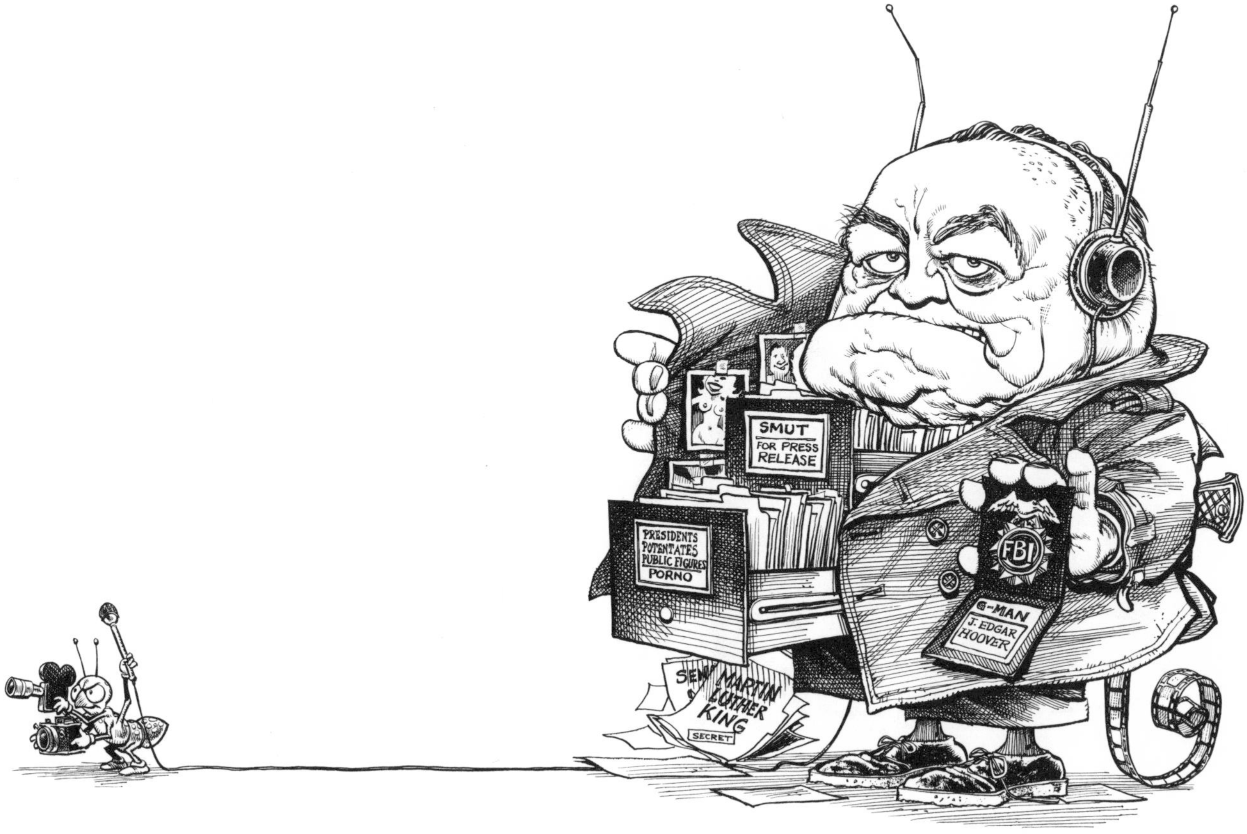
SMUT
FOR PRESS RELEASE
PRESIDENTS
POTENTATES
PUBLIC FIGURES
PORNO
FBI
G-MAN
J. EDGAR HOOVER
MARTIN LUTHER KING
SECRET

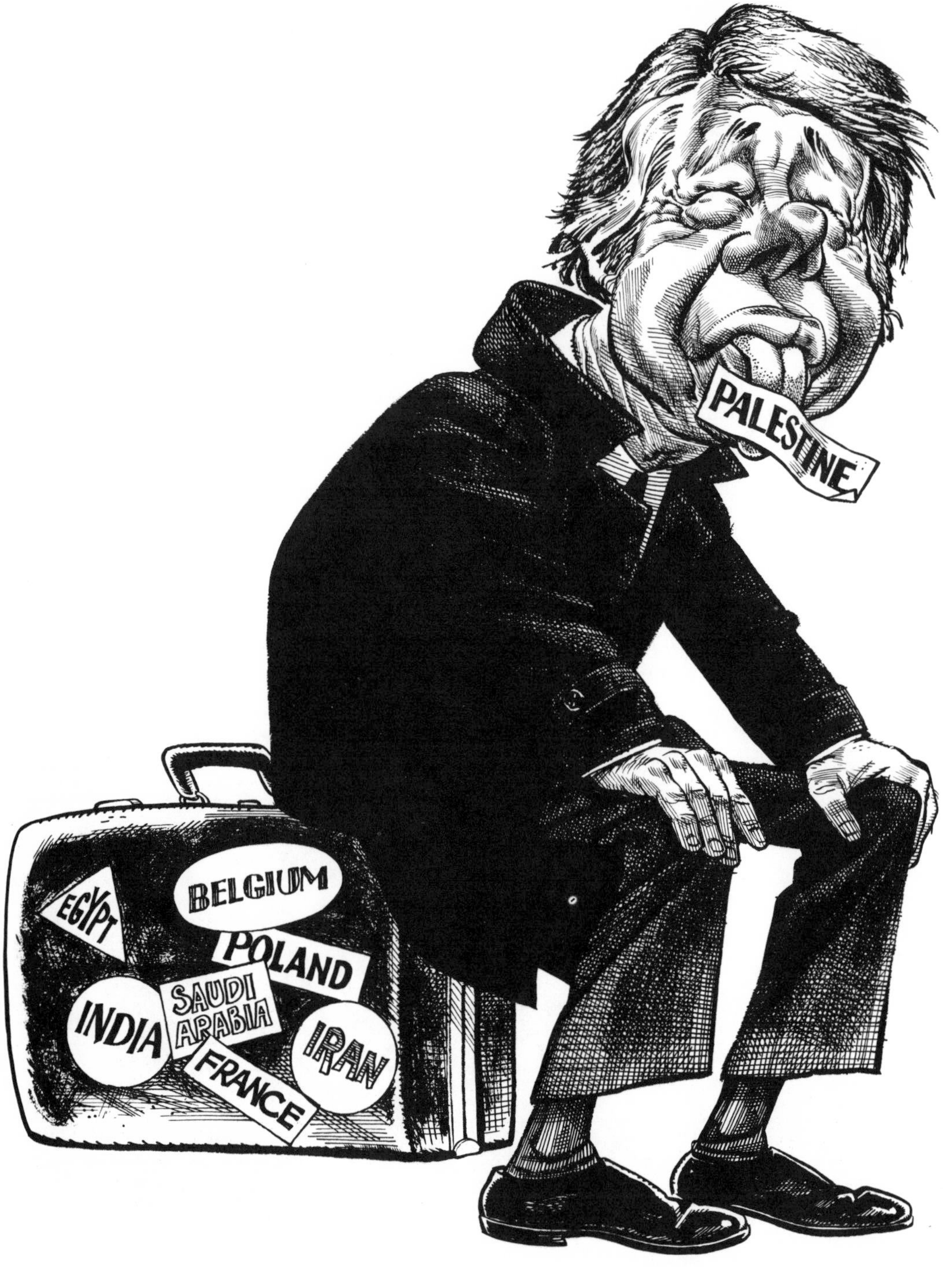
PALESTINE
BELGIUM
EGYPT
POLAND
SAUDI ARABIA
INDIA
IRAN
FRANCE

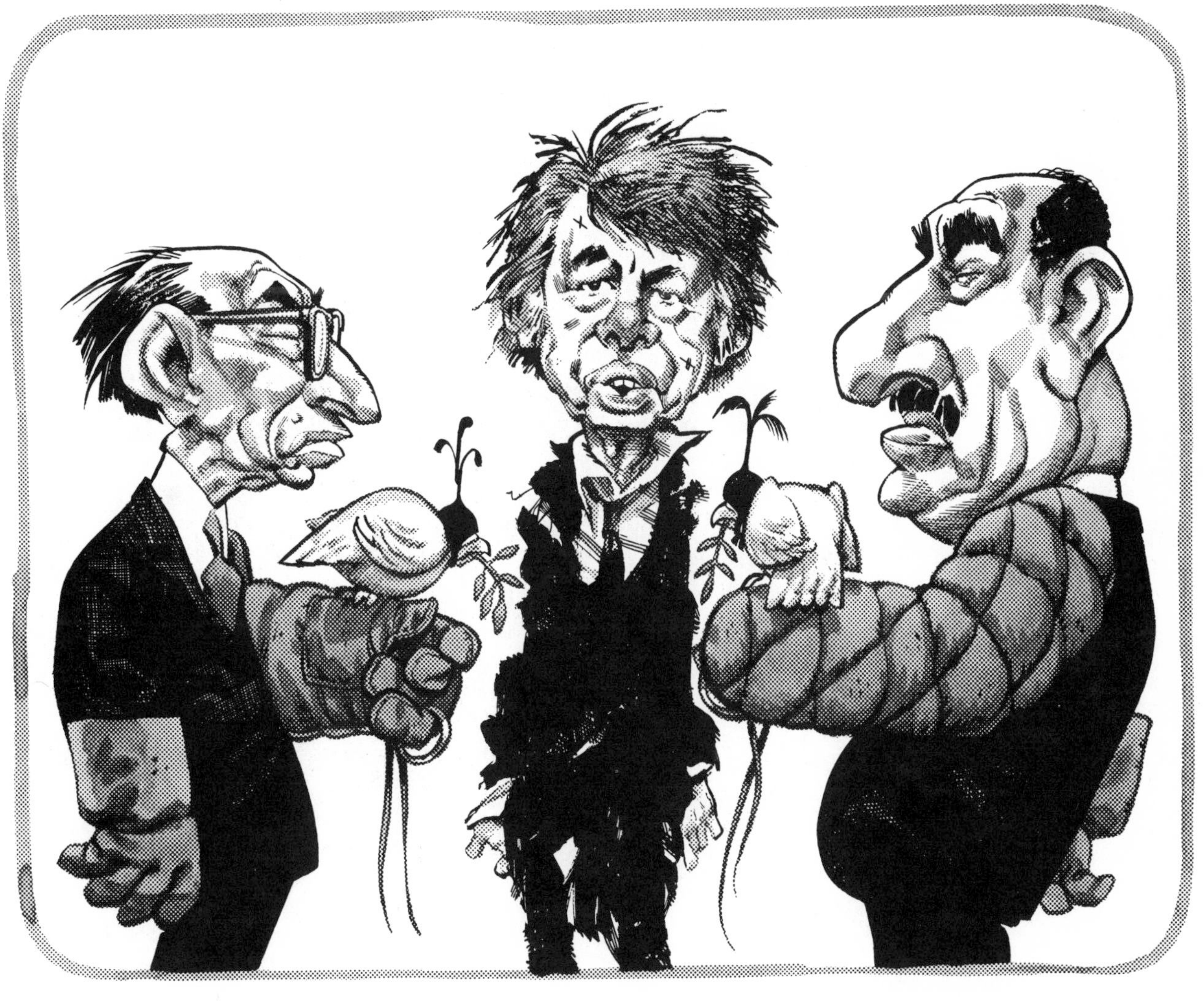

"Both parties have confirmed that our determined search for peace has escalated into an aggressive hunt for peace."

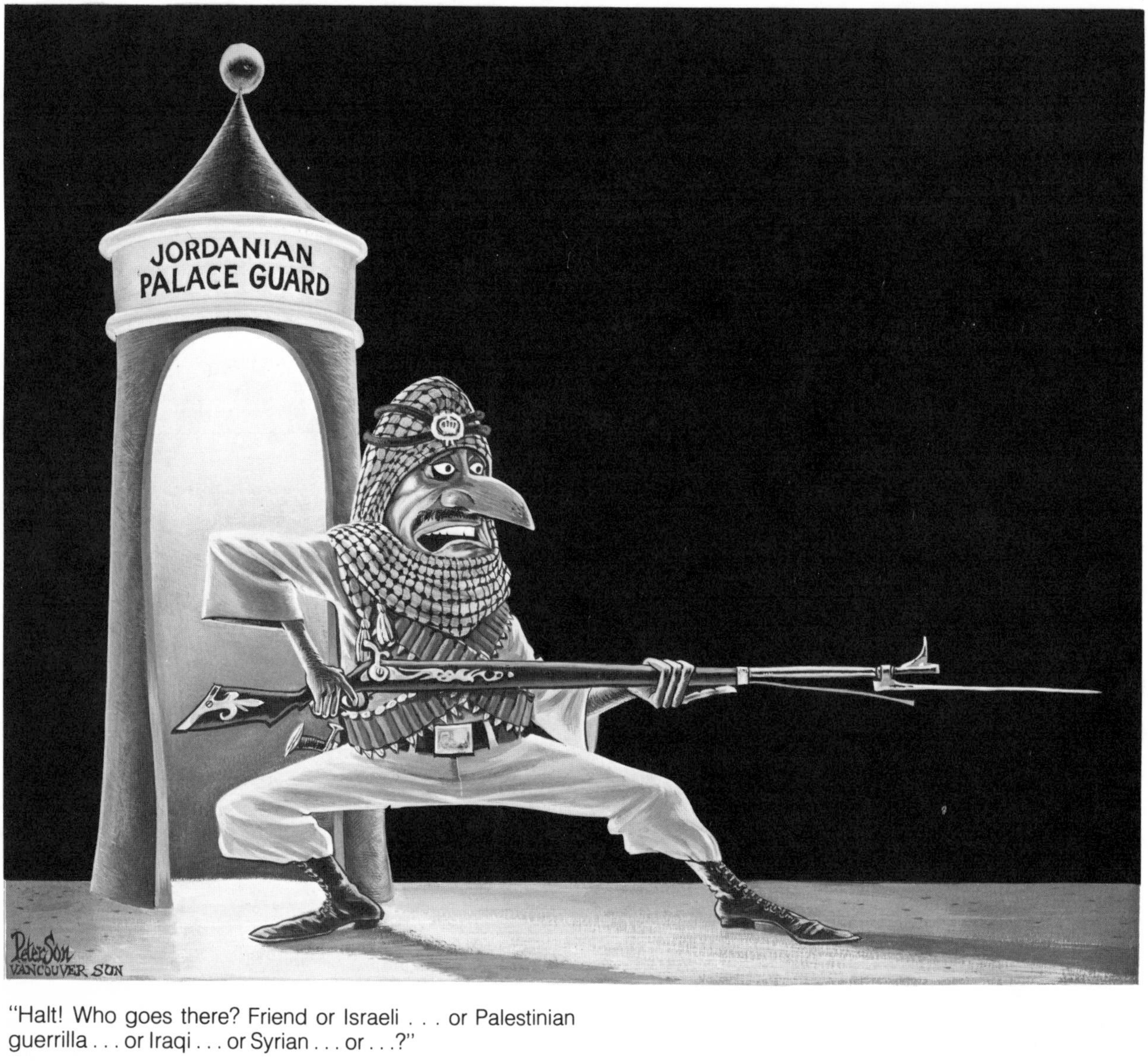
JORDANIAN
PALACE GUARD
Peterson
VANCOUVER SUN

"Halt! Who goes there? Friend or Israeli . . . or Palestinian guerrilla . . . or Iraqi . . . or Syrian . . . or . . .?"

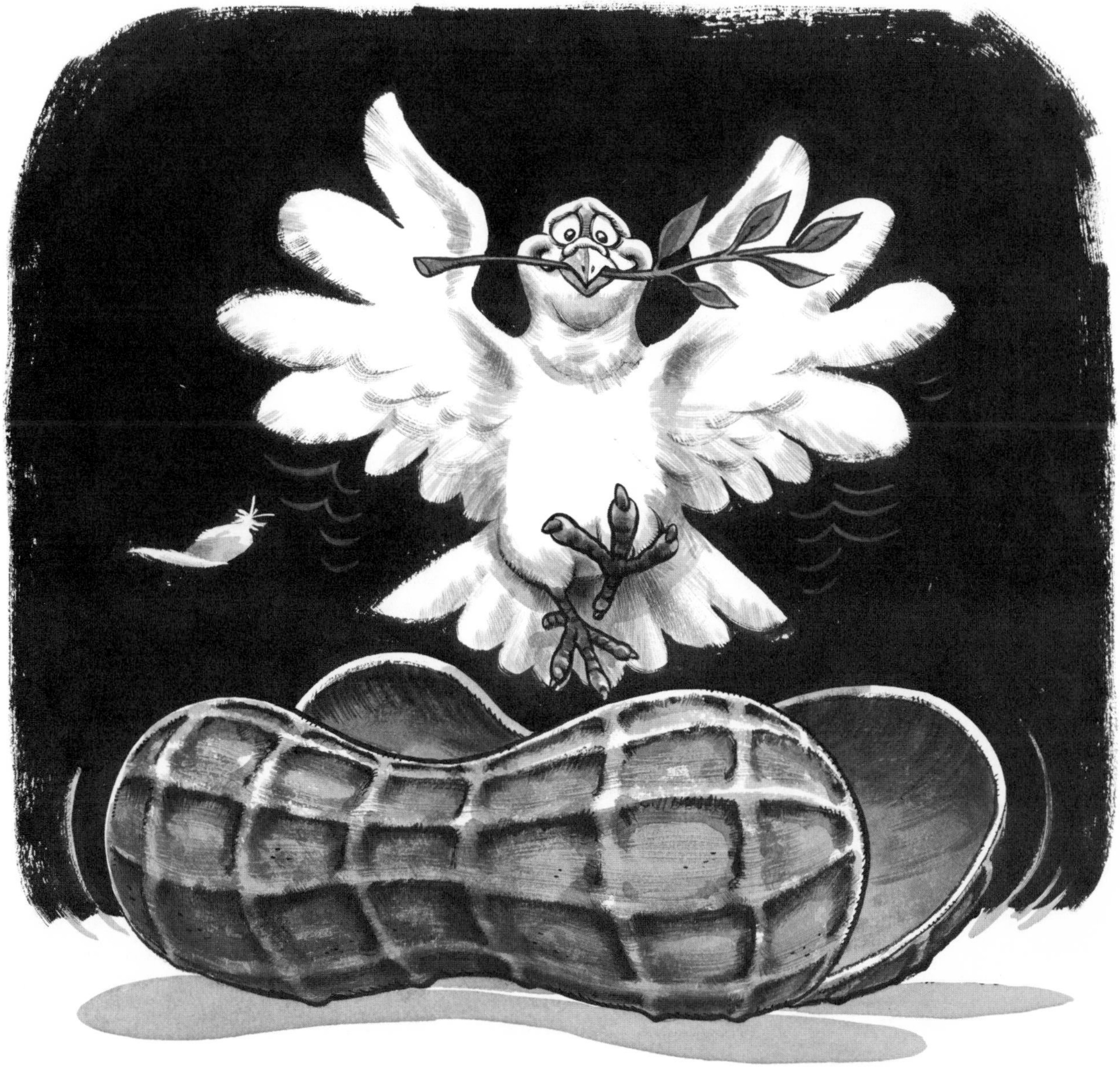

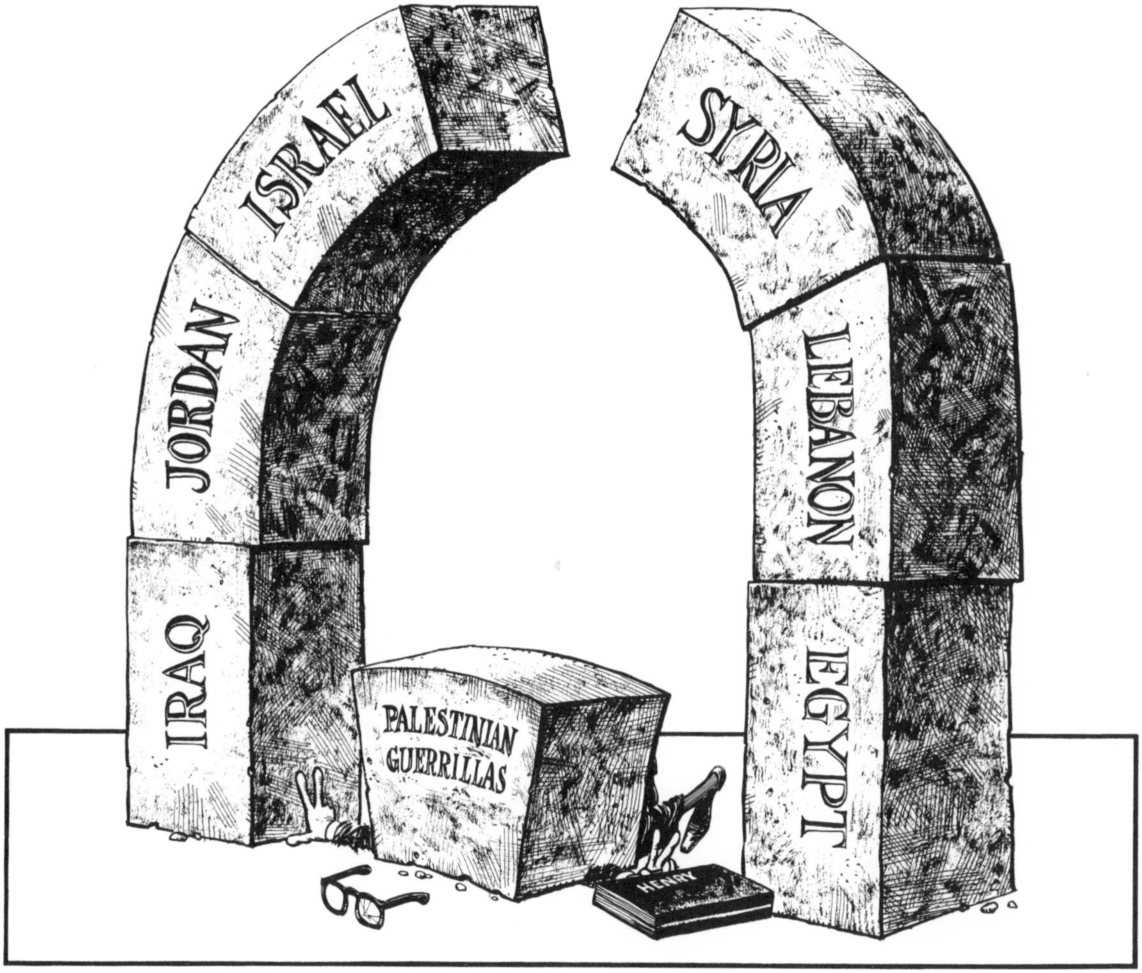
ISRAEL
JORDAN
IRAQ
SYRIA
LEBANON
EGYPT
PALESTINIAN
GUERRILLAS
HENRY

Peace Arch

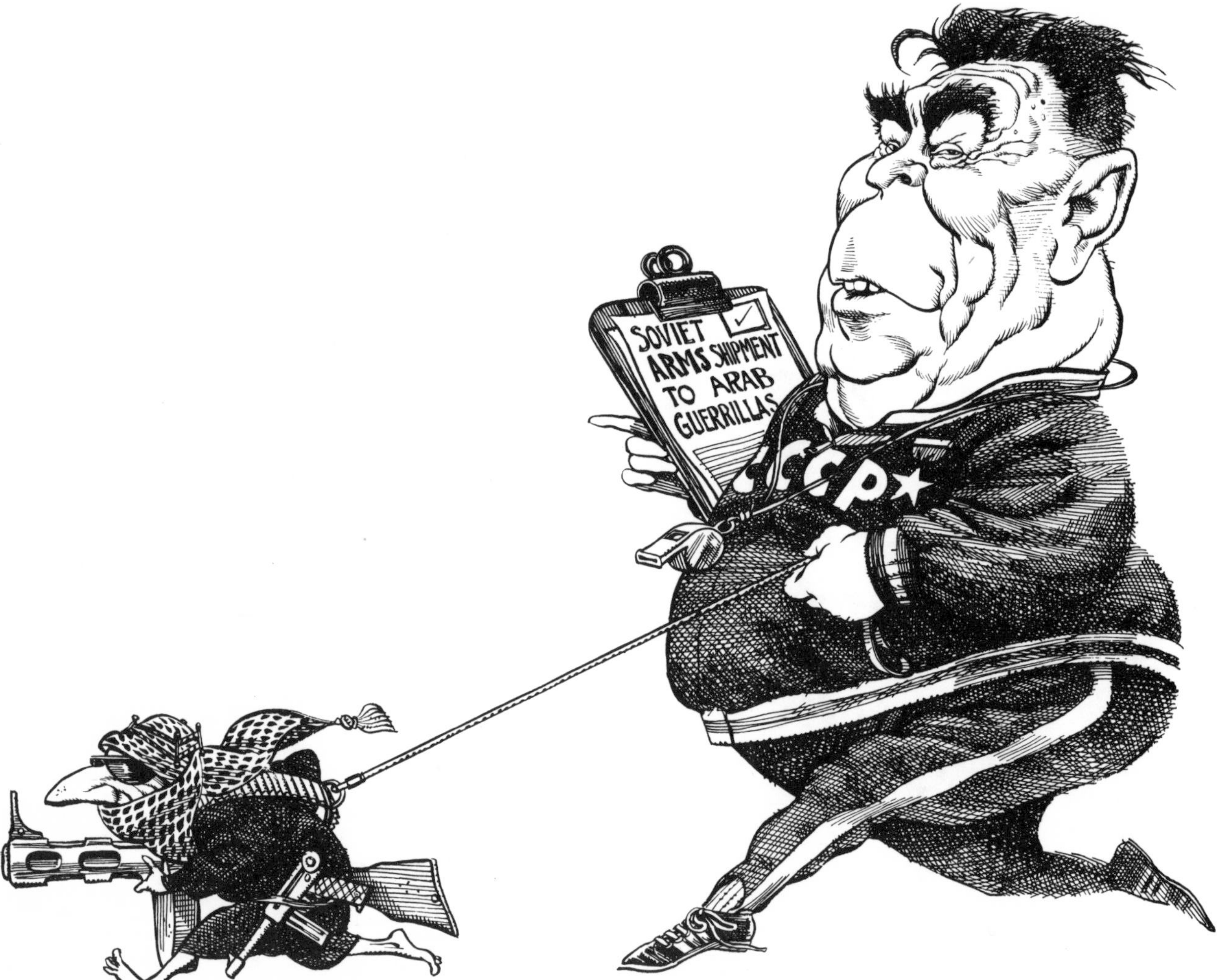
SOVIET ARMS SHIPMENT TO ARAB GUERRILLAS
CCCP

"Professional or amateur, one must stay in shape between Olympics, too . . ."

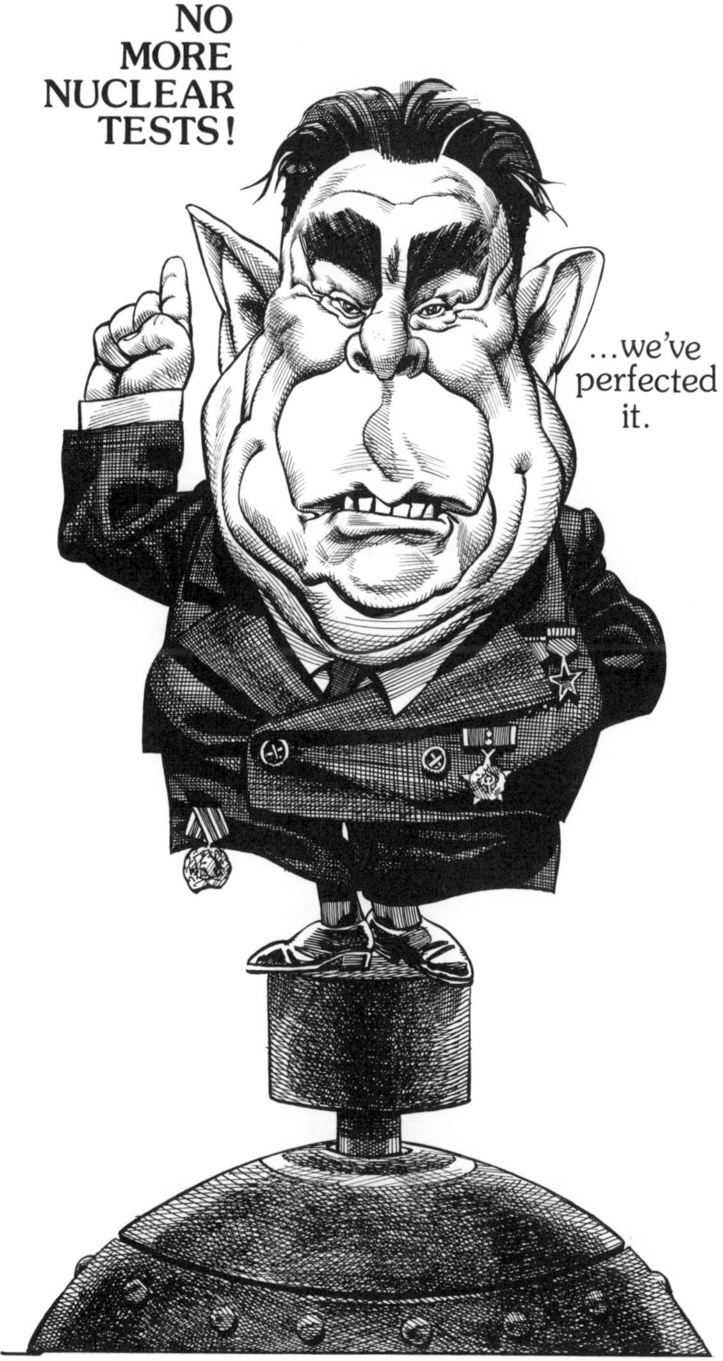
NO MORE NUCLEAR TESTS!
...we've perfected it.

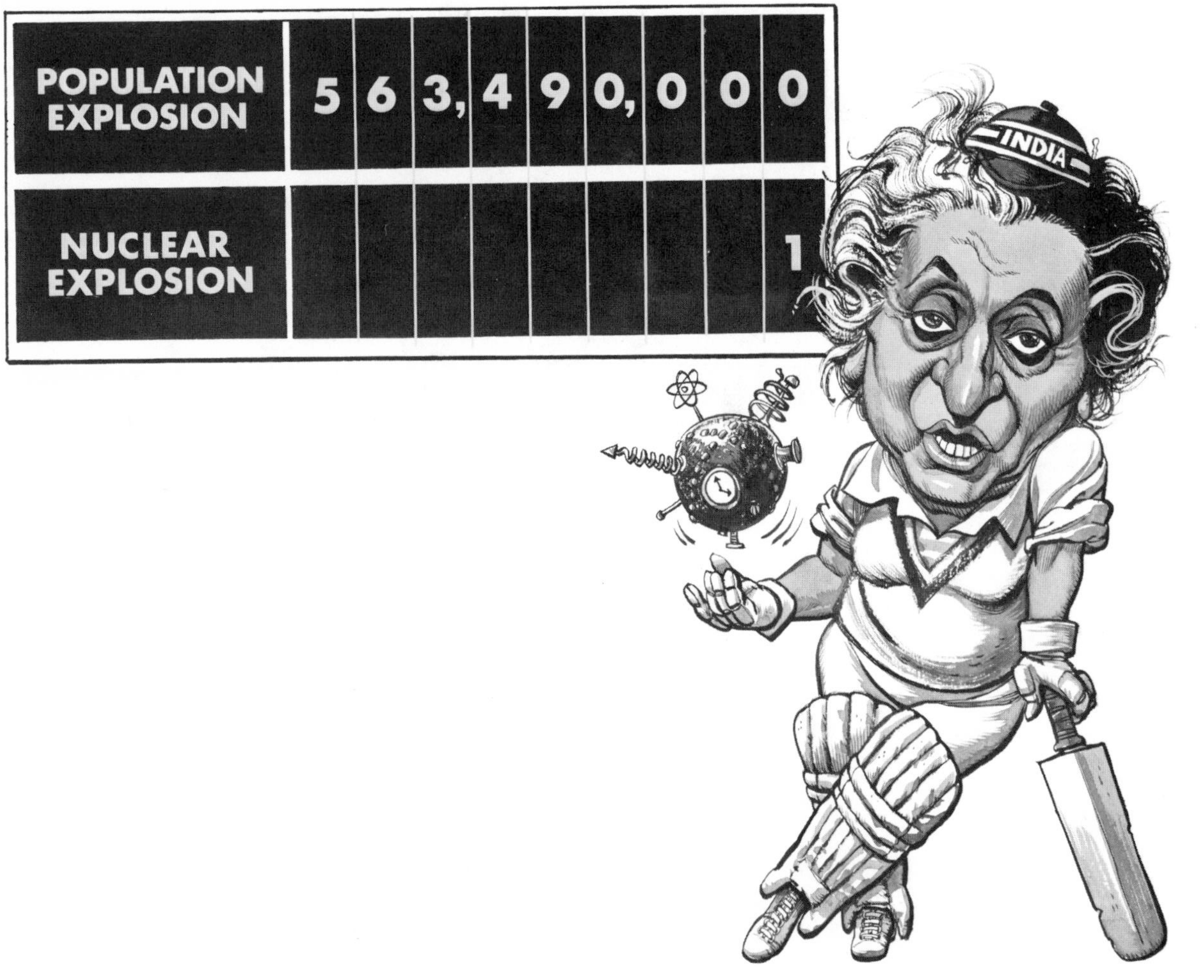
POPULATION EXPLOSION
563,490,000
NUCLEAR EXPLOSION
1
INDIA

"Who says it's not cricket?"

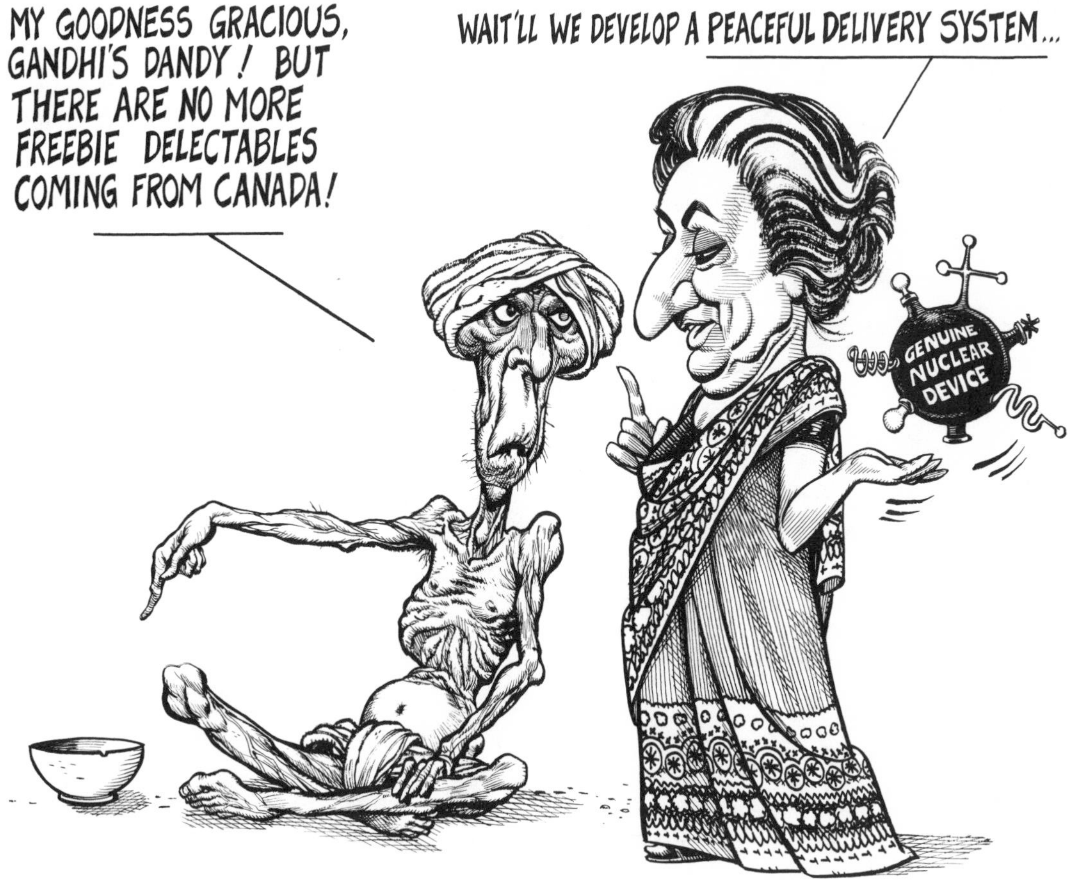
MY GOODNESS GRACIOUS, GANDHI'S DANDY! BUT THERE ARE NO MORE FREEBIE DELECTABLES COMING FROM CANADA!
WAIT'LL WE DEVELOP A PEACEFUL DELIVERY SYSTEM...
GENUINE NUCLEAR DEVICE

Nuclear Reaction

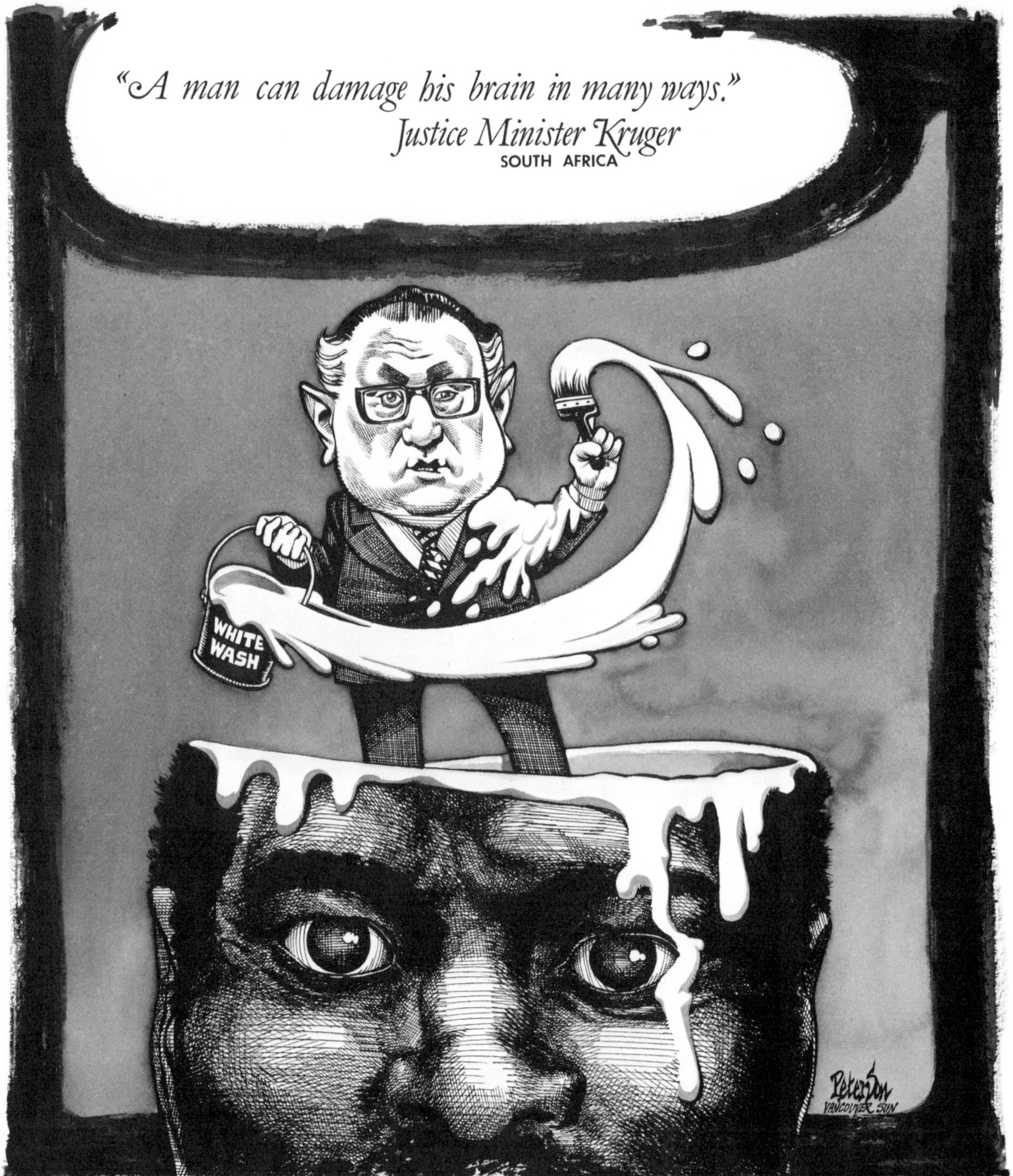
"A man can damage his brain in many ways."
Justice Minister Kruger
SOUTH AFRICA
WHITE WASH
Peterson
VANCOUVER SUN

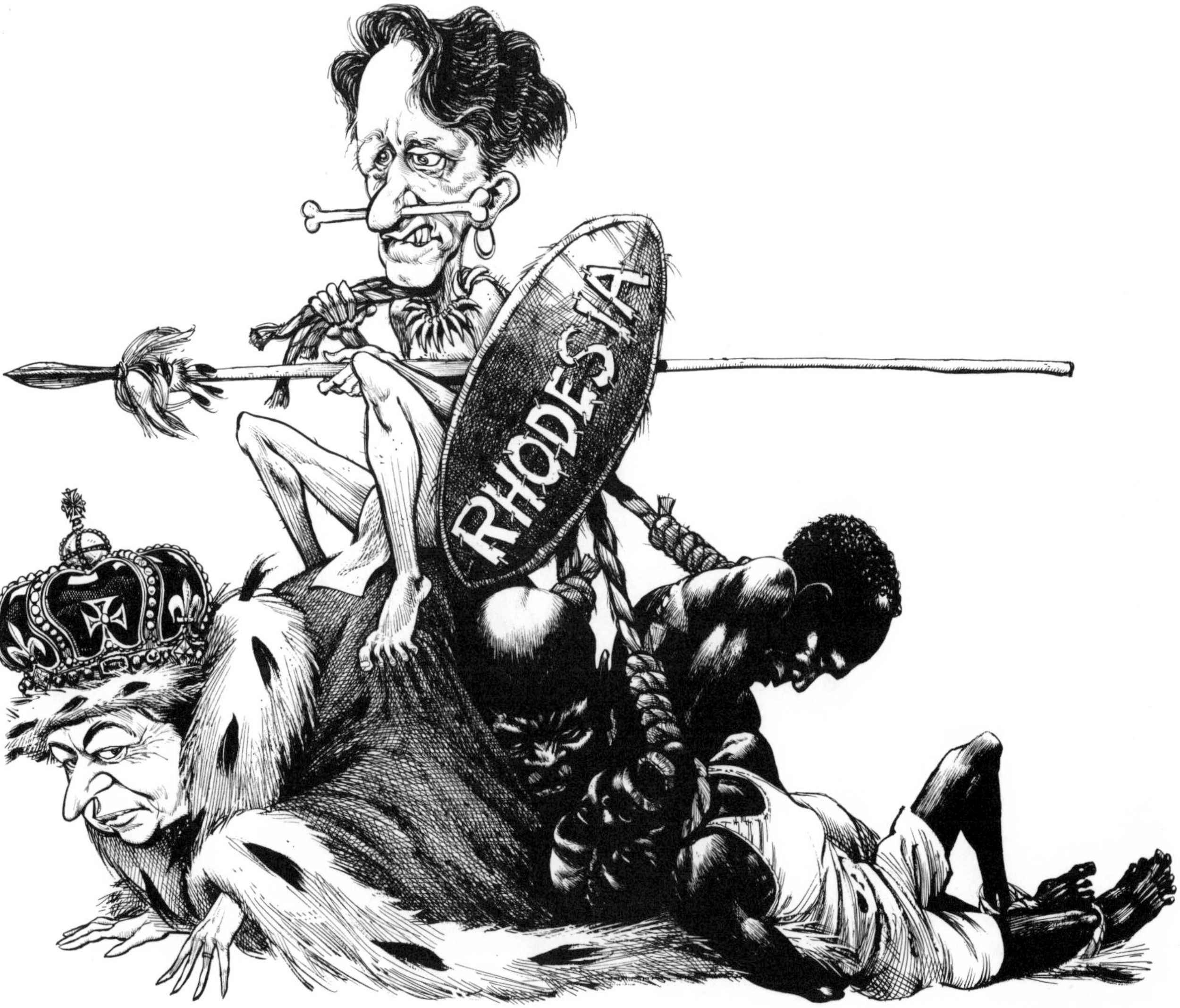
RHODESIA

The White Man Burden

Winner in the last race: Retail Price Index, by 'Inflation,' out of 'Control.'

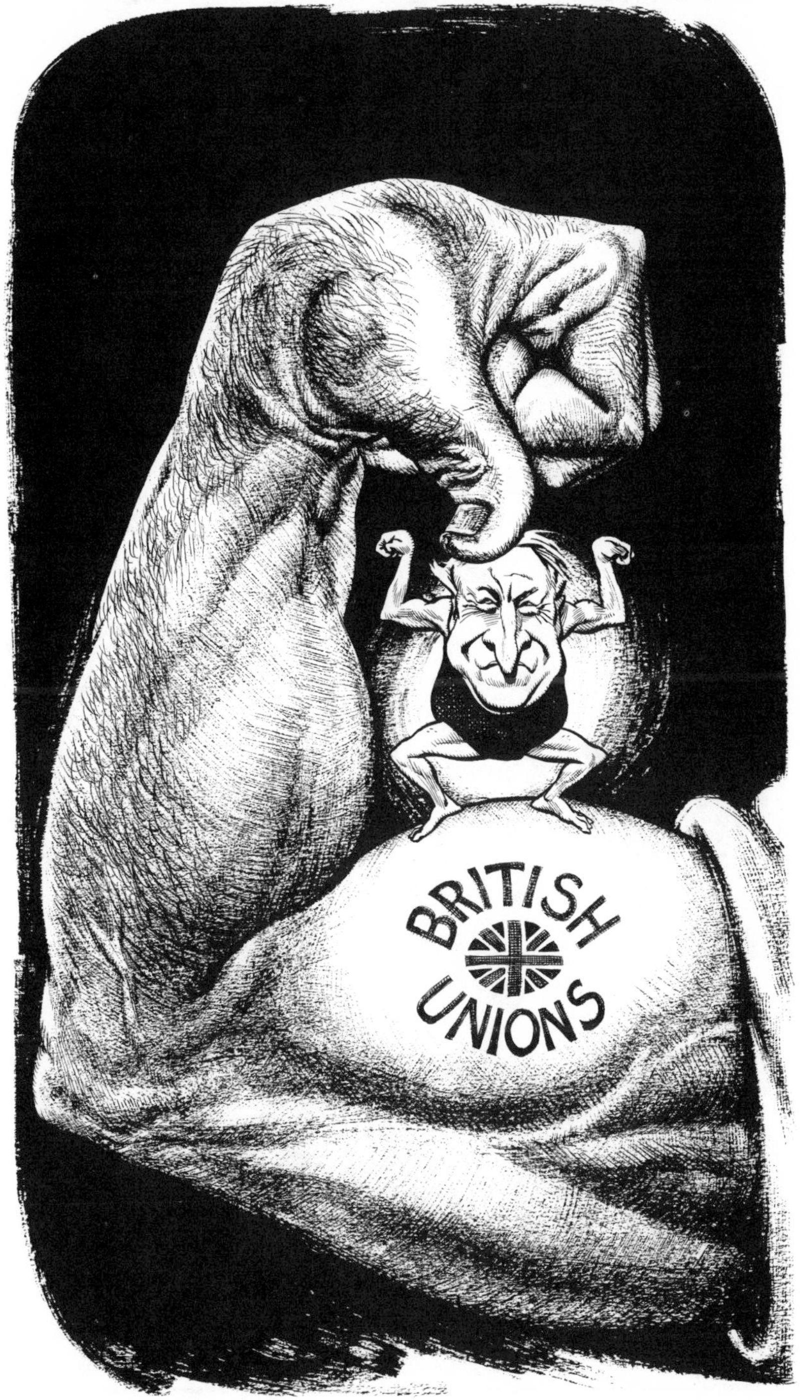
BRITISH
UNIONS

Ruling Britannia

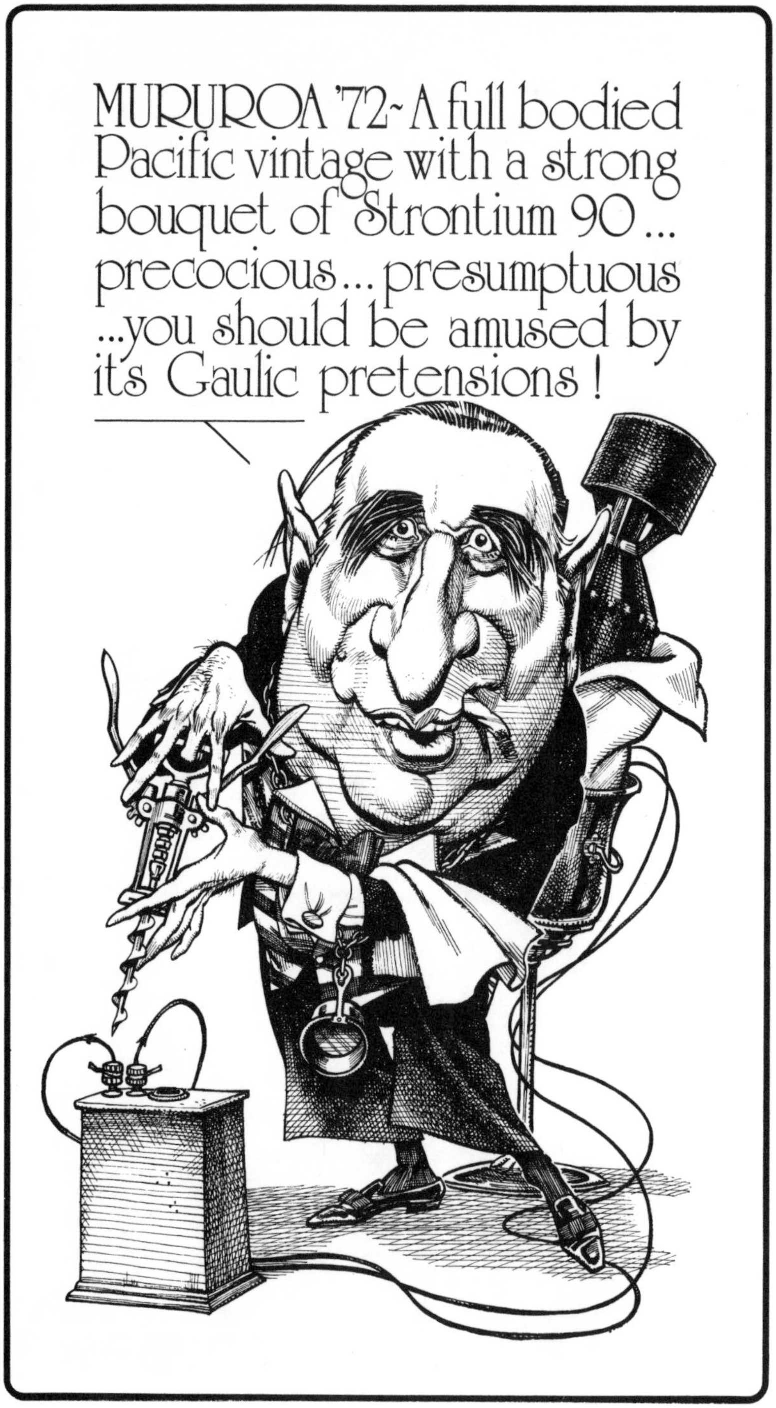
MURUROA '72~ A full bodied
Pacific vintage with a strong
bouquet of Strontium 90 ...
precocious ... presumptuous
...you should be amused by
its Gaulic pretensions !

Le Sommelier Grotesque

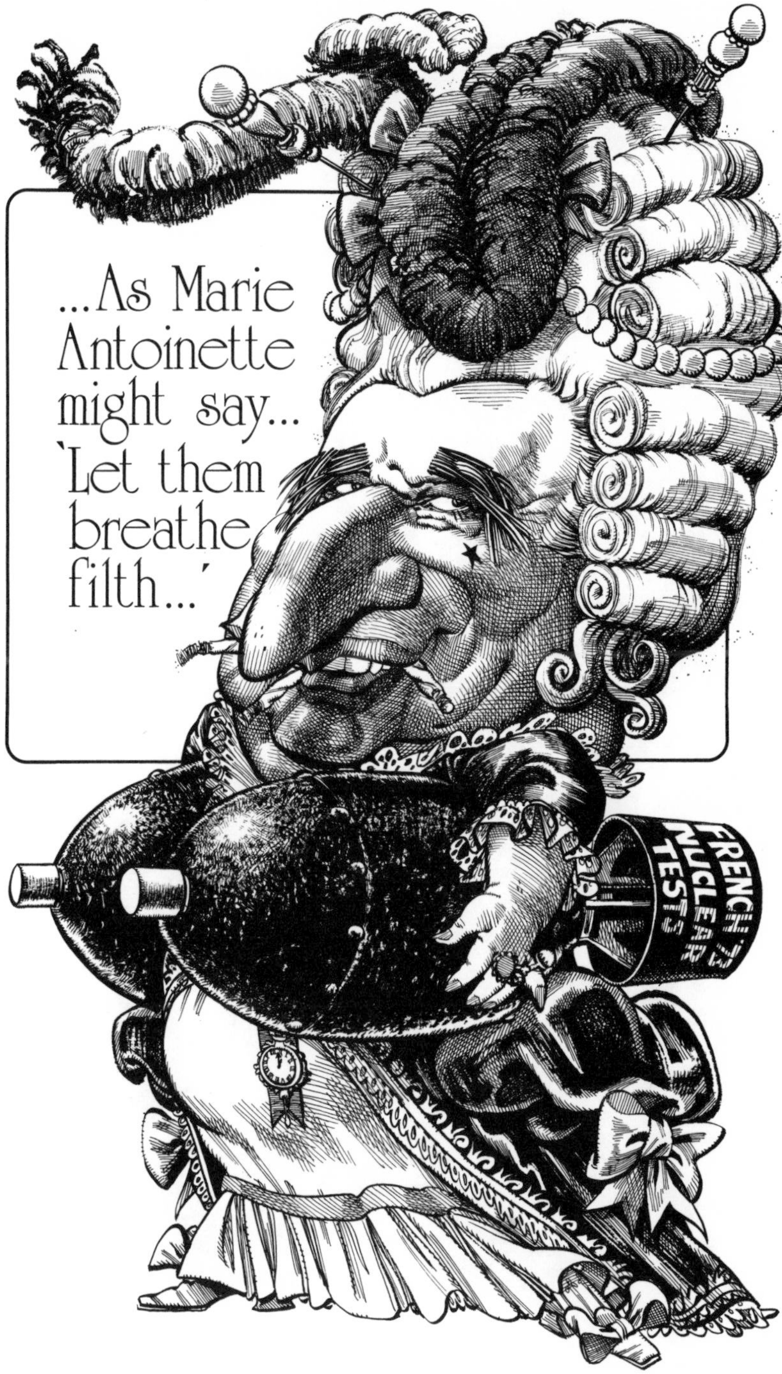
...As Marie Antoinette might say... 'Let them breathe filth...'
FRENCH '73 NUCLEAR TESTS

Madame de Pompidou

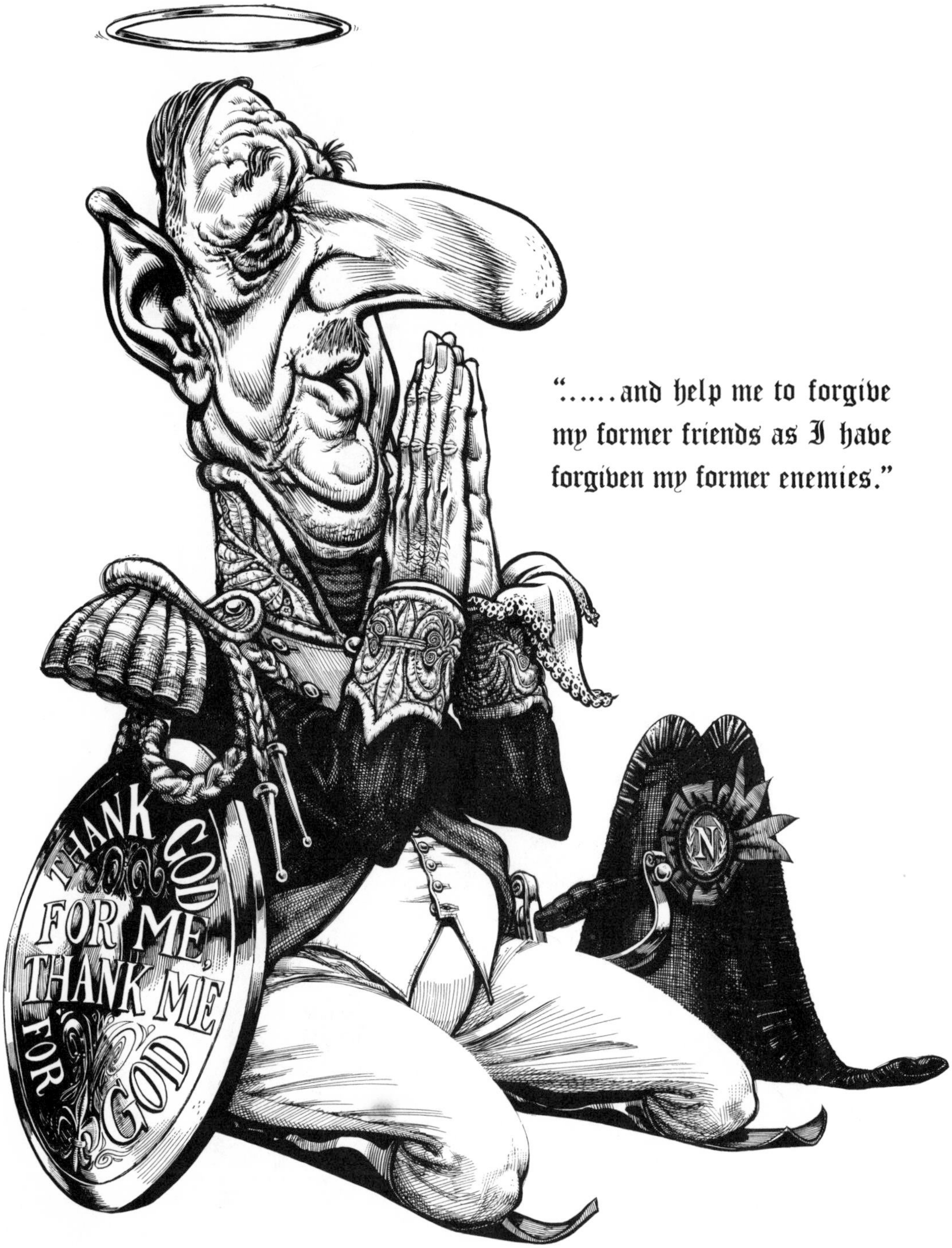
THANK GOD
FOR ME,
THANK ME
FOR GOD

"......and help me to forgive my former friends as I have forgiven my former enemies."

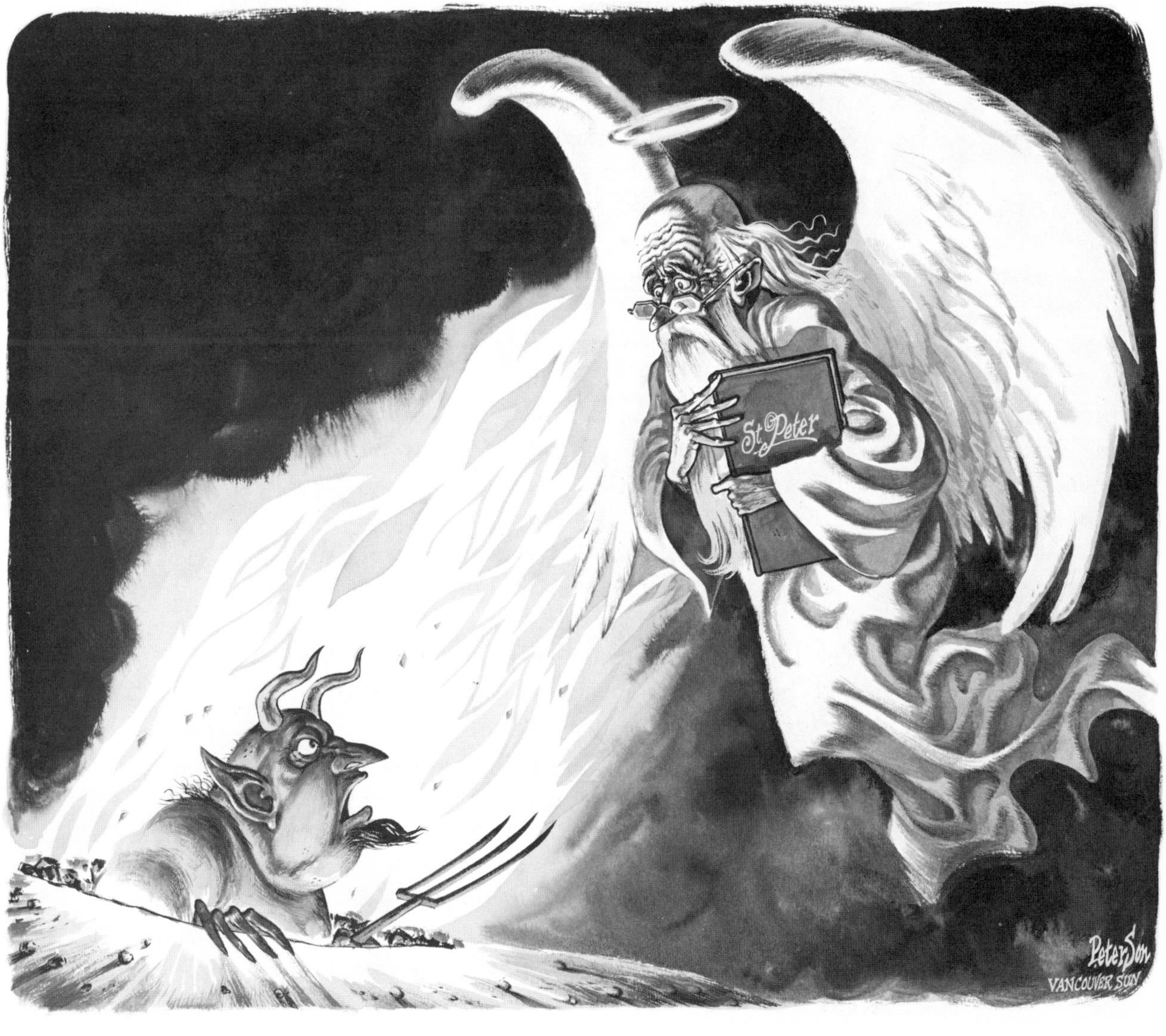
St Peter
PeterSon
VANCOUVER SUN

"It's been Earth on Hell since you sent down that last batch of Protestants and Catholics from Ireland!!!"

A World Unto Himself

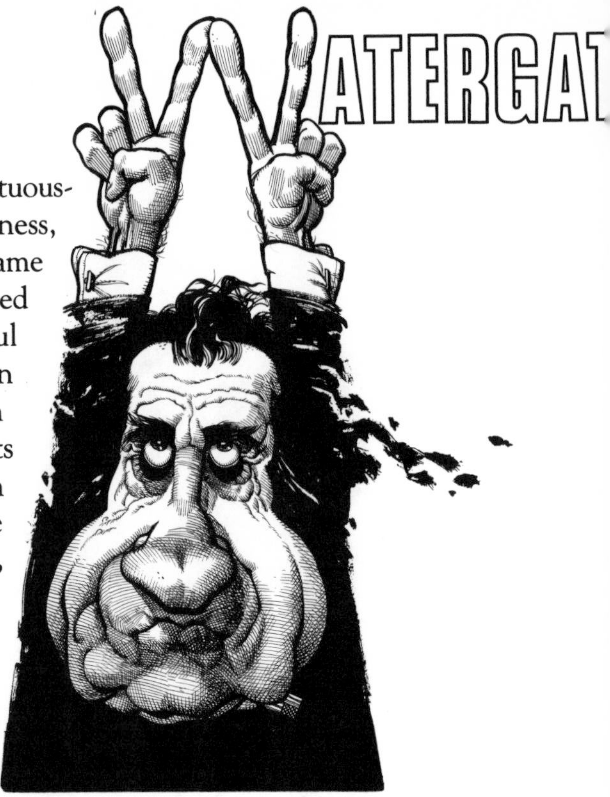
ATERGAT

Richard Nixon's major sin was that he gave a bad name to unctuousness. If he had fostered, from the start, an image of high-handedness, arrogance and ruthlessness (all those things that in the end we came to love him for), his audience might have forgiven him, accepted him, for being himself. But he persisted, throughout his pitiful career that even now will not go away, in that dreadful imitation of Uriah Heep-on-the-make, a smarmy jumped-up Californian who could not even assimilate that state's natural talent (for all its excesses) that one assumes is fed directly into the bloodstream of all its natives: a breezy openness and optimism, a certain naive cheerfulness. (California is a great place to live, said Fred Allen, if you're an orange.)

Richard Milhous somehow seems always a product of a bitter mill town in Pennsylvania, or the bad side of Chicago, perhaps a down-at-the-desire section of the south (a good law school in the northeast could always clean up the accent). Whittier, California, can't have been too far removed from Plains, Georgia, but Nixon throughout his life has always tried to hide his dark side striving to emulate a rectitude that comes so naturally to Jimmy Carter (and makes *him* so boring).

If Nixon, quite the nastiest piece of goods to wobble across the political scene on this side of the pond for eons, had been honest to his soul and from his apprenticeship had shown his true side, who wouldn't argue that things might have been different? There is always a market in the political spectrum for the autocrat. But Nixon, the master of smarm, *didn't* give the impression of a Huey Long, a Boss Tweed, a Richard Daley—even a vain Duplessis or an ordained-by-intelligence C.D. Howe. (You didn't have to like Howe; just accept him as an honest autocrat irritated by democracy. As he said one day in the Commons, "I do not think this should be allowed to degenerate into a debate.") Nixon of course was more than an autocrat. He was a crook, but an unctuous crook. God save us from those.

His other serious crime (history will skim over his vainglorious stupidity in not burning his own tapes) is that he had neither wit nor sense of humour. There is a difference between the two—though the absence of both always unveils the demagogue. As the English can tell you, the Irish have wit: Wilde and Shaw and Behan and the rest. But they have no sense of humour. They can't laugh at themselves. Pierre Trudeau has wit (his oft-misquoted "Where's Biafra?" was a dig at reporters to see if *they* knew), but he has no sense of humour. Robert Stanfield, who has, annually wiped the floor with Trudeau at the off-the-record Parliamentary Press Gallery dinner. Stanfield, as devastating in private as he was stultifying in public, could poke fun at himself. Trudeau can't. One of the unknown facts about Joe Clark is that, in private, he has a very nice, dry, sardonic sense of humour—especially about himself. As with Stanfield, this aspect of his brain somehow freezes once he is exposed to the public, his attempts at wit coming off as arch or feeble. He apparently doesn't think the public is capable of handling the same perceptions that he tosses off in private. (Trudeau's problem has been the opposite: he blithely hurls overboard sophomoric smart-assisms that would better have been left in the Common Room.)

Adlai Stevenson doomed himself with his wit: "The job of an editor is to separate the wheat from the chaff—and then print the chaff." George Romney's presidential aspirations were impaled on one descriptive phrase: "Deep down, he's shallow." Churchill is one of the rare successful politicians whose wit has survived him: "Clement Attlee is a sheep in sheep's clothing." Lyndon Johnson was deadly in his backroom barbs. (What he actually said was that "Gerald Ford is so dumb he can't fart and chew gum at the same time.")

Is there a single recorded instance of a witty line from Mackenzie King? Such is the seriousness of Alberta in shaking off Depression humiliation that the self-important Peter Lougheed displays no sense of humour whatever. René Lévesque has that worldly, bittersweet air of the jaded boulevardier. Perhaps, like Stevenson, it has doomed them, but the socialists of Canada have been the masters of wit: Tommy Douglas, the greatest platform performer of them all; Dave Barrett, a born clown; one of the aspects Ed Broadbent's handlers try to hide from the public is a withering sarcasm. (The right-wing *Toronto Sun's* right-wing columnist Claire Hoy, said Ed, "made Goebbels look like Albert Camus," a typical throwaway line that almost produced a restaurant punch-up between Broadbent and Hoy during the campaign.)

Richard Nixon will undoubtedly be forgiven his unctuousness in his own peculiar heaven. But he can't be forgiven his second lapse. Even today he cannot see how funny he is.

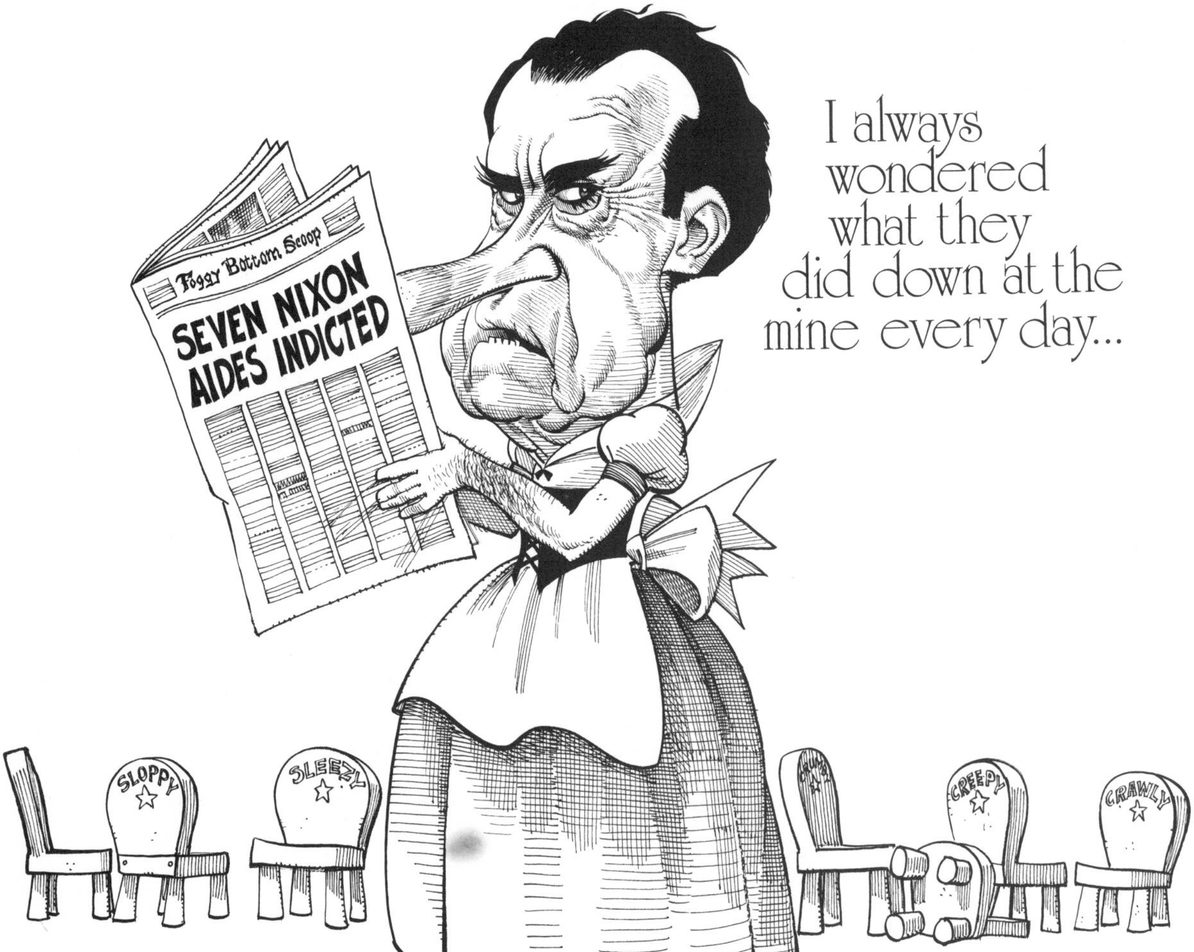
Foggy Bottom Scoop
SEVEN NIXON AIDES INDICTED
SLOPPY
SLEEZY
CREEPY
CRAWLY
I always wondered what they did down at the mine every day...

Snow White

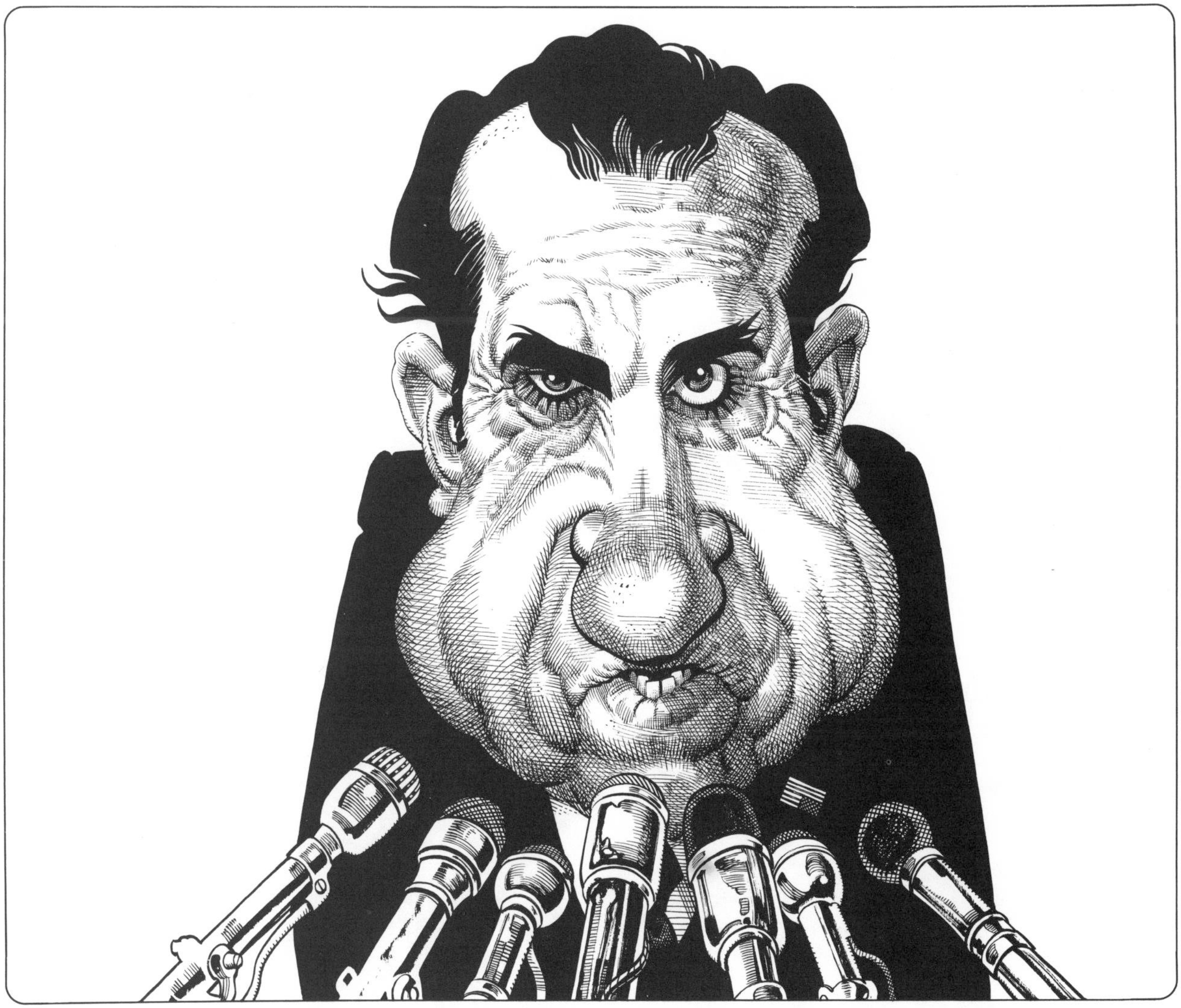

"Unaccustomed as I am to PUBLIC speaking . . ."

March on, march on, since we are up in arms;
If not to fight with foreign enemies,
Yet... to beat down these rebels here at home!

King Richard III
Act IV-Scene IV

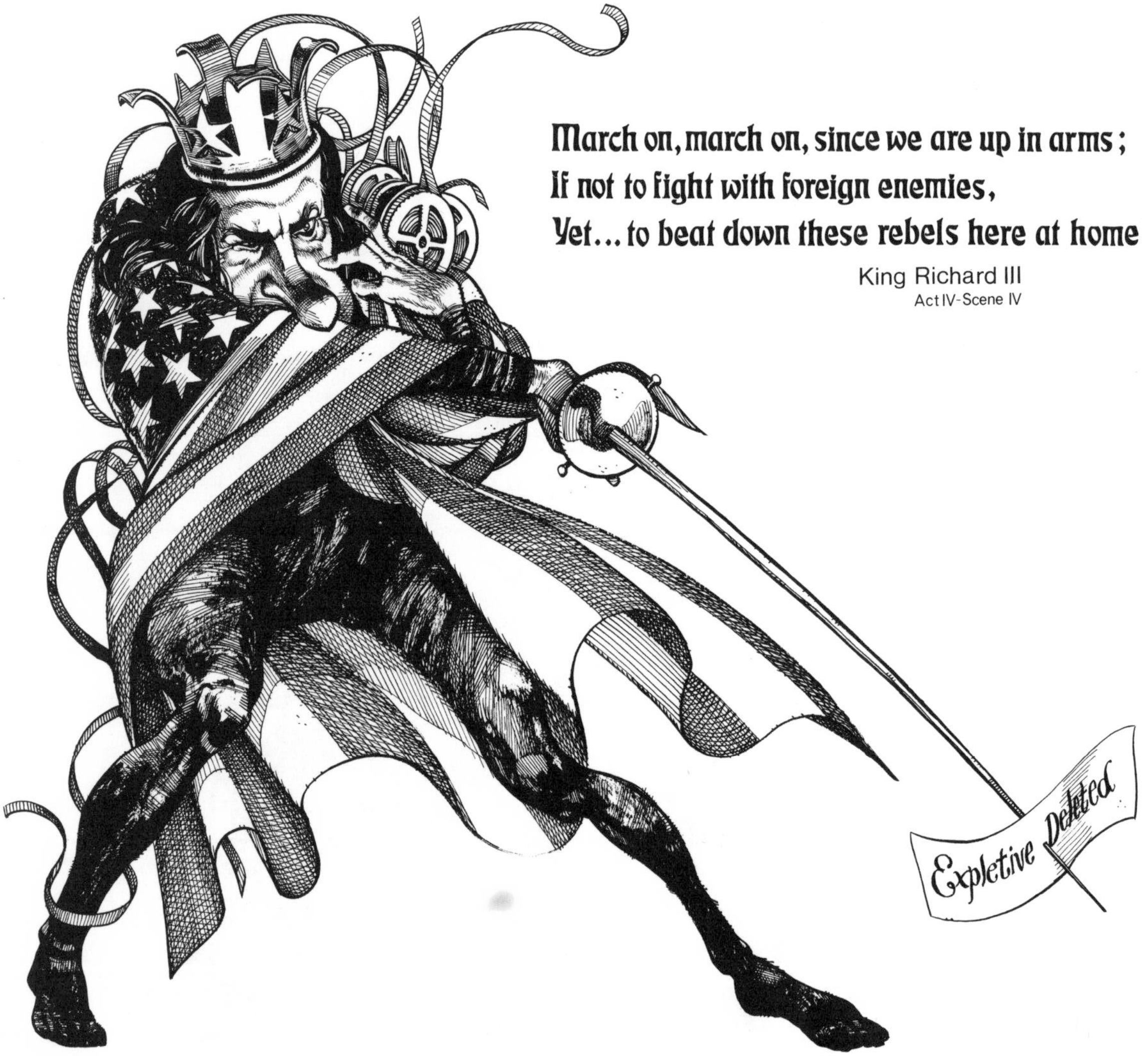
Expletive Deleted

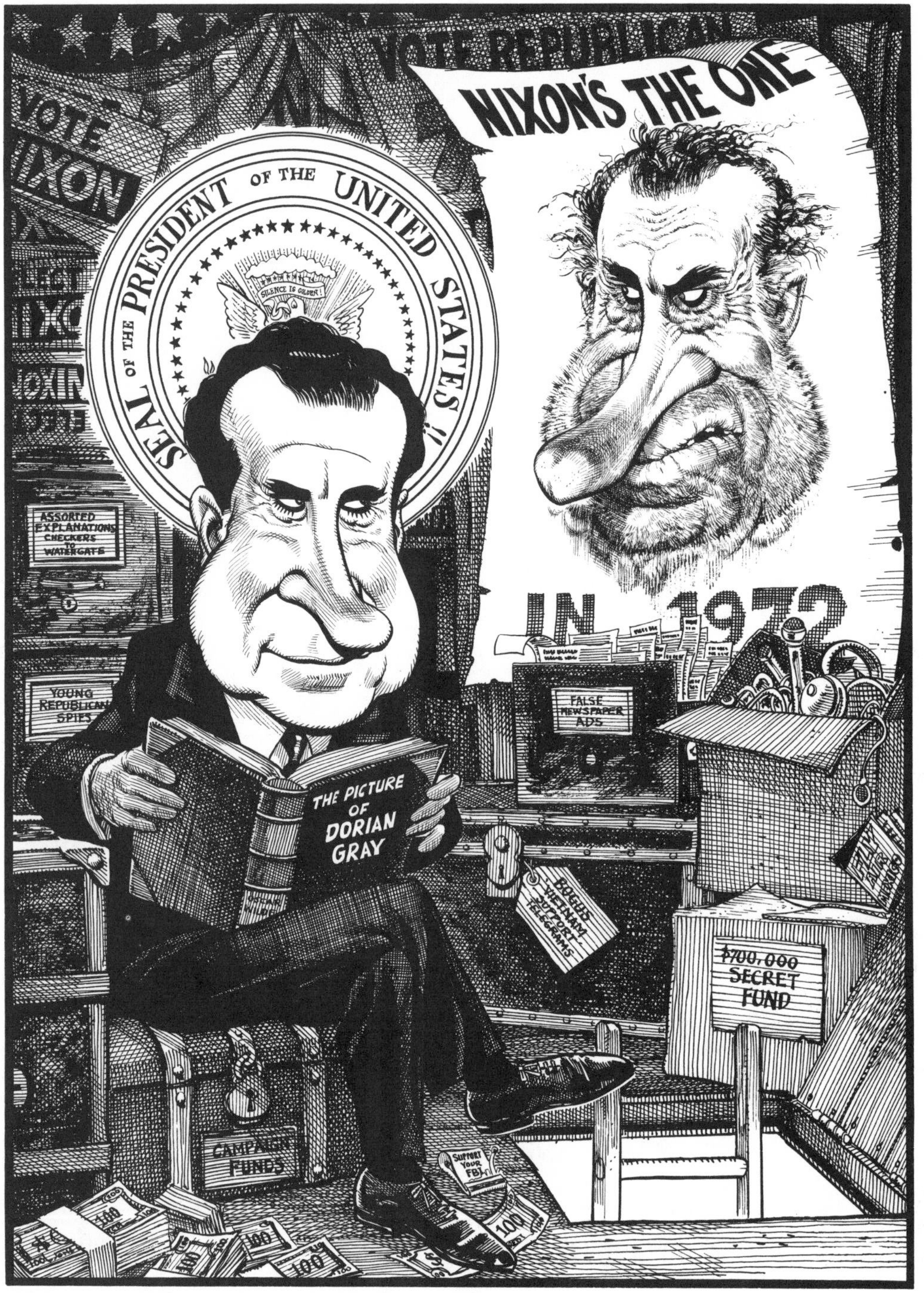
VOTE REPUBLICAN
VOTE NIXON
NIXON'S THE ONE
IN 1972
SEAL OF THE PRESIDENT OF THE UNITED STATES !!
SILENCE IS GOLDEN!
ASSORTED EXPLANATIONS CHECKERS TO WATERGATE
YOUNG REPUBLICAN SPIES
THE PICTURE OF DORIAN GRAY
FALSE NEWSPAPER ADS
BOGUS VIETNAM SUPPORT TELEGRAMS
$700,000 SECRET FUND
CAMPAIGN FUNDS
SUPPORT YOUR FBI

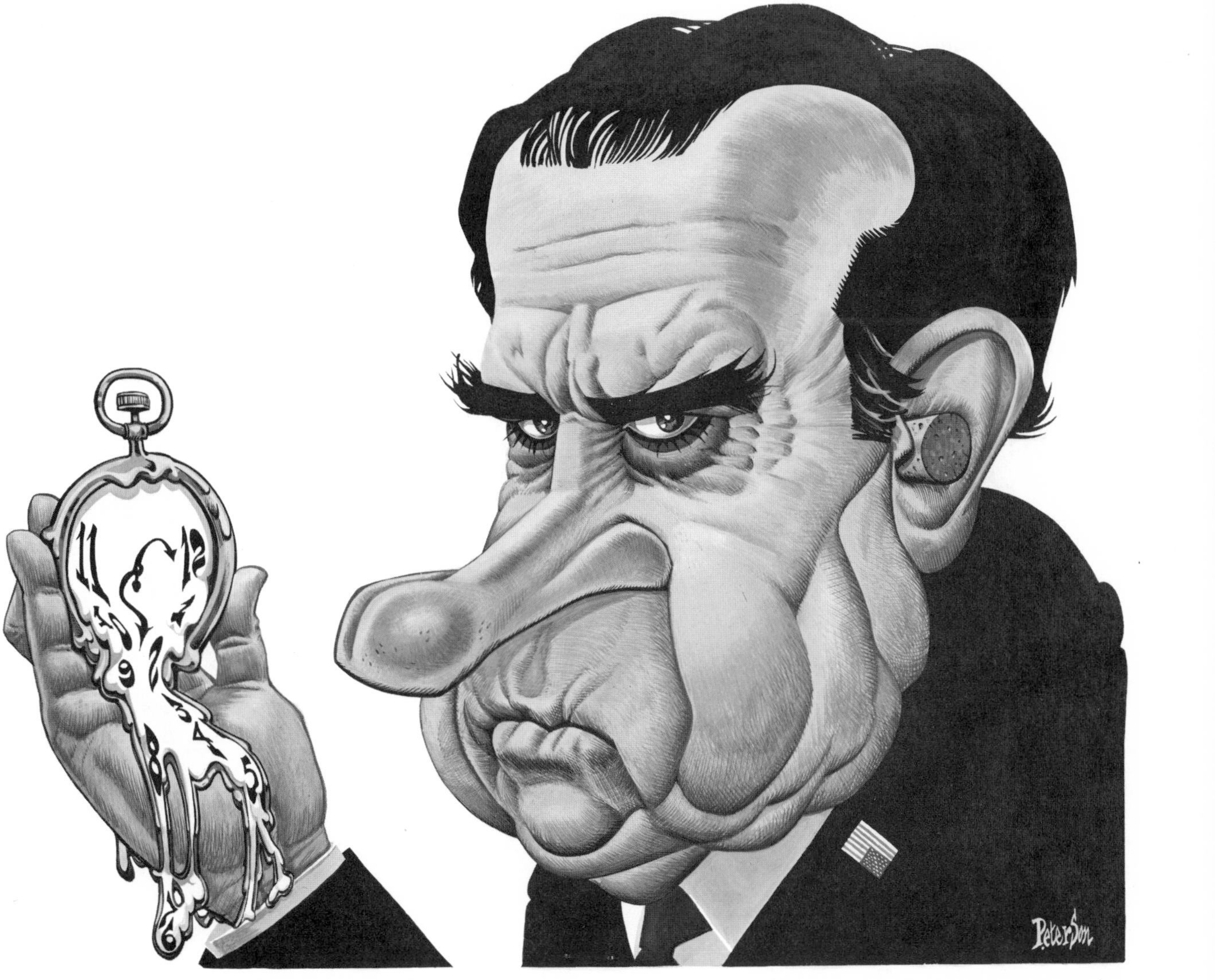
Peterson

The World in a Nutshell

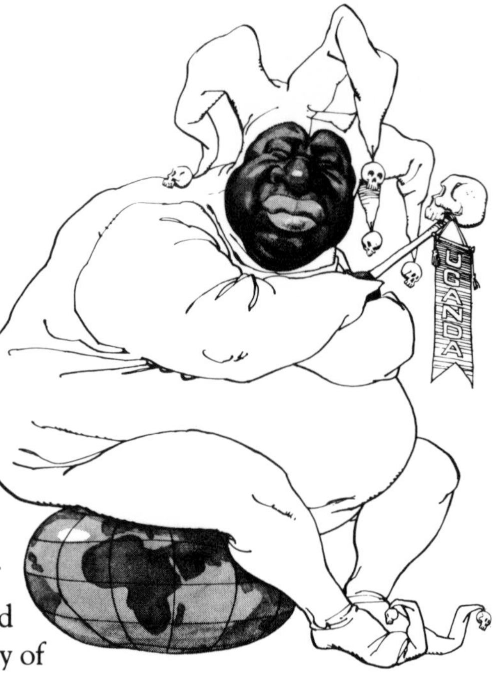
UGANDA

The essence of the art of the cartoonist is to make the caption superfluous. If the message performs the required massage, there is no need for an explanatory commercial. The best of art delivers its own story, with no need for a nudge nudge, wink wink. The brush alone makes the statement. The typewriter line is redundant.

In 1975 Roy Peterson introduced a new idea as part of his work for the *Vancouver Sun.* Each Saturday he would produce an uncaptioned work that summed up the major story of the week. He called it "The Peterson Portfolio." It is a tribute to his brilliance that years later these weekly summaries stand up with such relevance and clarity, whatever the news-peg at the time. Newspapers have been defined as "history in a hurry." Peterson slows down the process.

The symbolism is superb. At the height of the Star Wars craze in 1977, who else could see René Lévesque as a lurking Darth Vader, with a wide-eyed Pierre Trudeau attempting to save the maiden Canada while the intergalactic rocket planes form the fleur-de-lis in space? John Diefenbaker, after being made to look foolish by a suddenly aroused Robert Stanfield, appears as Victor, the giraffe at the London Zoo who flitted across the world's wirephotos for a week after he collapsed spraddle-legged in the midst of an amorous bout and could not be erected again.

The mournful Stanfield, rooted in his loneliness, watches his tenure wind down as the eager knives of his restless Tory caucus reach out for him. Peterson in his examination of Stanfield over the years somehow captures the morose nature of the man—not just the customary dourness of a Maritimer trapped out of his territory, but a certain feeling that here was a politician, decent and honest, who was out of synch with the age of television—a man voters would shy from at the last moment in the polling booth while extolling his virtues. Stanfield left his rose garden and came to

Ottawa reluctantly under the pressures of the Tory image-makers who would save us from Dief: Stanfield's face, translated by Peterson, tells us that he himself knew all along that it would never work.

Gerald Ford comes across as genuinely stupid, the man who freed Poland, and who perhaps did, as alleged, play one too many football games minus his helmet. The legacy of Nixon is shown by the two men he chose to back him up: Spiro Agnew, articulate shyster, a barefaced charlatan; and Ford, too slow to be anything but honest, epitomizing the Peter Principle in his role as golf course buffoon for Bob Hope and corporate vice-presidents.

Jimmy Carter, hiding behind his teeth, comes upon the cavity of Bert Lance. Ian Smith in the Peterson view is always slightly demented, an unknowing grin on his face, secure in his righteousness, oblivious to the inevitable. Skateboarding on the back of blacks, he is a sad product of bravado as that beautiful sunny country, which waited too long to change, twists in the wind.

Harold Wilson, with that infernal pipe as prop to disguise his lack of resolution, is revealed as the petty man we now know him to have been. Bryce Mackasey, who set a world record by resigning from the cabinet twice in one day, has his head chopped off. Trudeau, about to blow an election bugle, is stymied when Francis Fox finds the wrong man's name leaking out of his ball point. Mr. Justice Tom Berger squeezes off the Mackenzie Valley oil bubble. Jack Horner desperately tries to scrub off his spots, a transparent piece of Liberal cynicism that Peterson (two years before the voters back him up) predicted would not work. Parti Québecois finance minister Jacques Parizeau, in a nasty shaft, becomes J. Parasite.

He says it all. Without a single word.

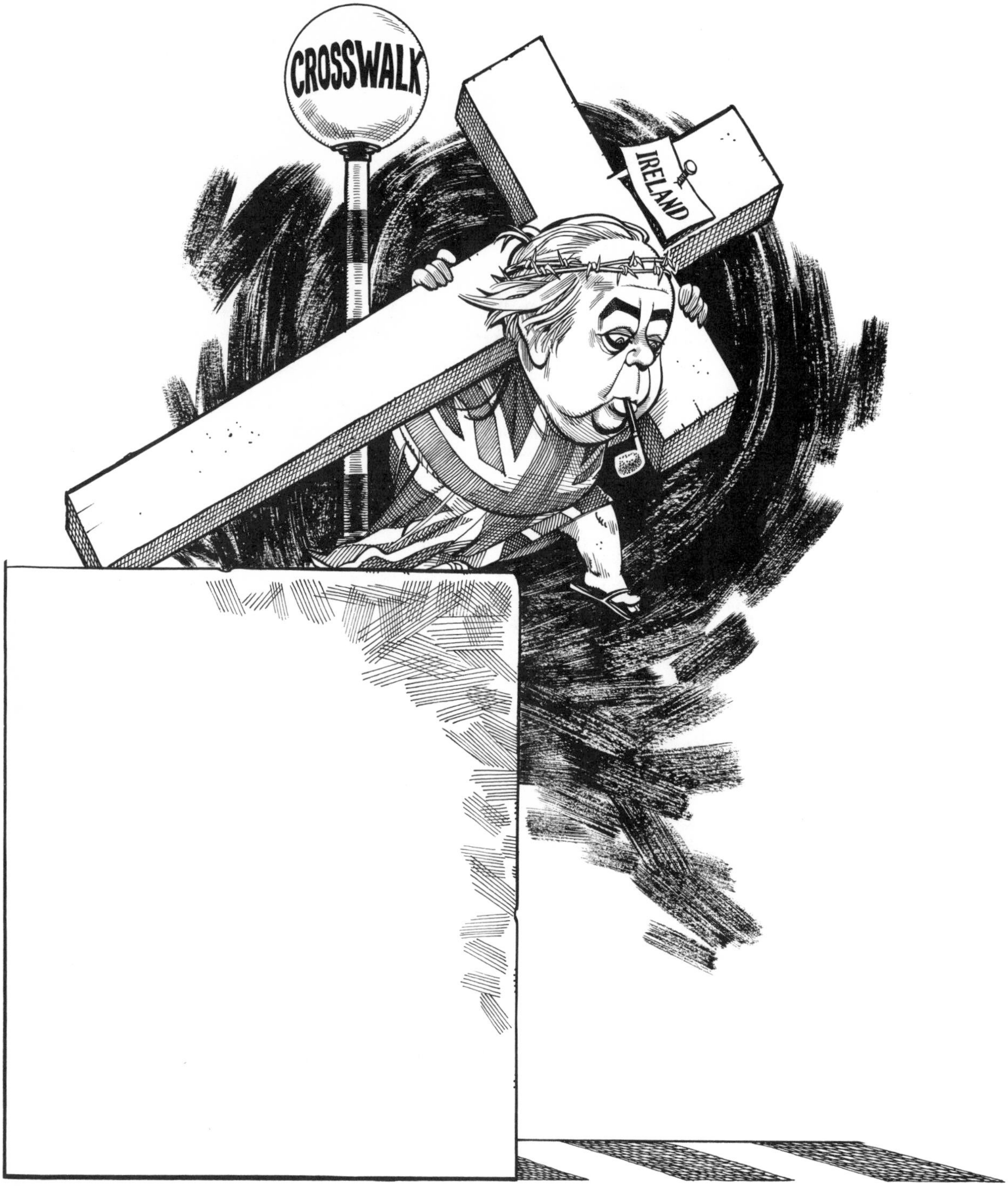
CROSSWALK
IRELAND

Harold Wilson

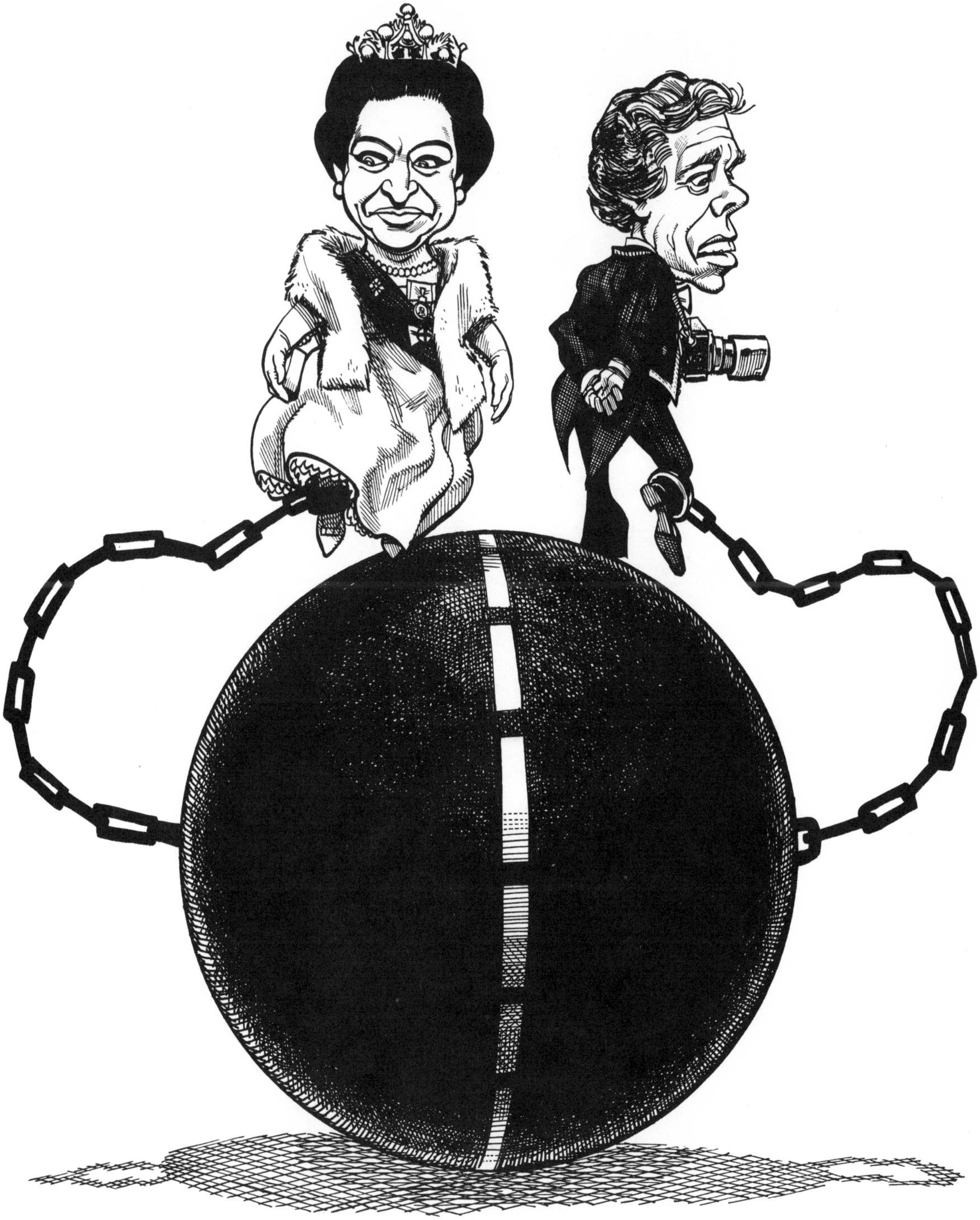

Princess Margaret and Lord Snowdon

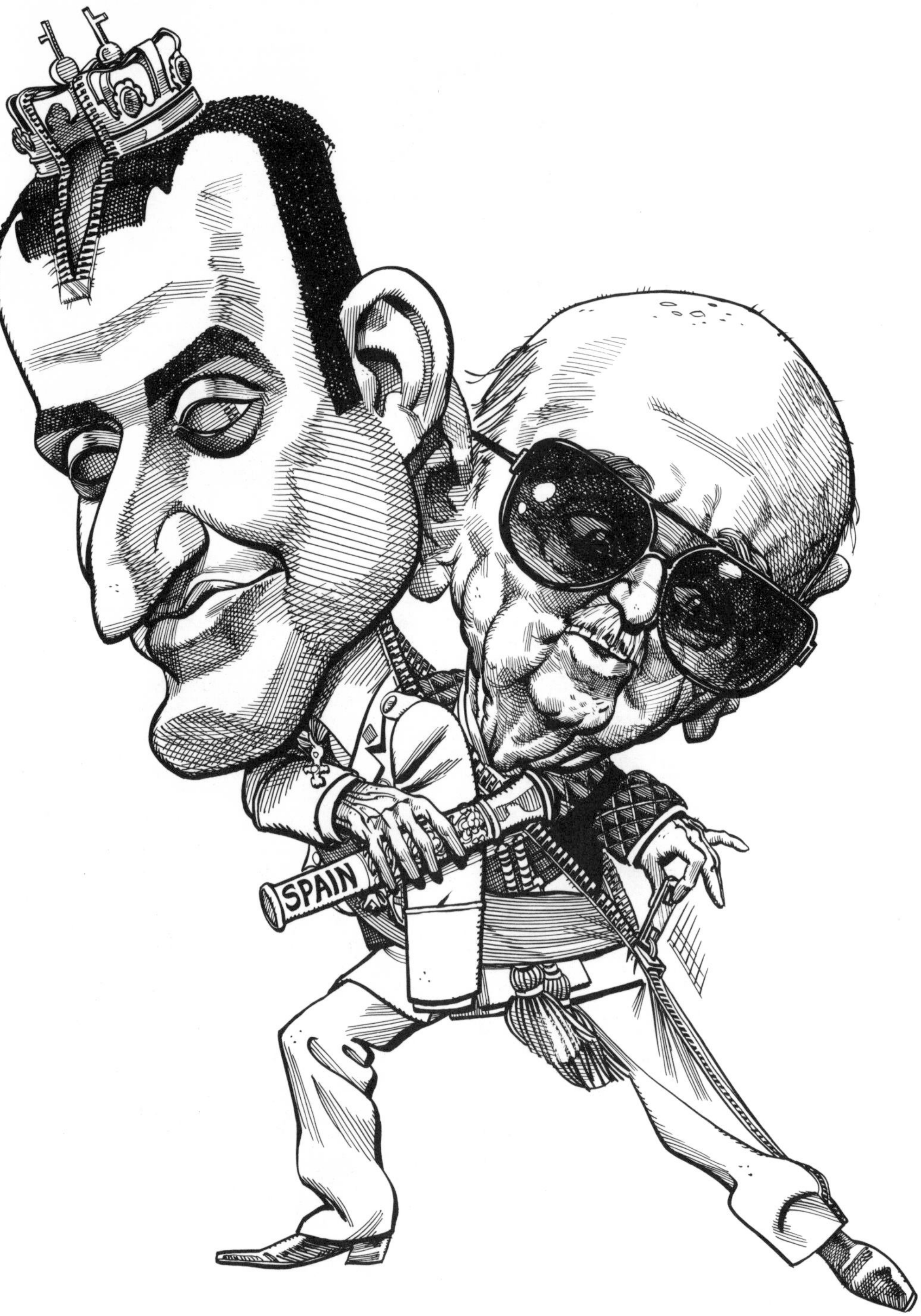
SPAIN

General Francisco Franco and Prince Juan Carlos

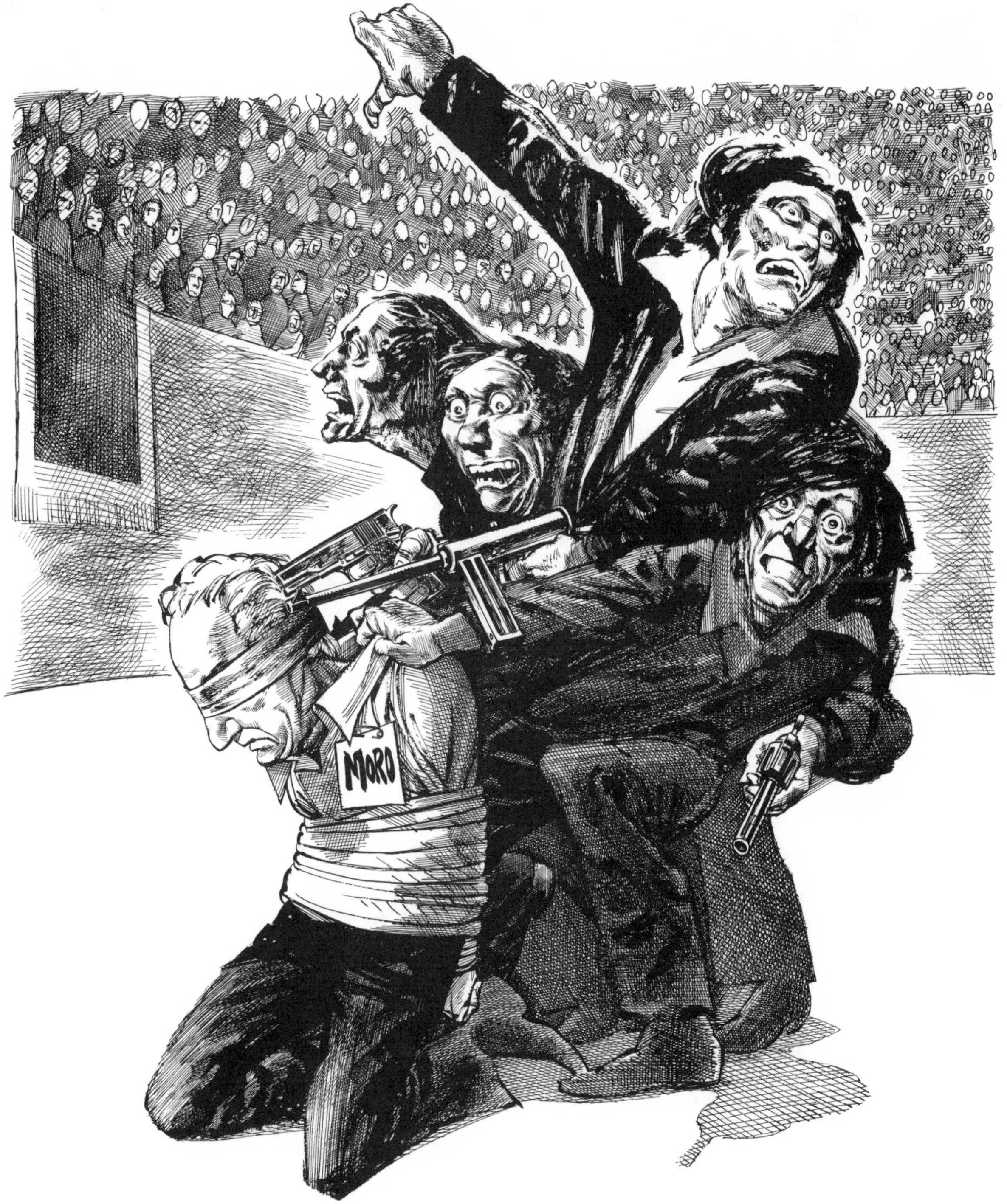
MORO

Aldo Moro

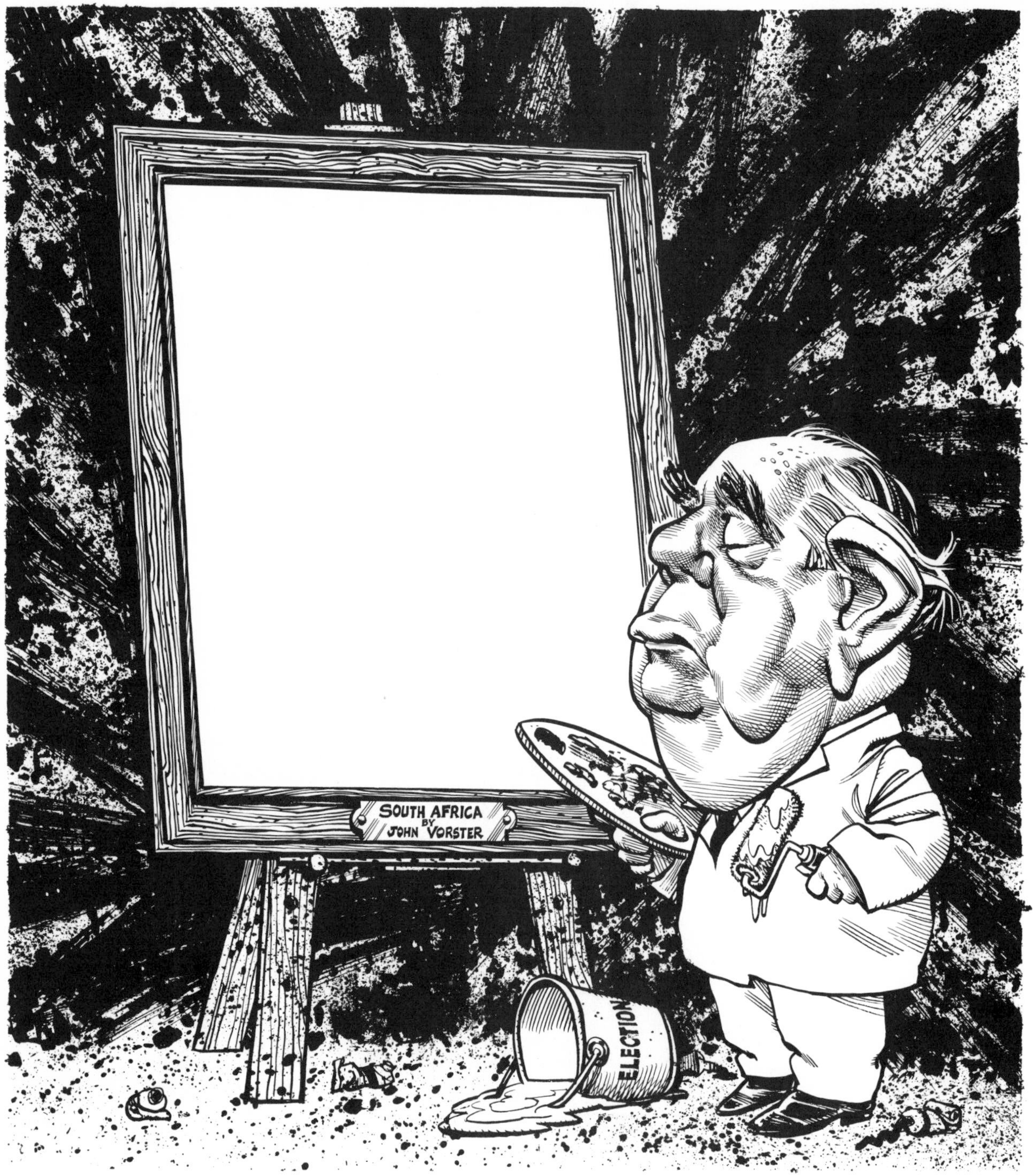
SOUTH AFRICA BY JOHN VORSTER
ELECTION

John Vorster

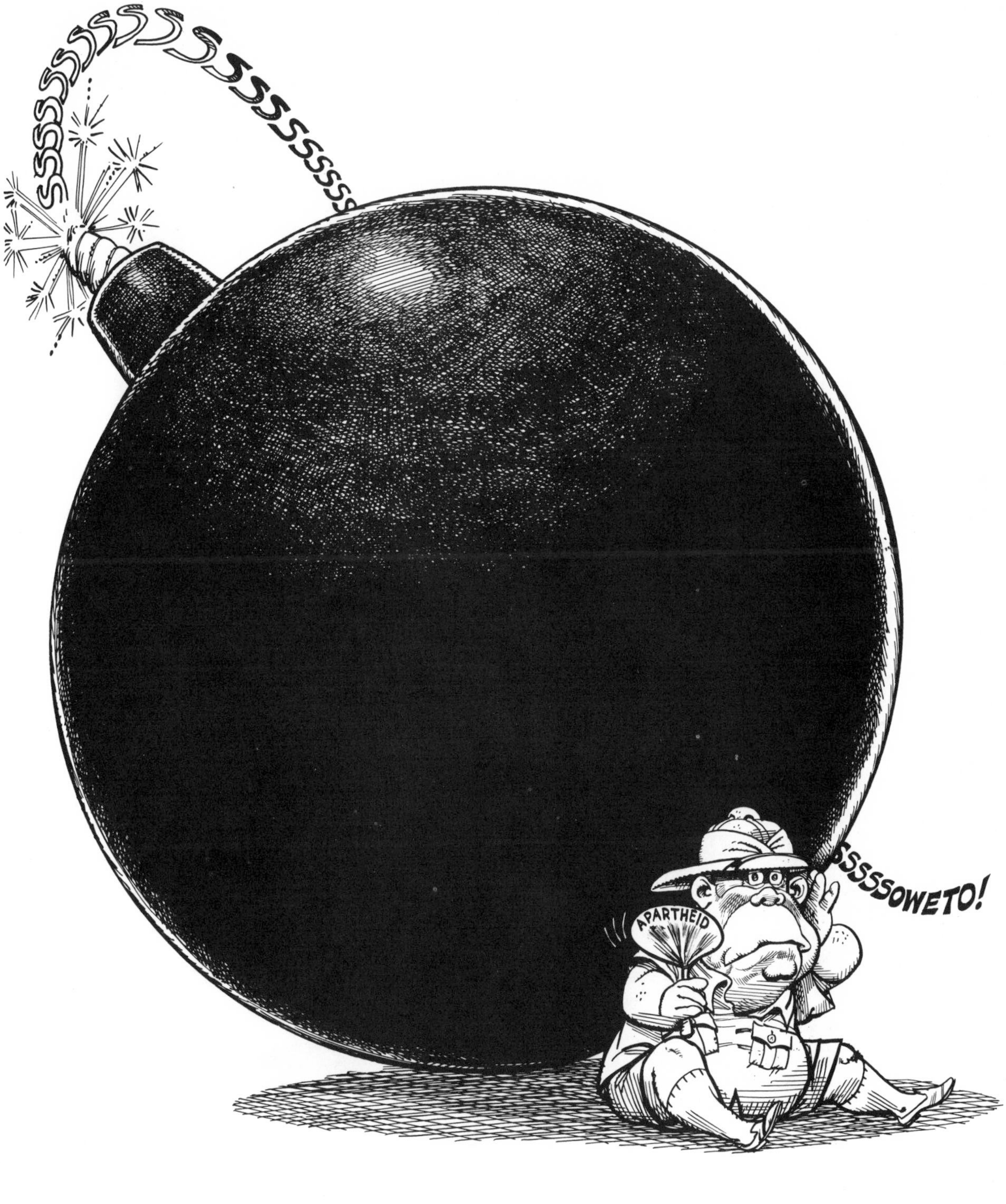
APARTHEID
SSSSSOWETO!

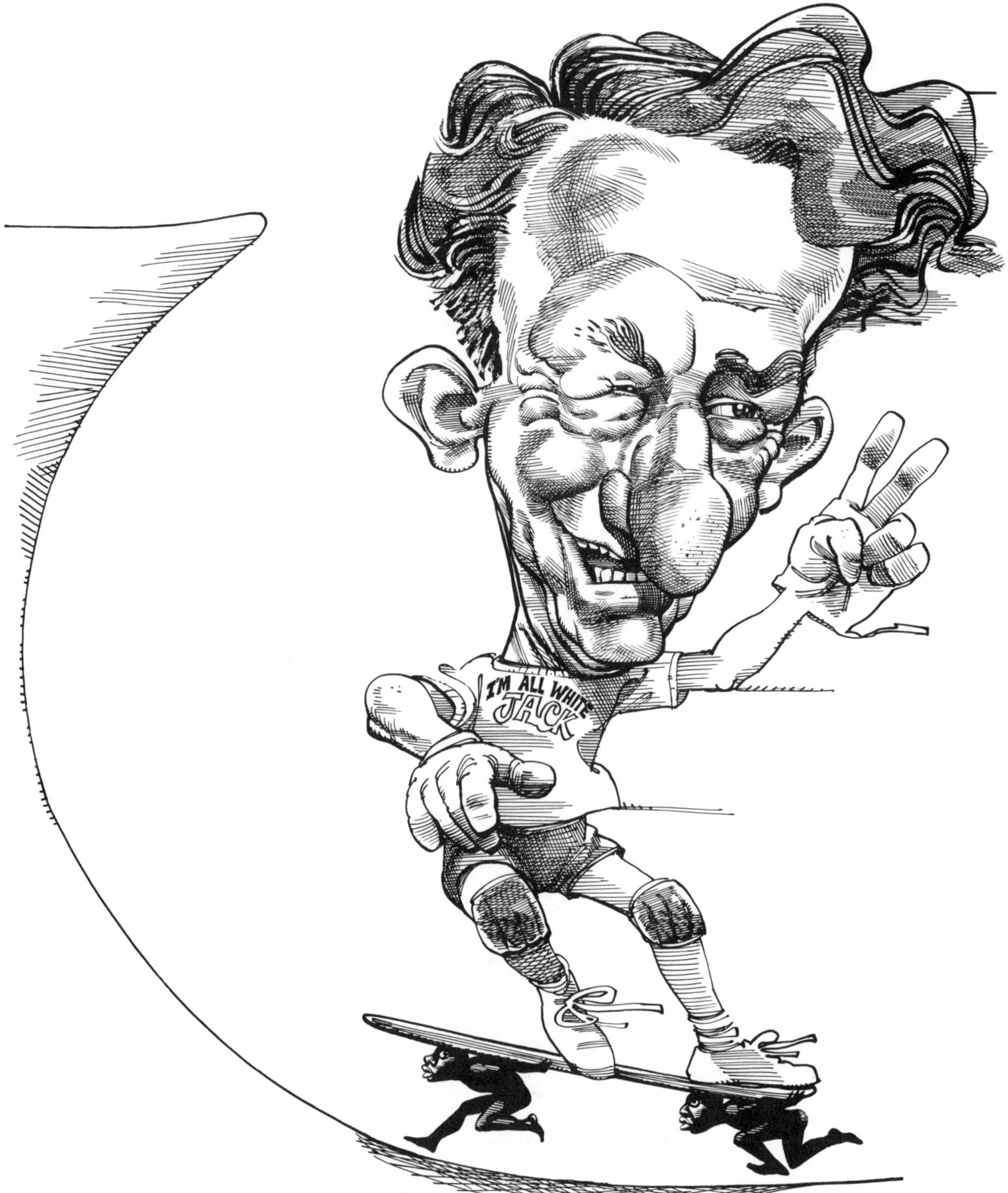
I'M ALL WHITE
JACK

Ian Smith

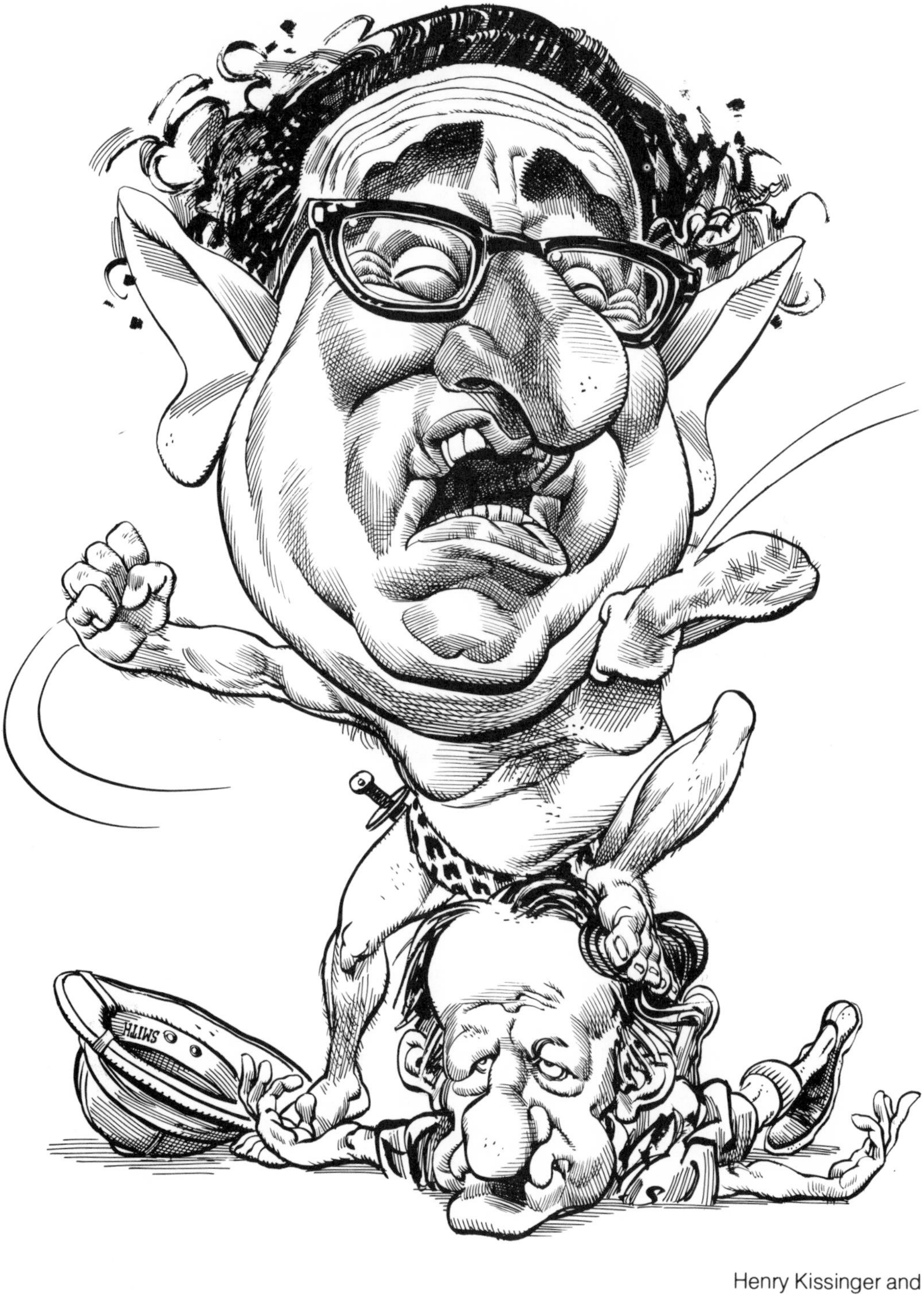
SMITH

Henry Kissinger and Ian Smith

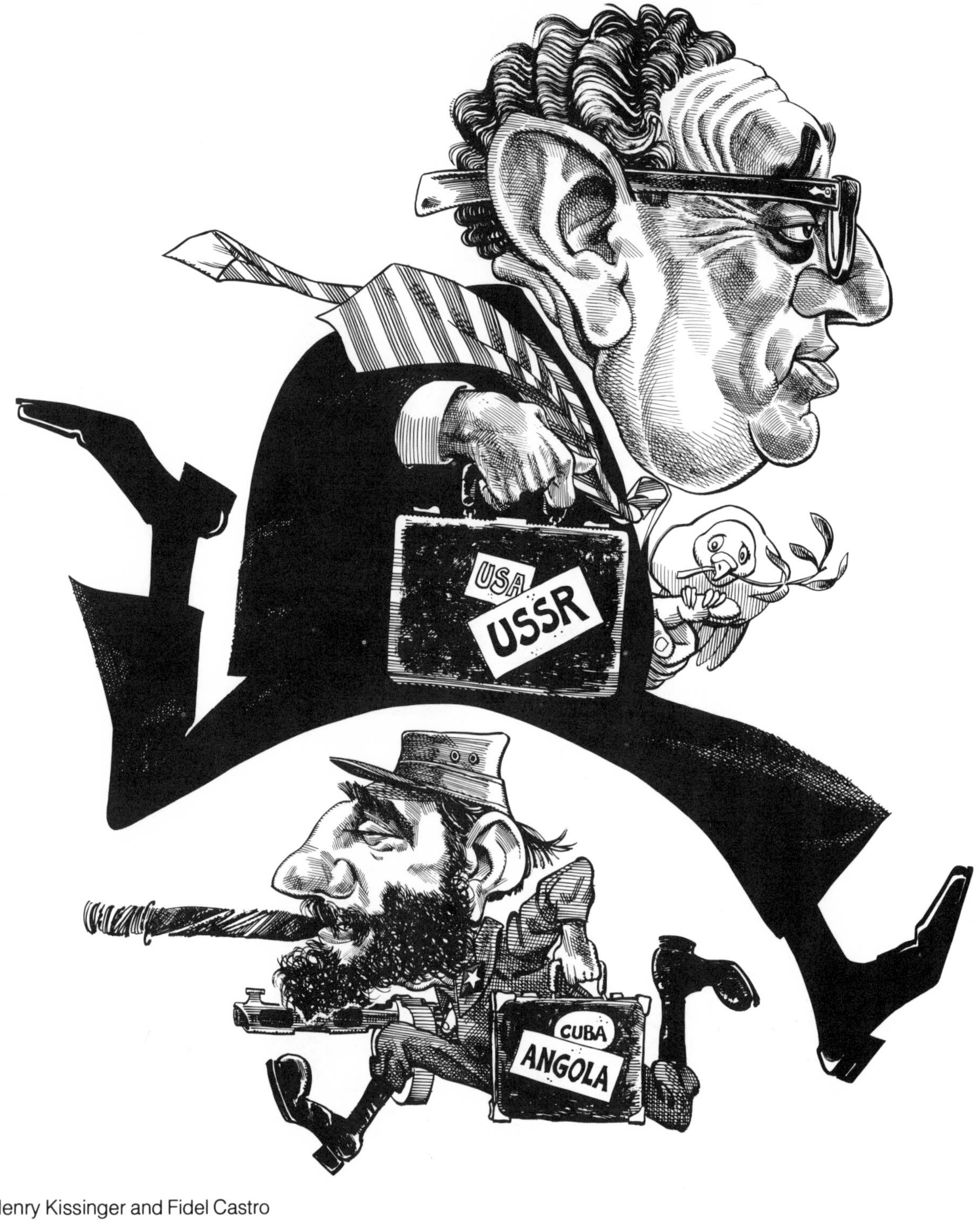
USA
USSR
CUBA
ANGOLA

Henry Kissinger and Fidel Castro

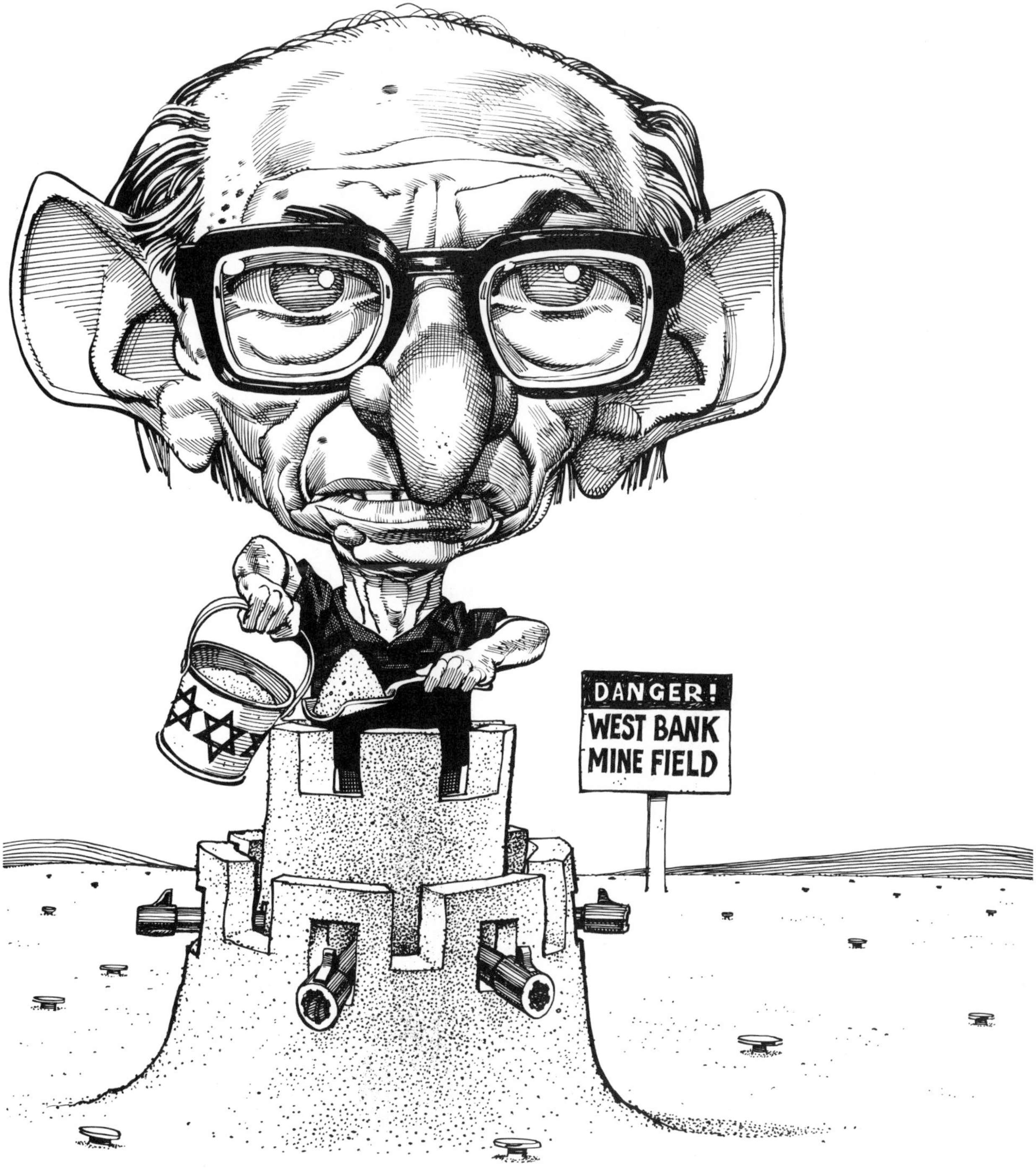
DANGER!
WEST BANK
MINE FIELD

Menachem Begin

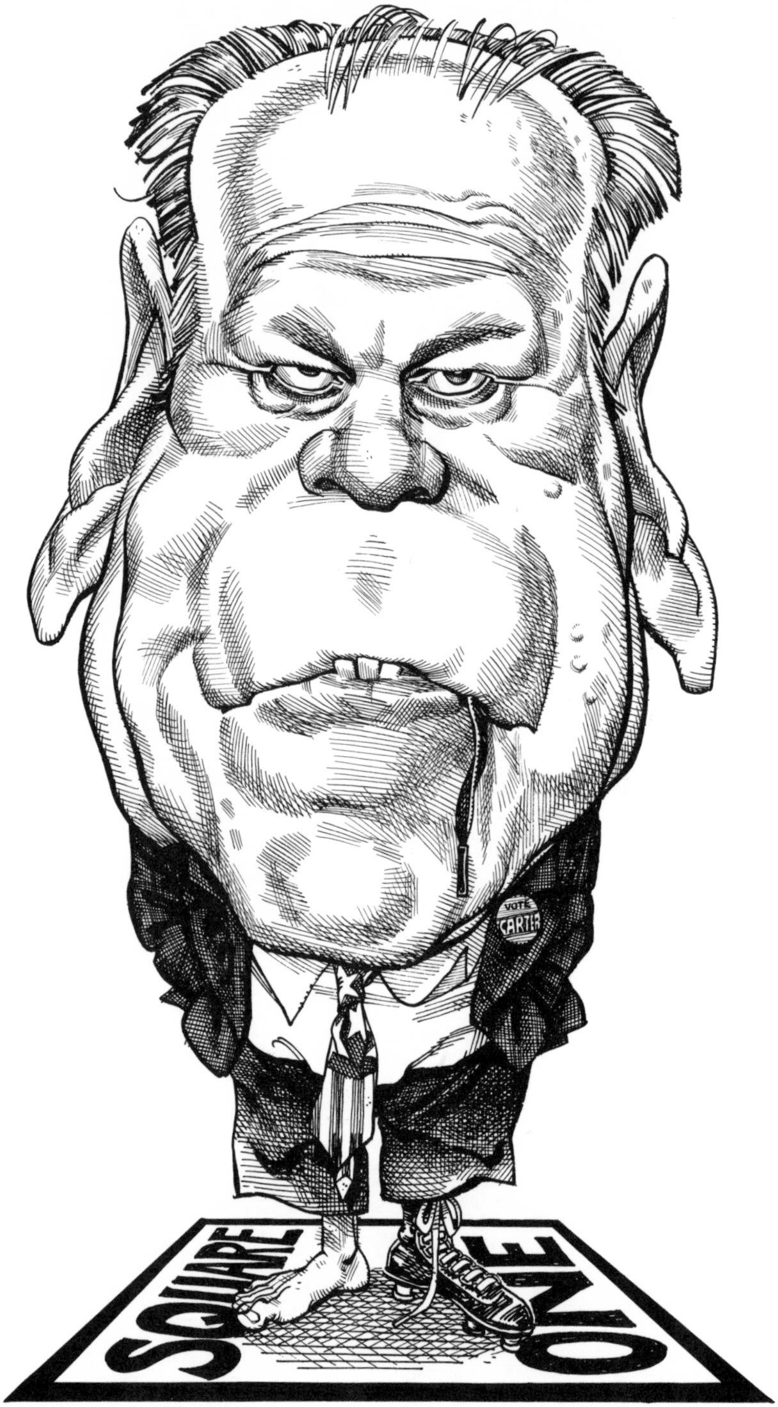
VOTE
CARTER
SQUARE
ONE

Gerald Ford

Jimmy Carter and Bert Lance

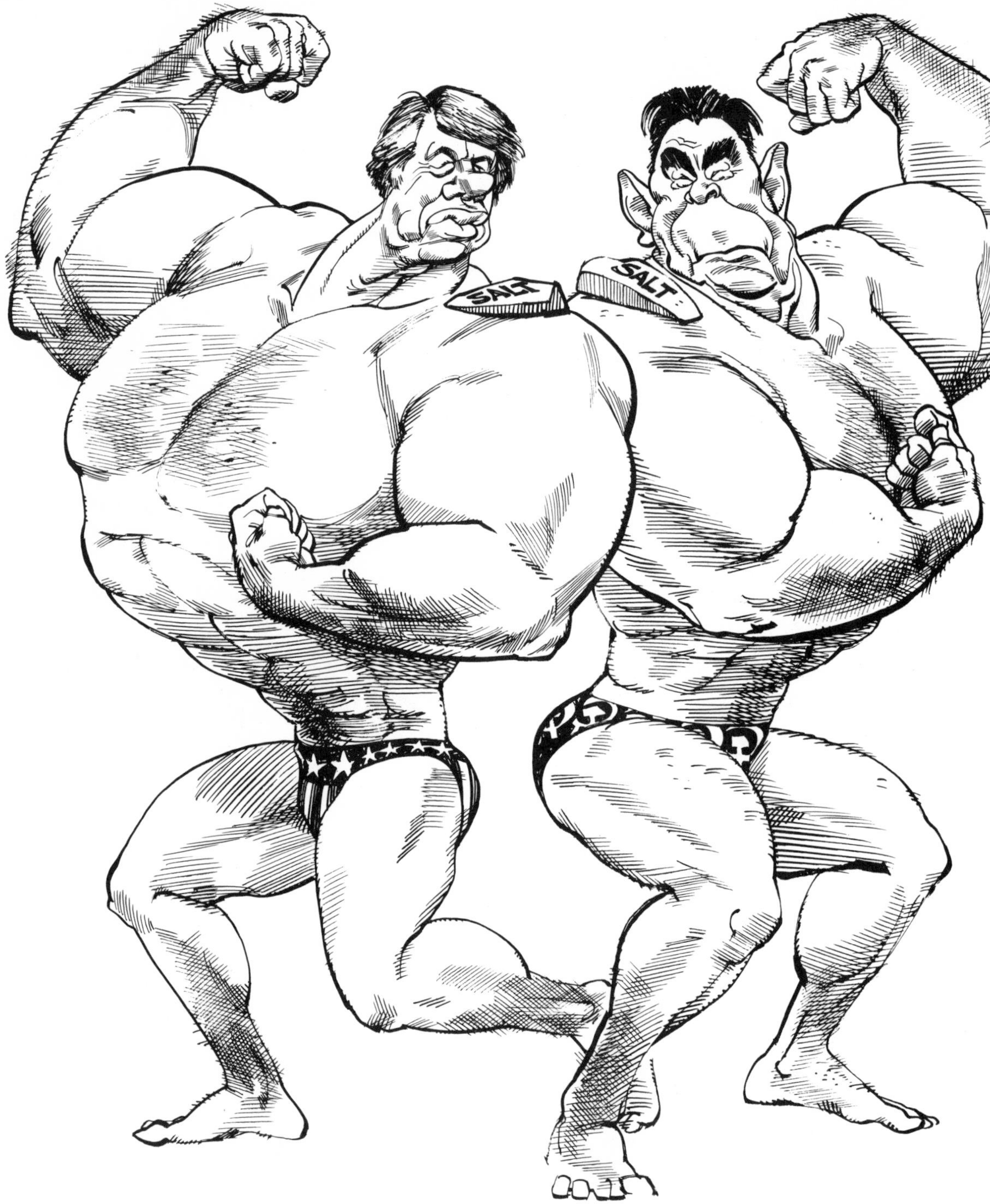
SALT
SALT

Jimmy Carter and Leonid Brezhnev

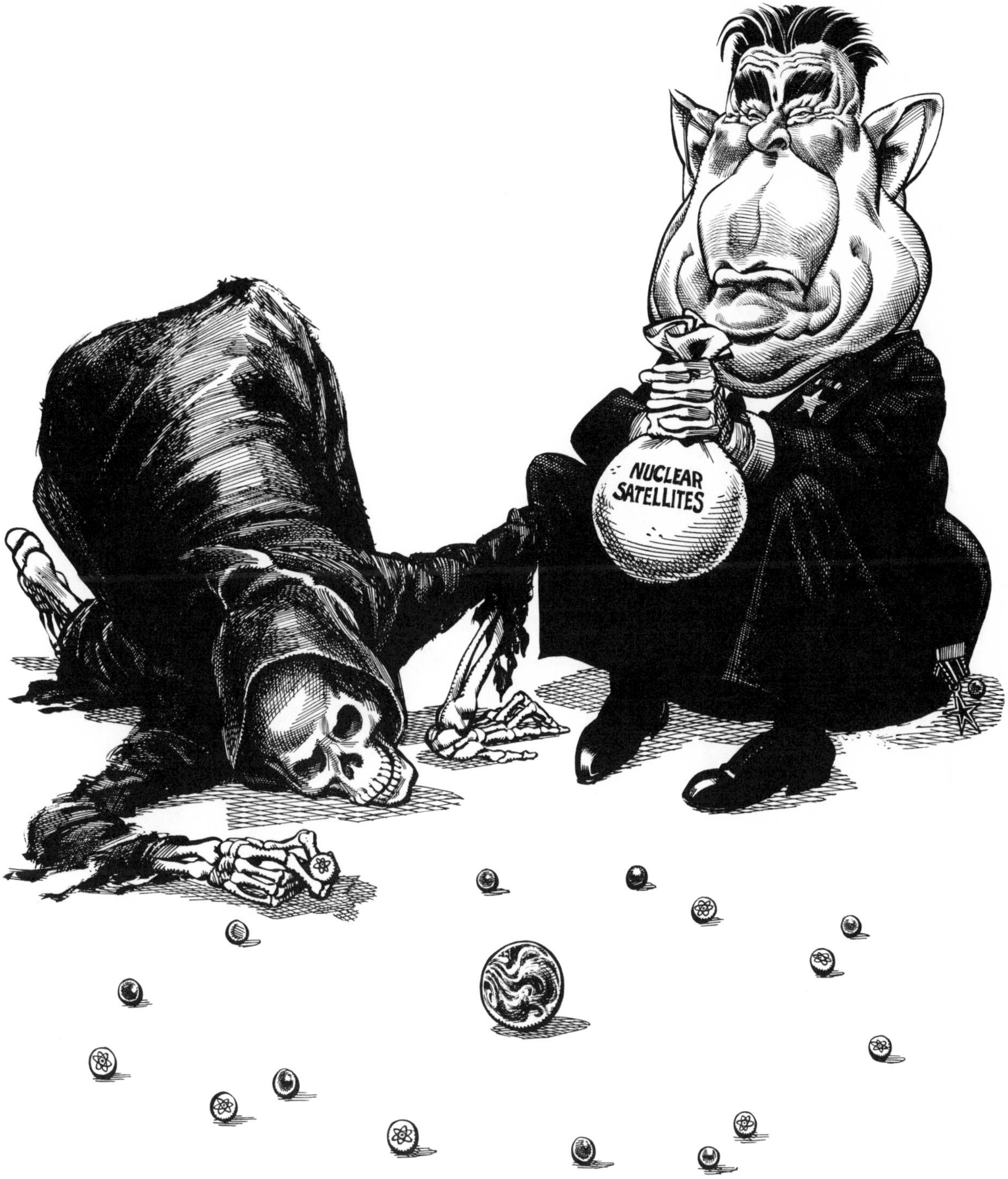
NUCLEAR SATELLITES

Leonid Brezhnev

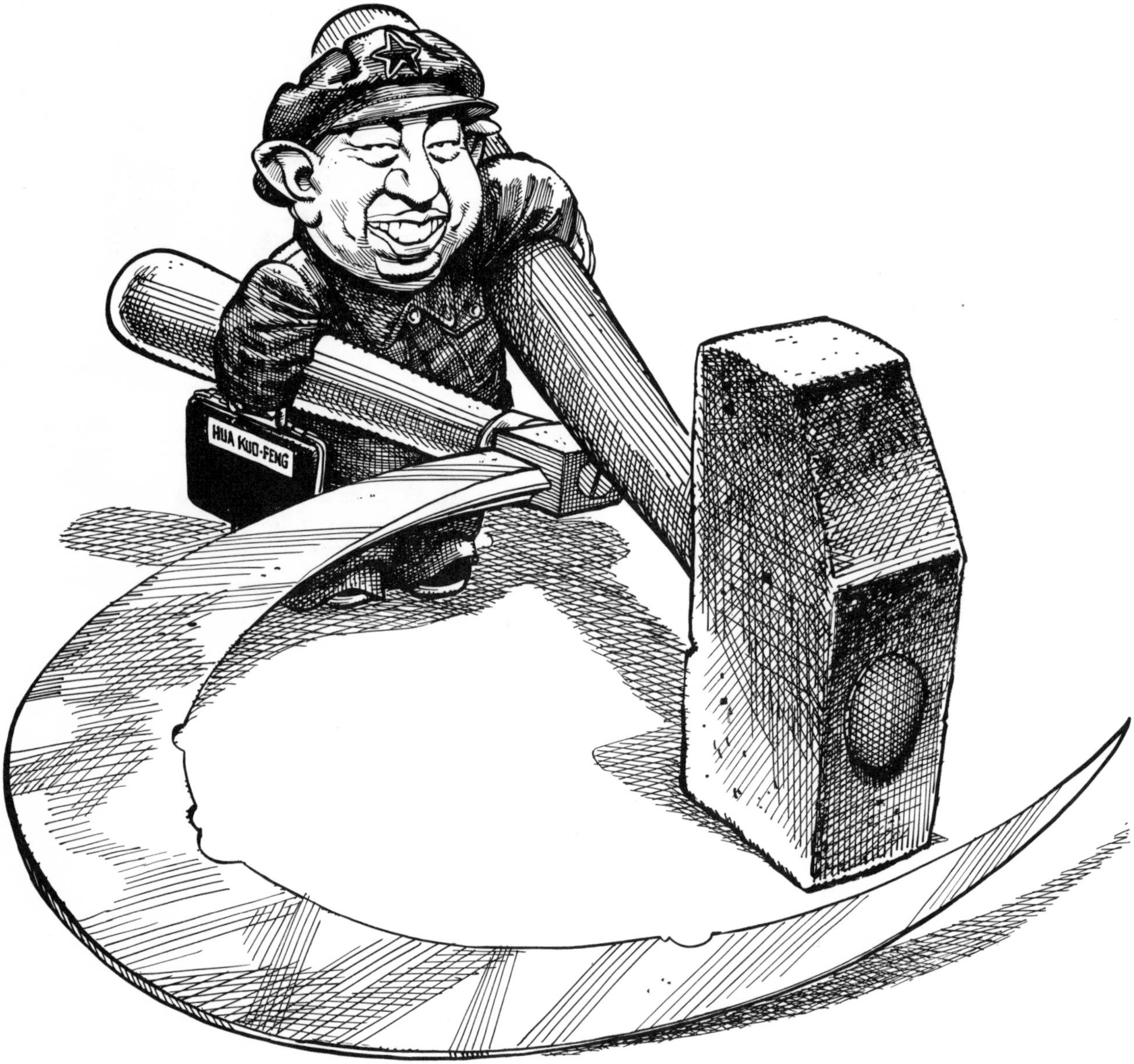
HUA KUO-FENG

Hua Kuo-feng

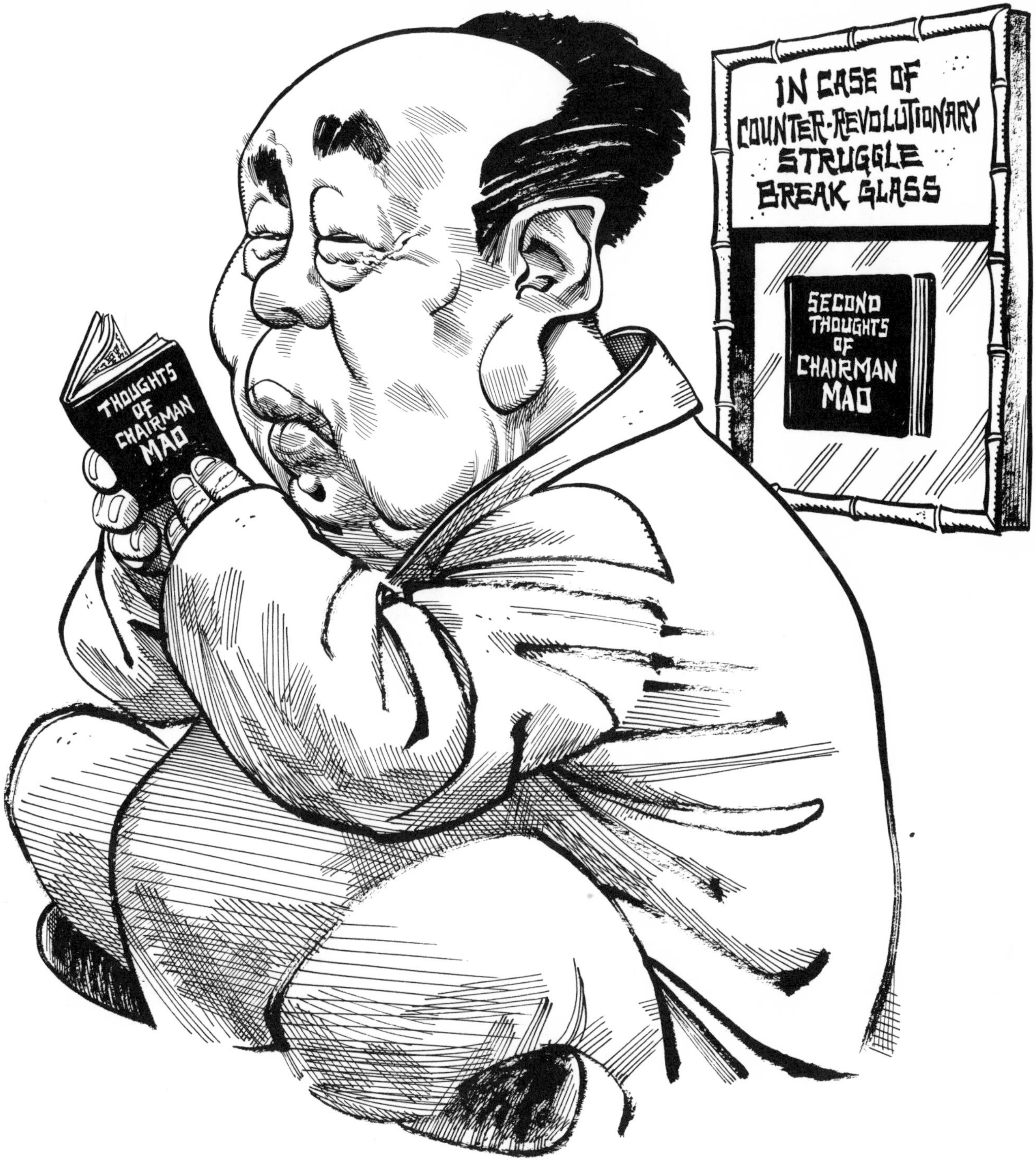
IN CASE OF
COUNTER-REVOLUTIONARY
STRUGGLE
BREAK GLASS
SECOND THOUGHTS OF CHAIRMAN MAO
THOUGHTS OF CHAIRMAN MAO

Mao Tse-tung

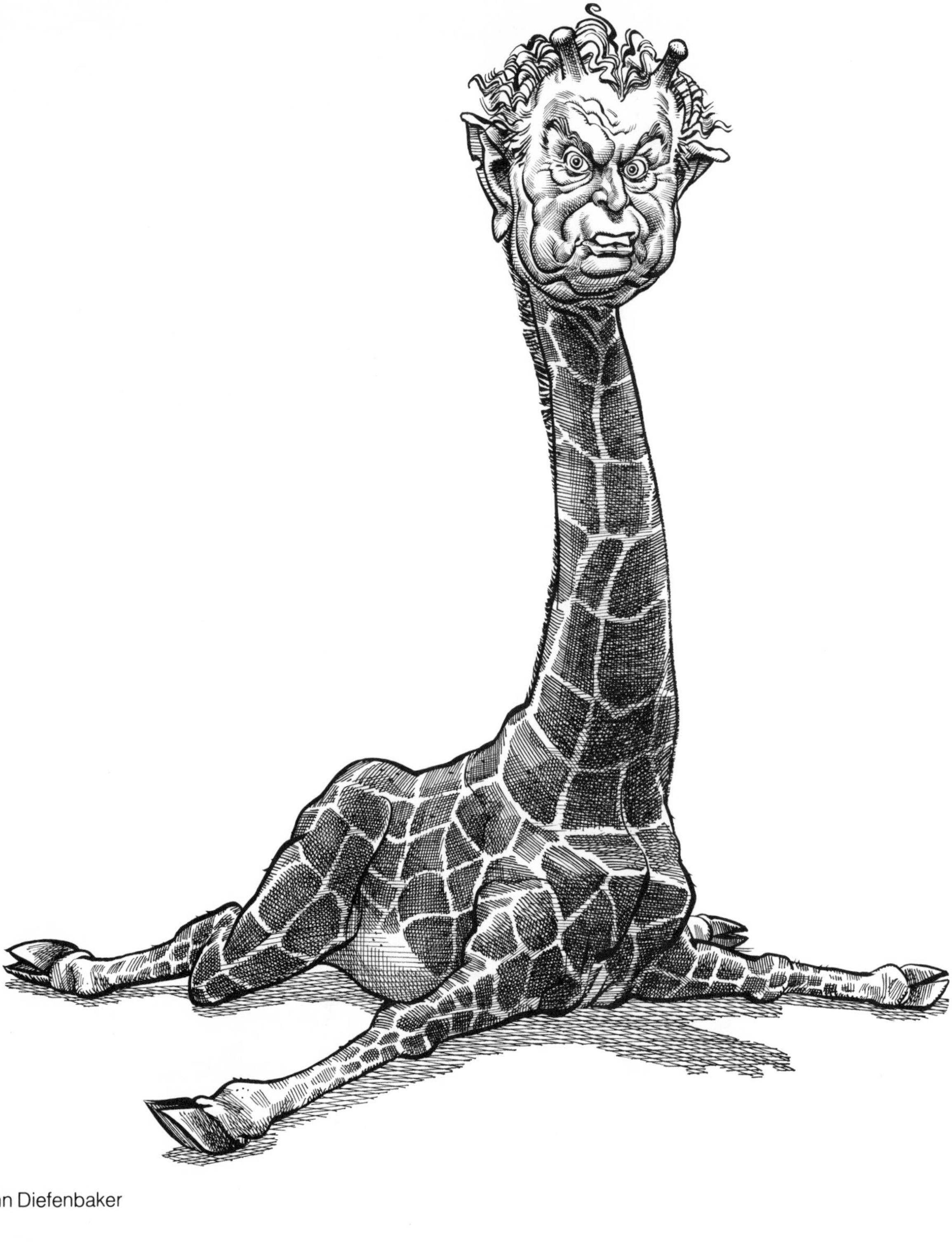

John Diefenbaker

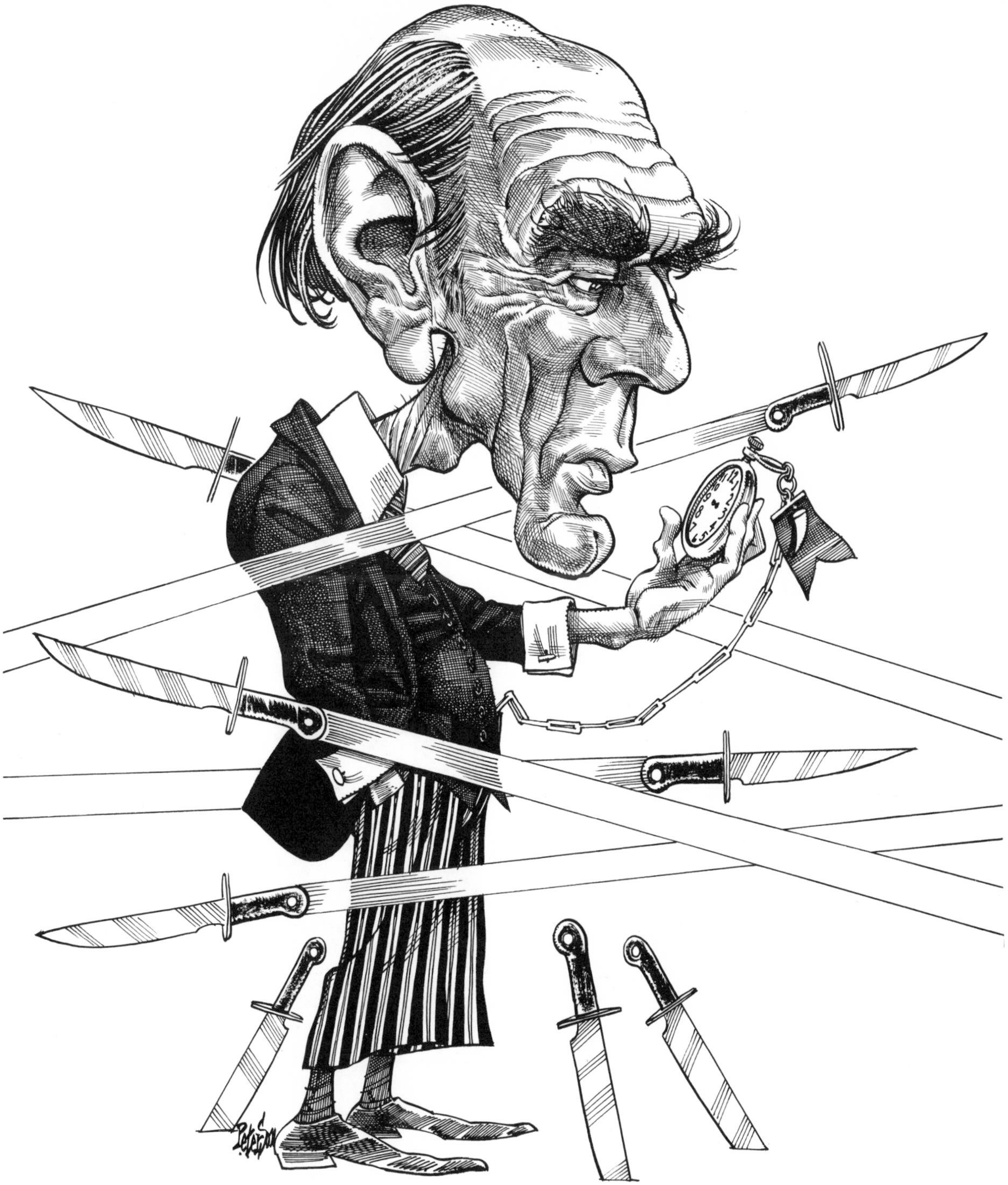

Robert Stanfield

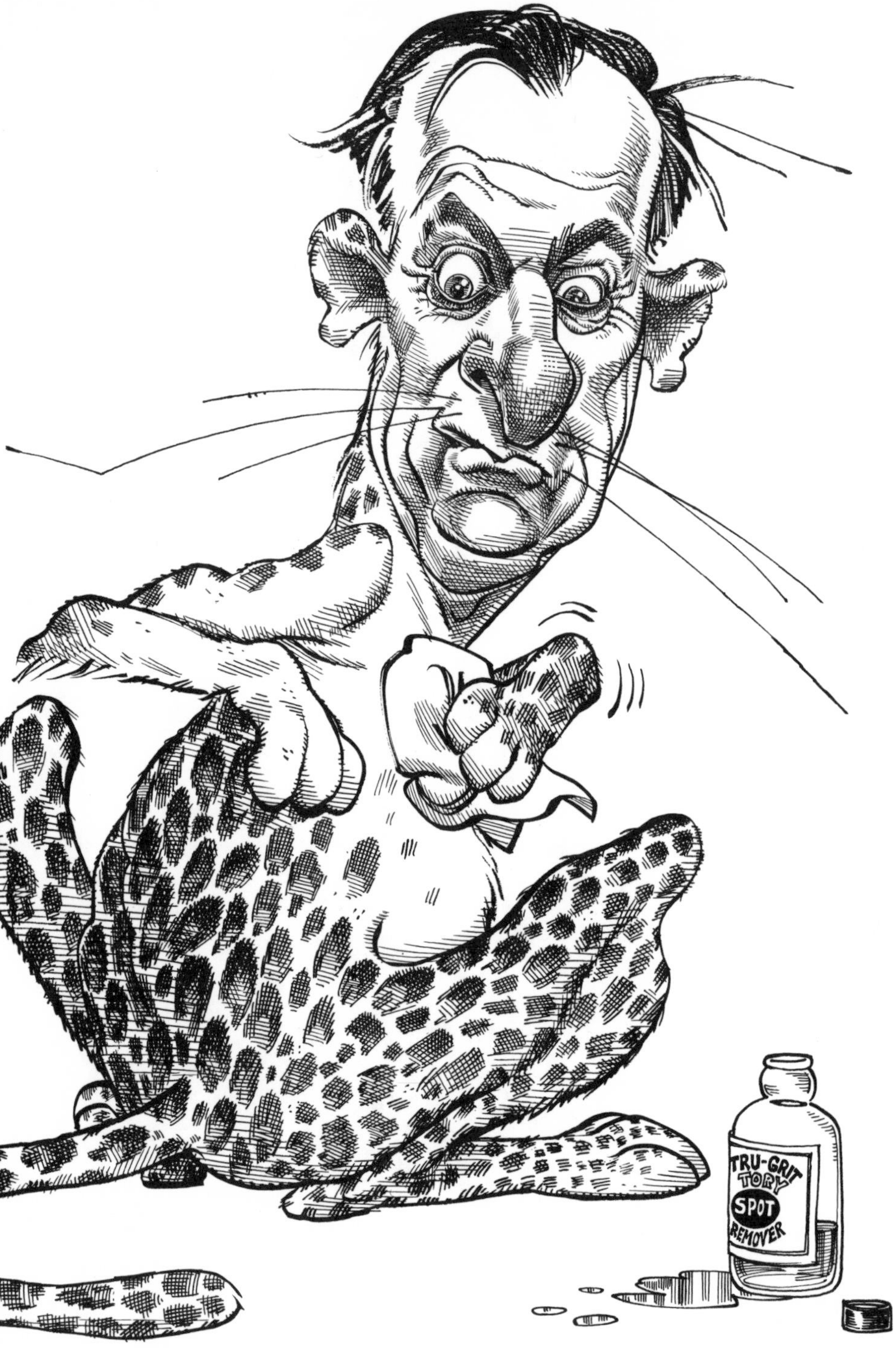
TRU-GRIT
TORY
SPOT
REMOVER

Jack Horner

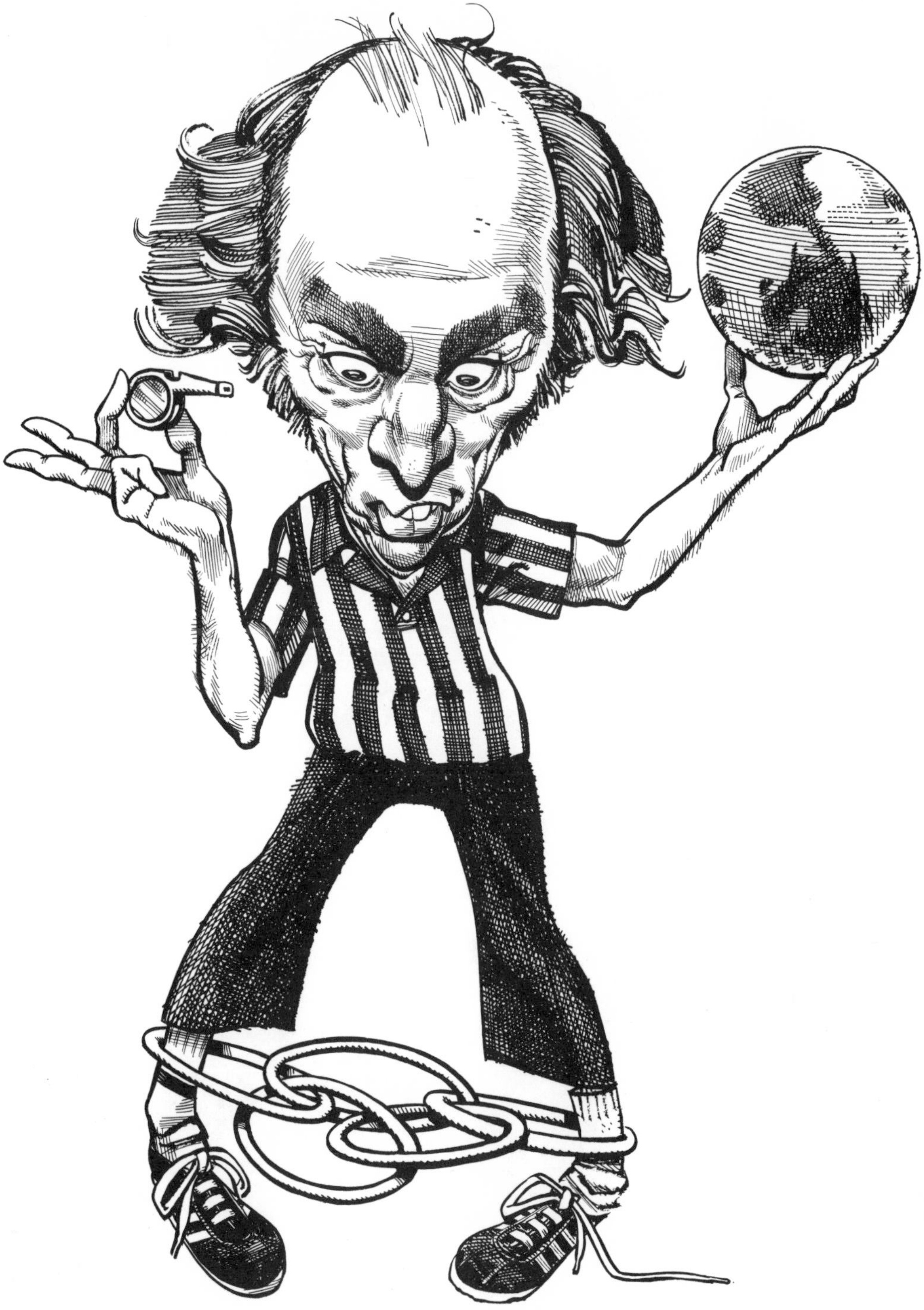

Pierre Trudeau

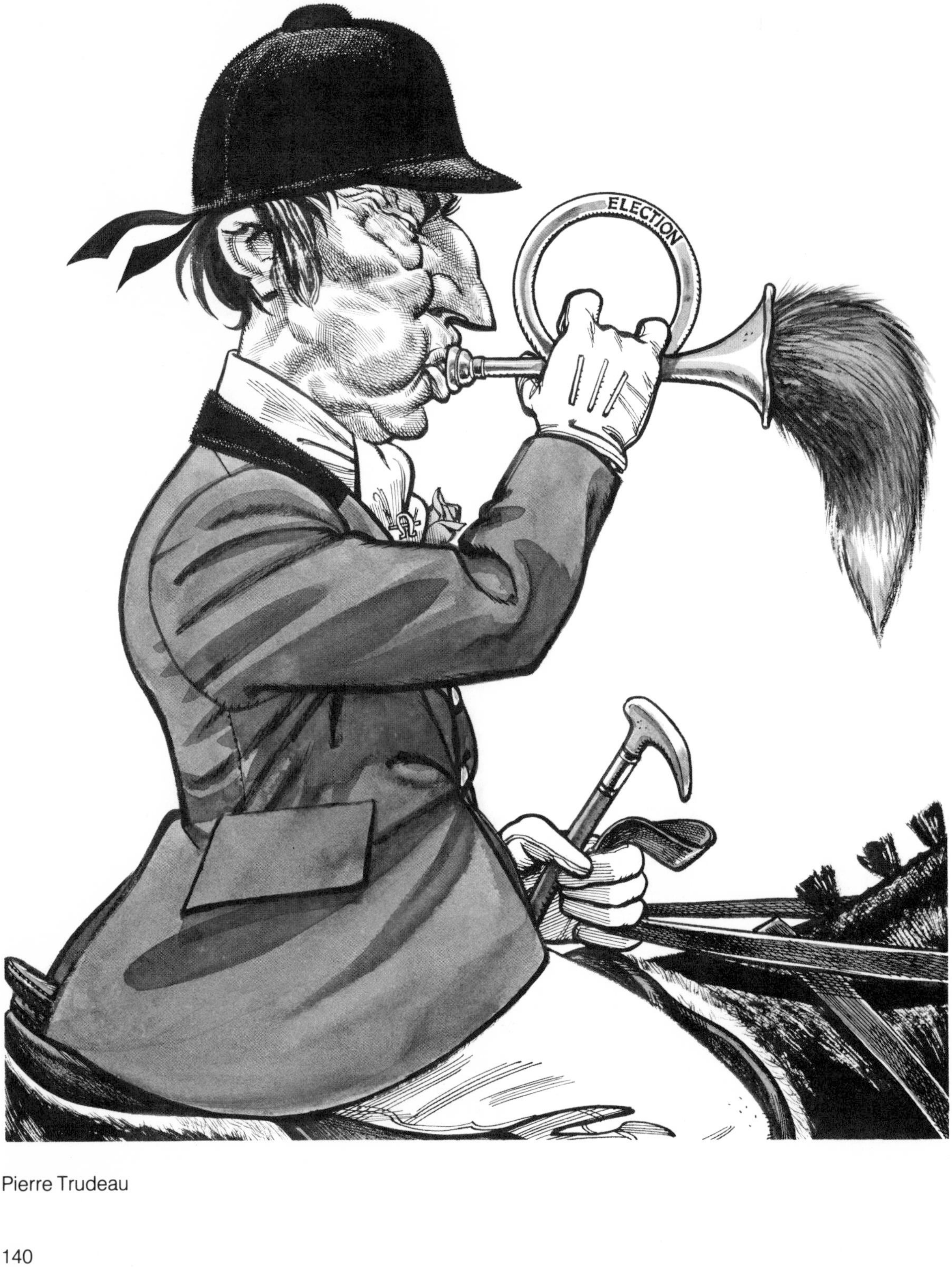
ELECTION

Pierre Trudeau

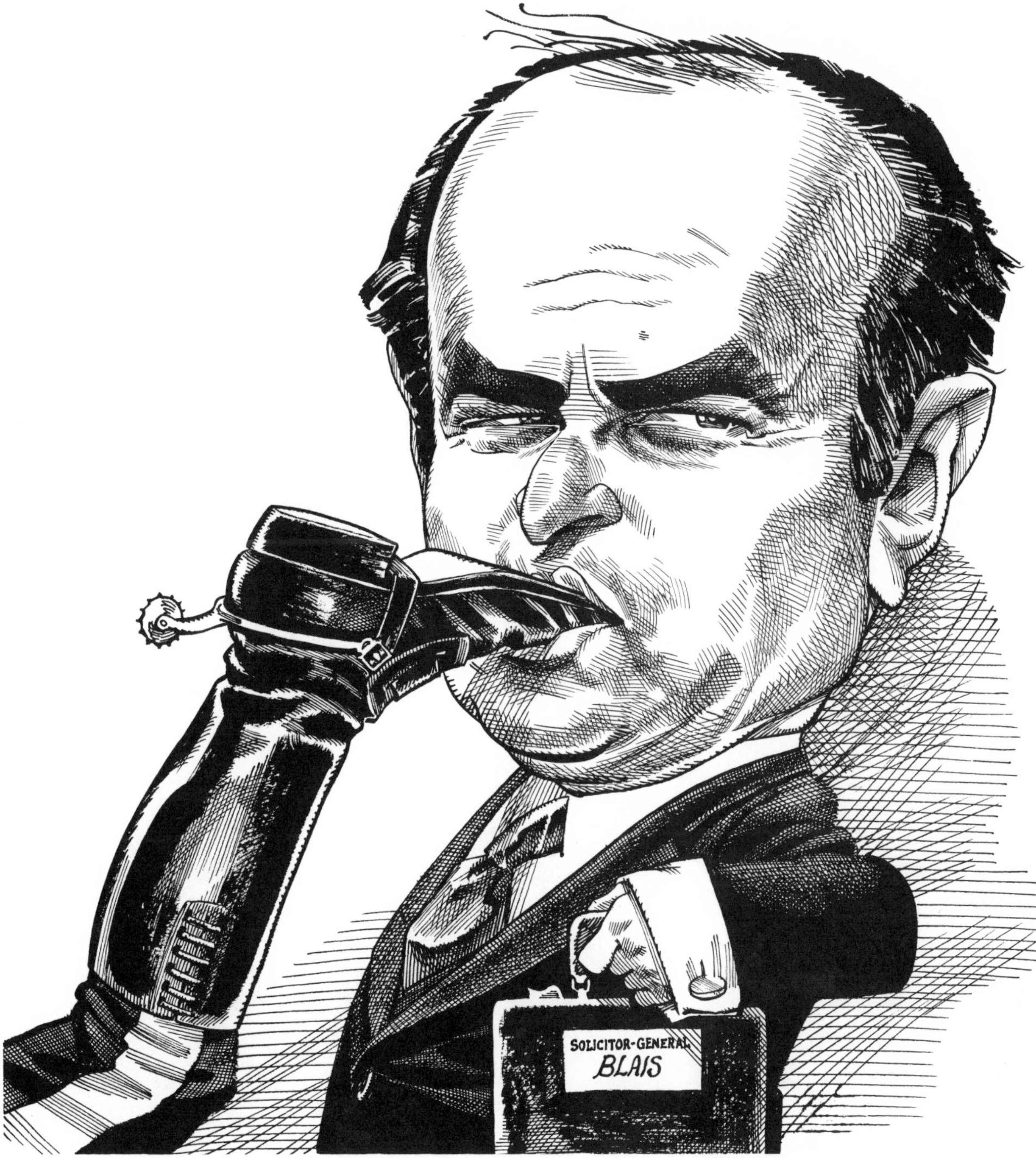
SOLICITOR-GENERAL
BLAIS

Jean-Jacques Blais

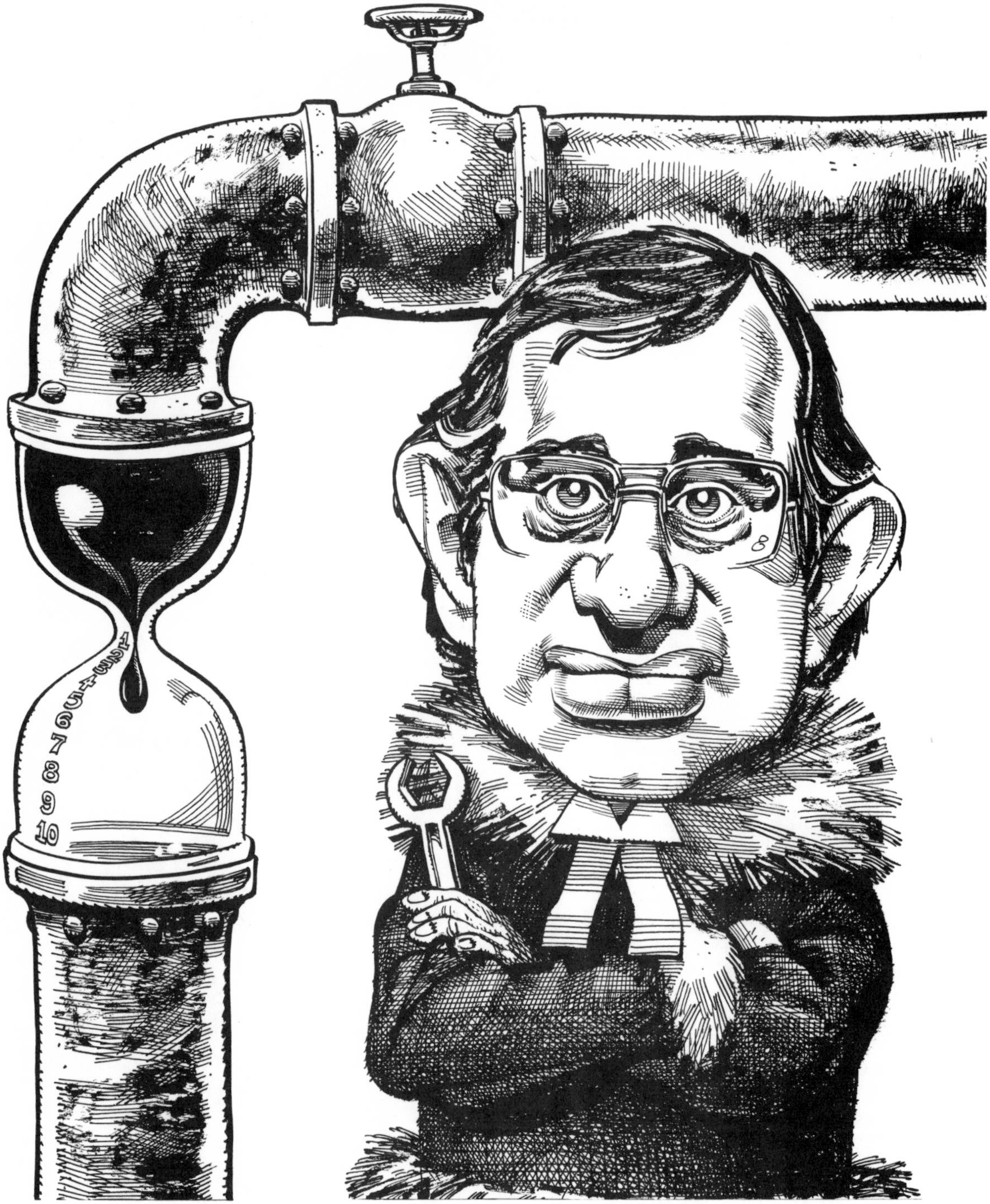
5
6
7
8
9
10

Tom Berger

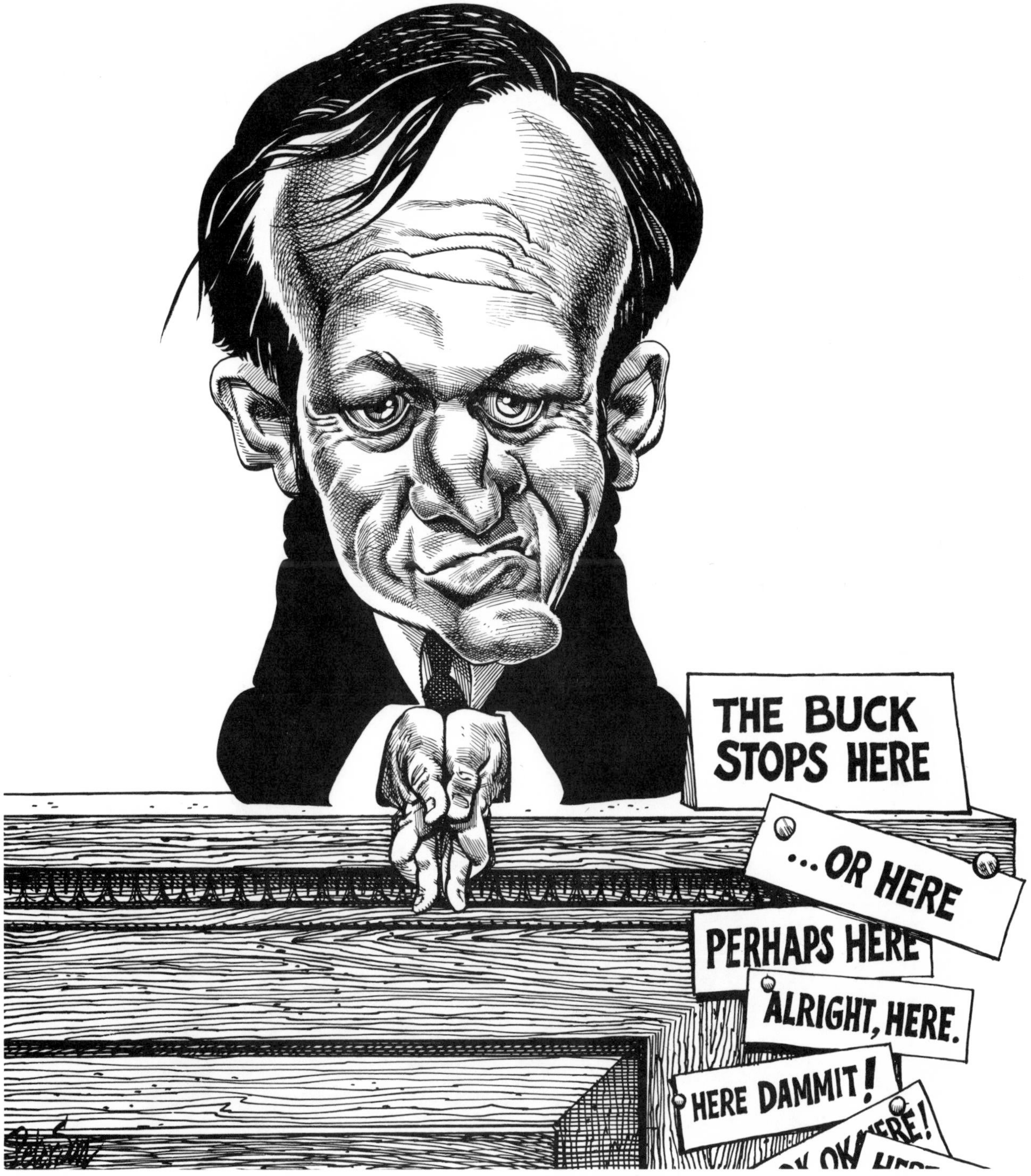
THE BUCK STOPS HERE
...OR HERE
PERHAPS HERE
ALRIGHT, HERE.
HERE DAMMIT!

Jean Chrétien

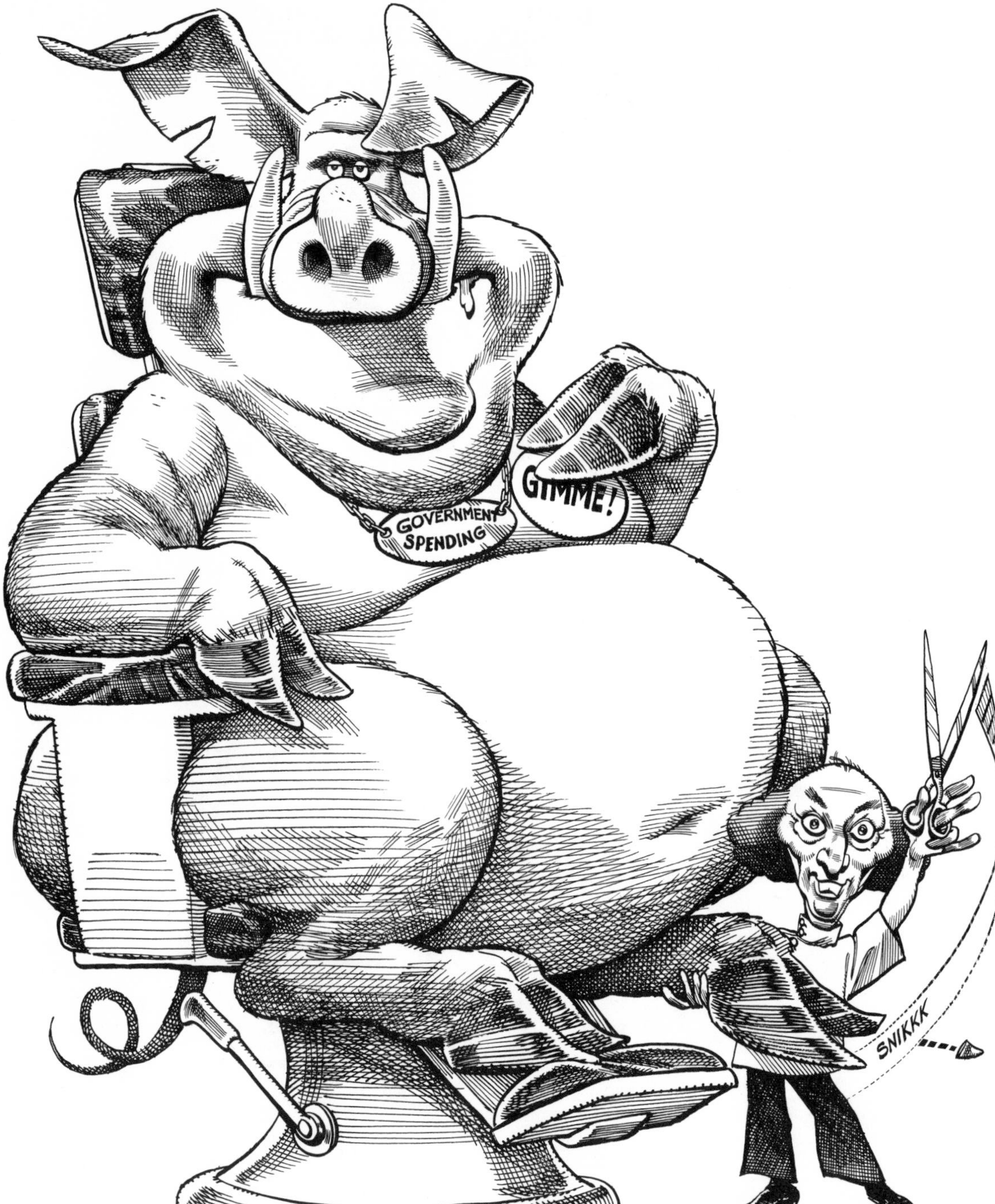
GOVERNMENT SPENDING
GIMME!
SNIKKK

Pierre Trudeau

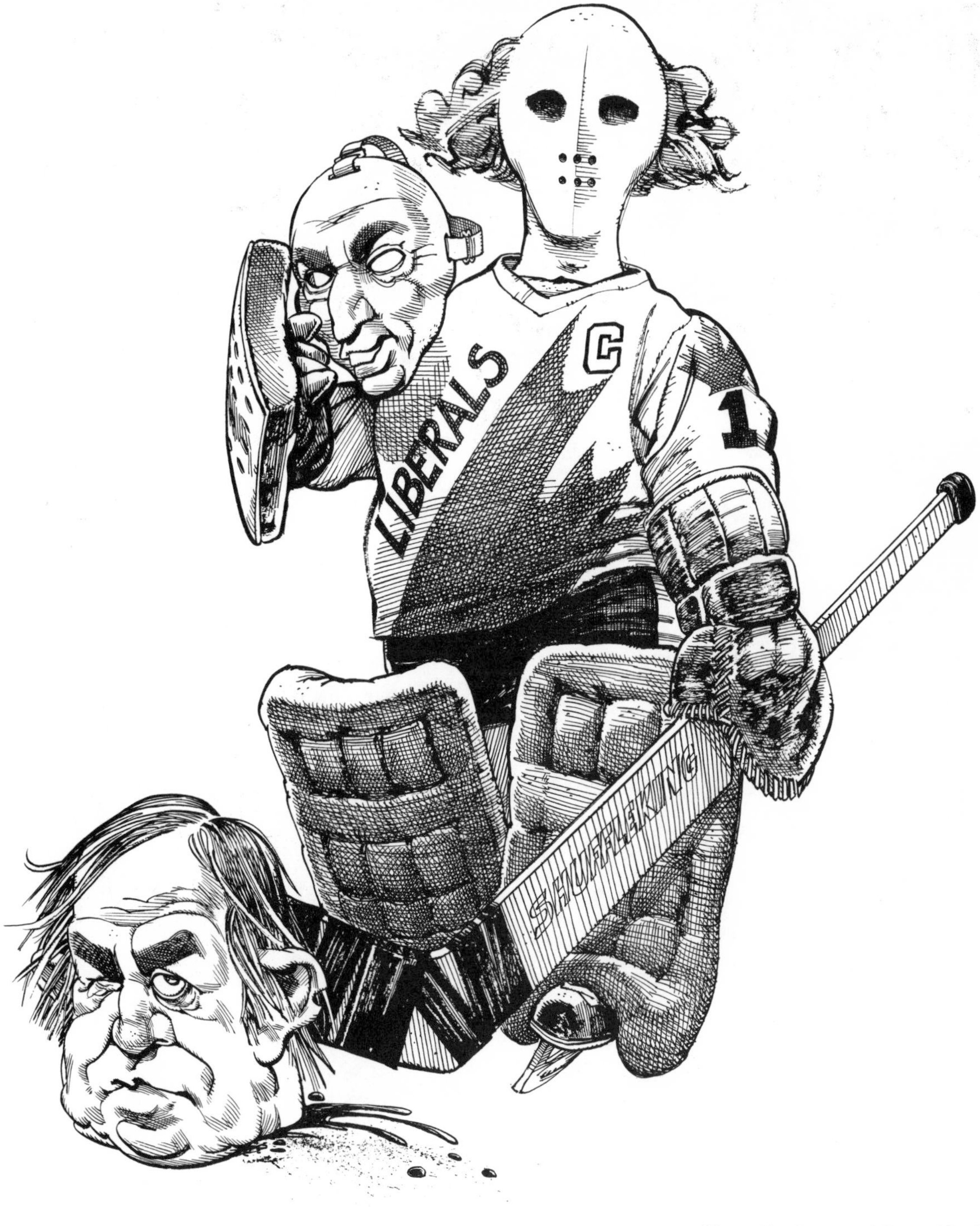
LIBERALS
C
1
SHUFFLEKING

Pierre Trudeau and Bryce Mackasey

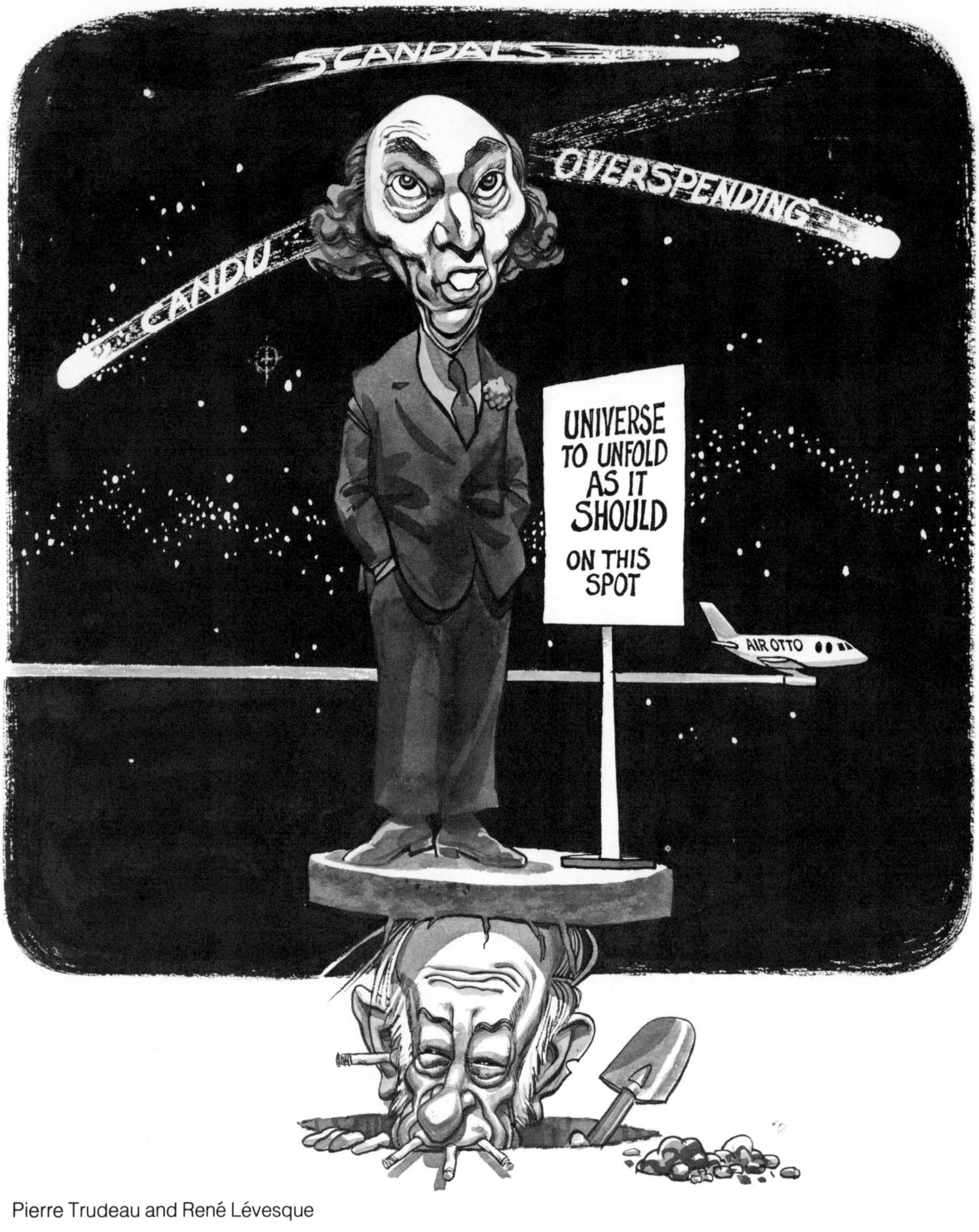
SCANDALS
OVERSPENDING
CANDU
UNIVERSE TO UNFOLD AS IT SHOULD
ON THIS SPOT
AIR OTTO

Pierre Trudeau and René Lévesque

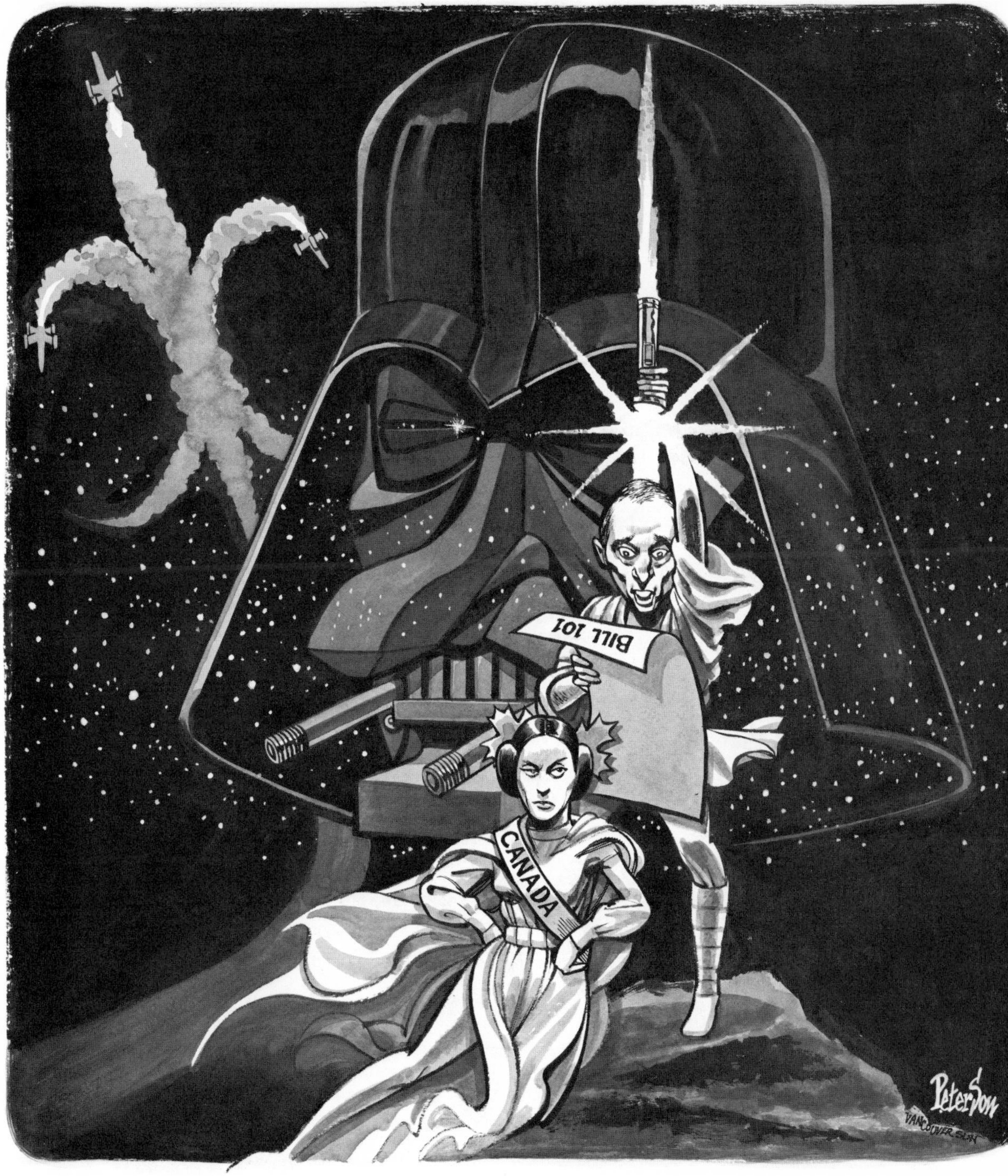
BILL 101
CANADA
PeterSon
VANCOUVER SUN

Pierre Trudeau and René Lévesque

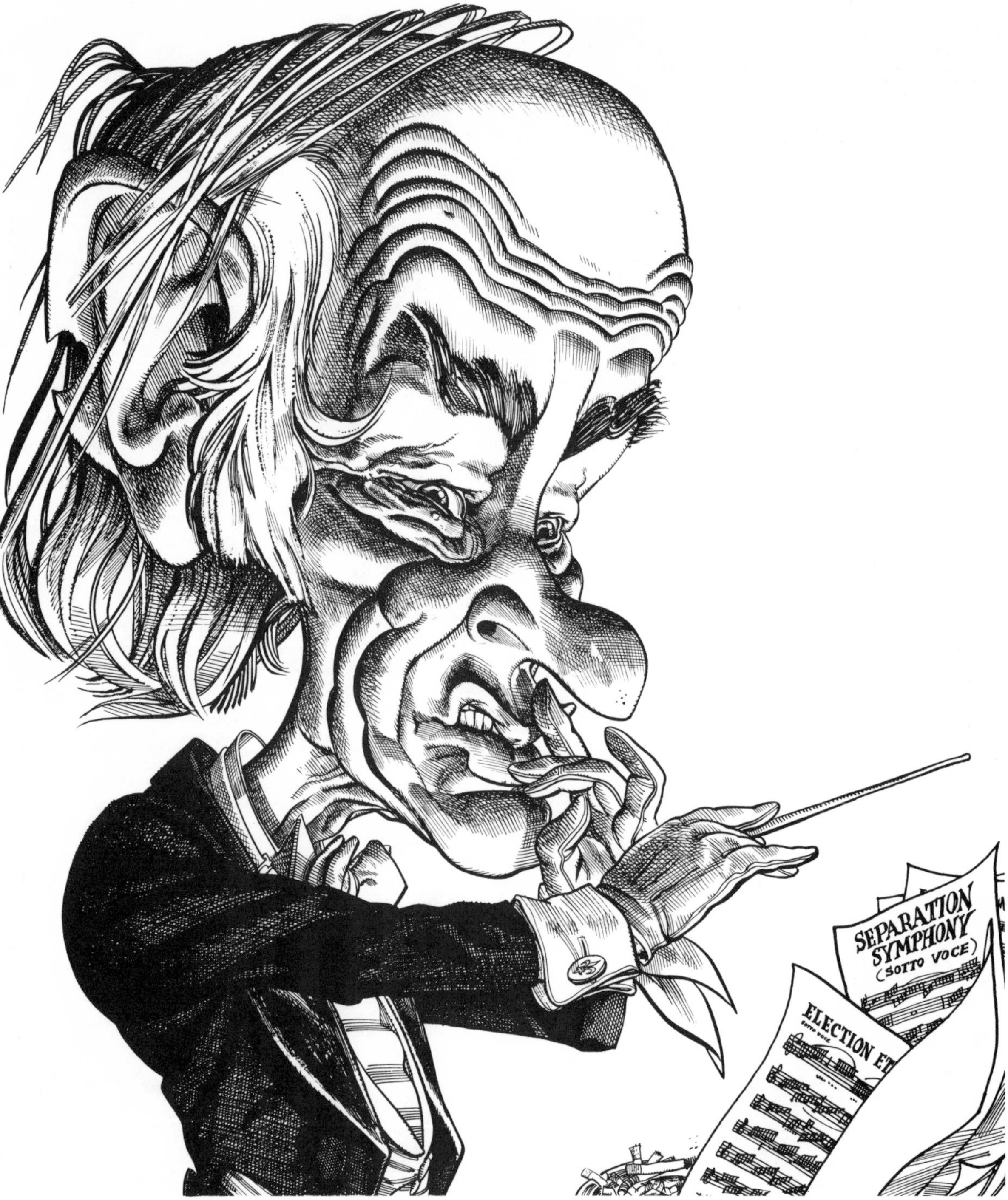
SEPARATION SYMPHONY
(SOTTO VOCE)
ELECTION ET

René Lévesque

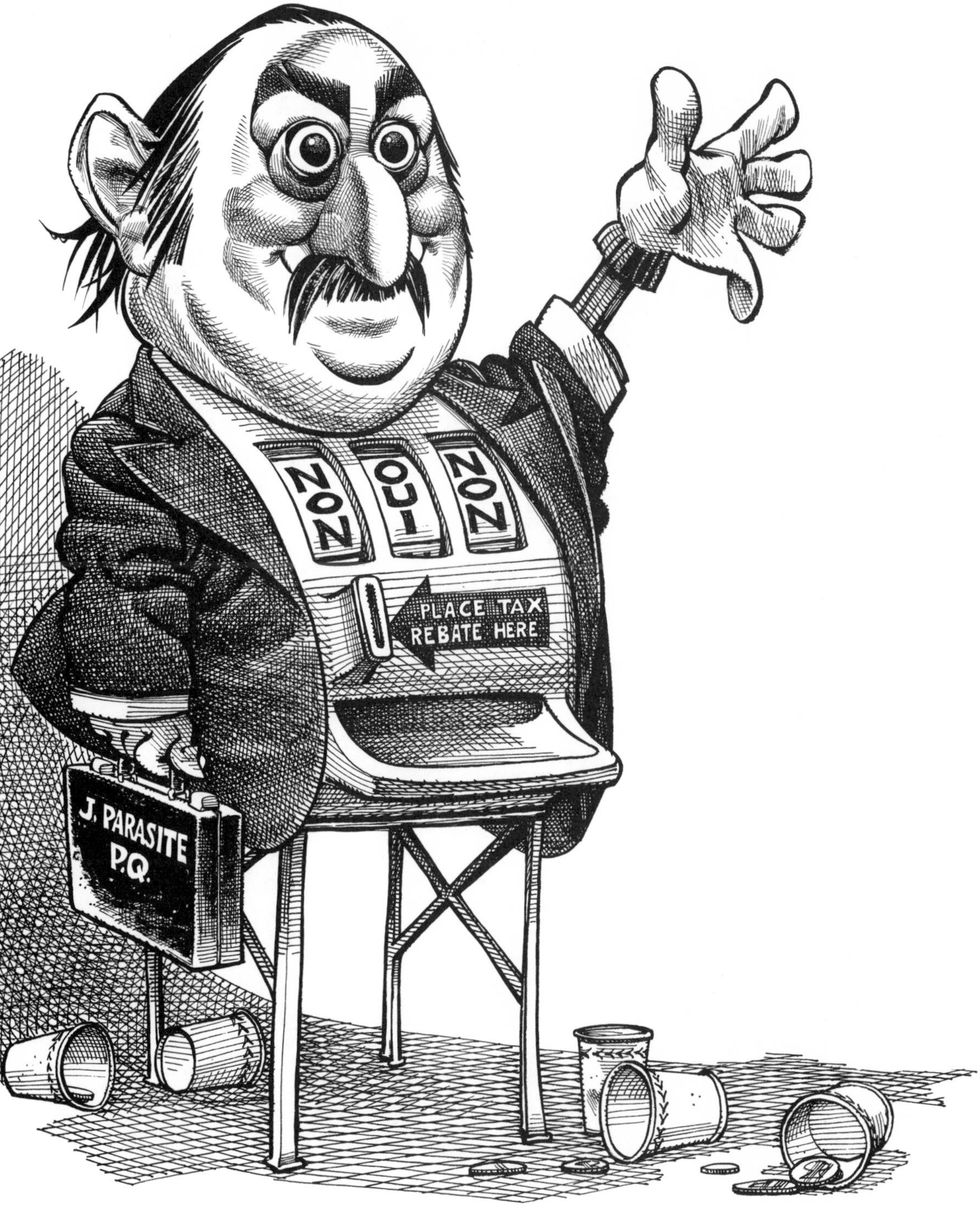
NON
OUI
NON
PLACE TAX
REBATE HERE
J. PARASITE
P.Q.

Jacques Parizeau

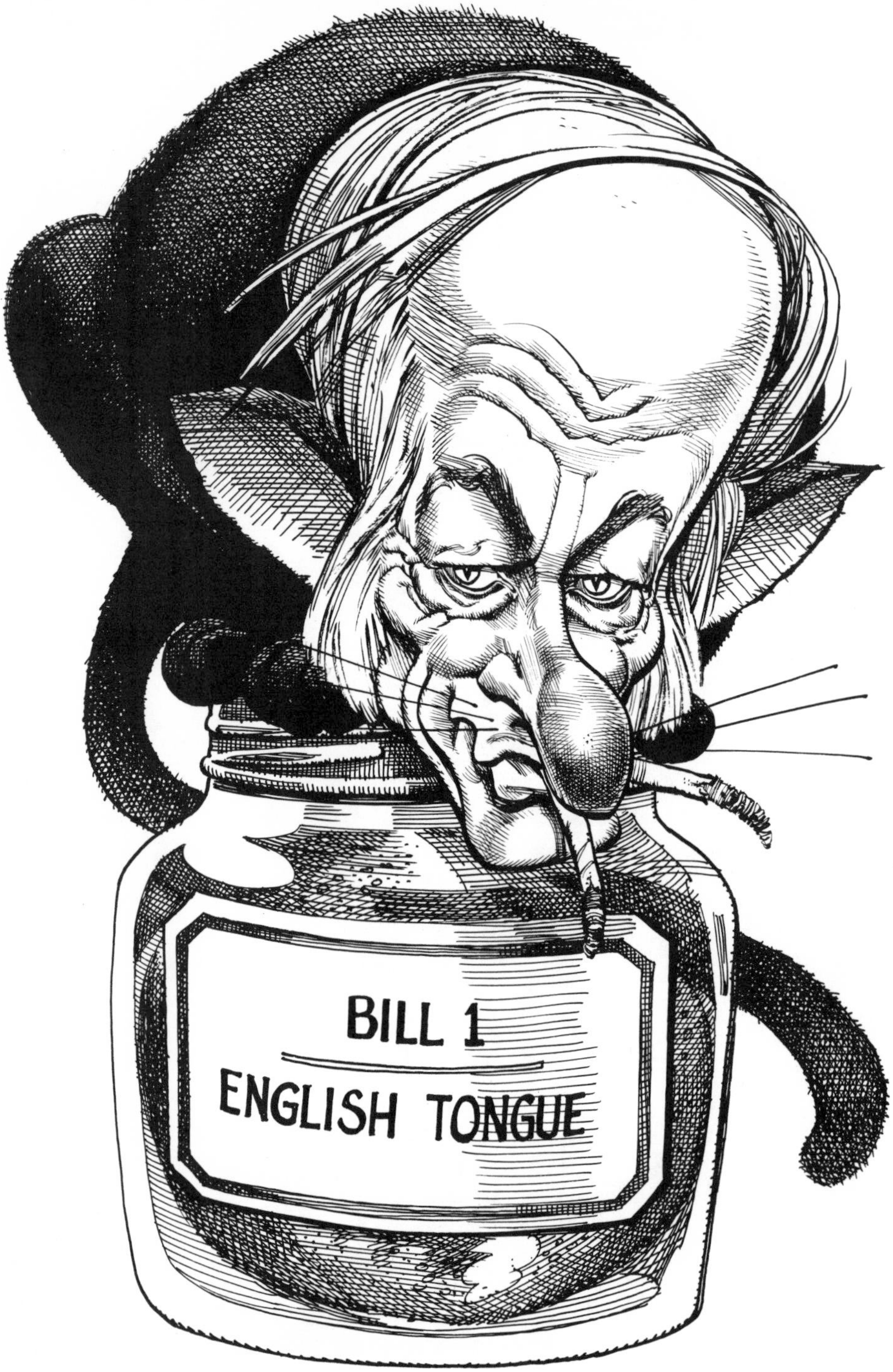
BILL 1
ENGLISH TONGUE

René Lévesque

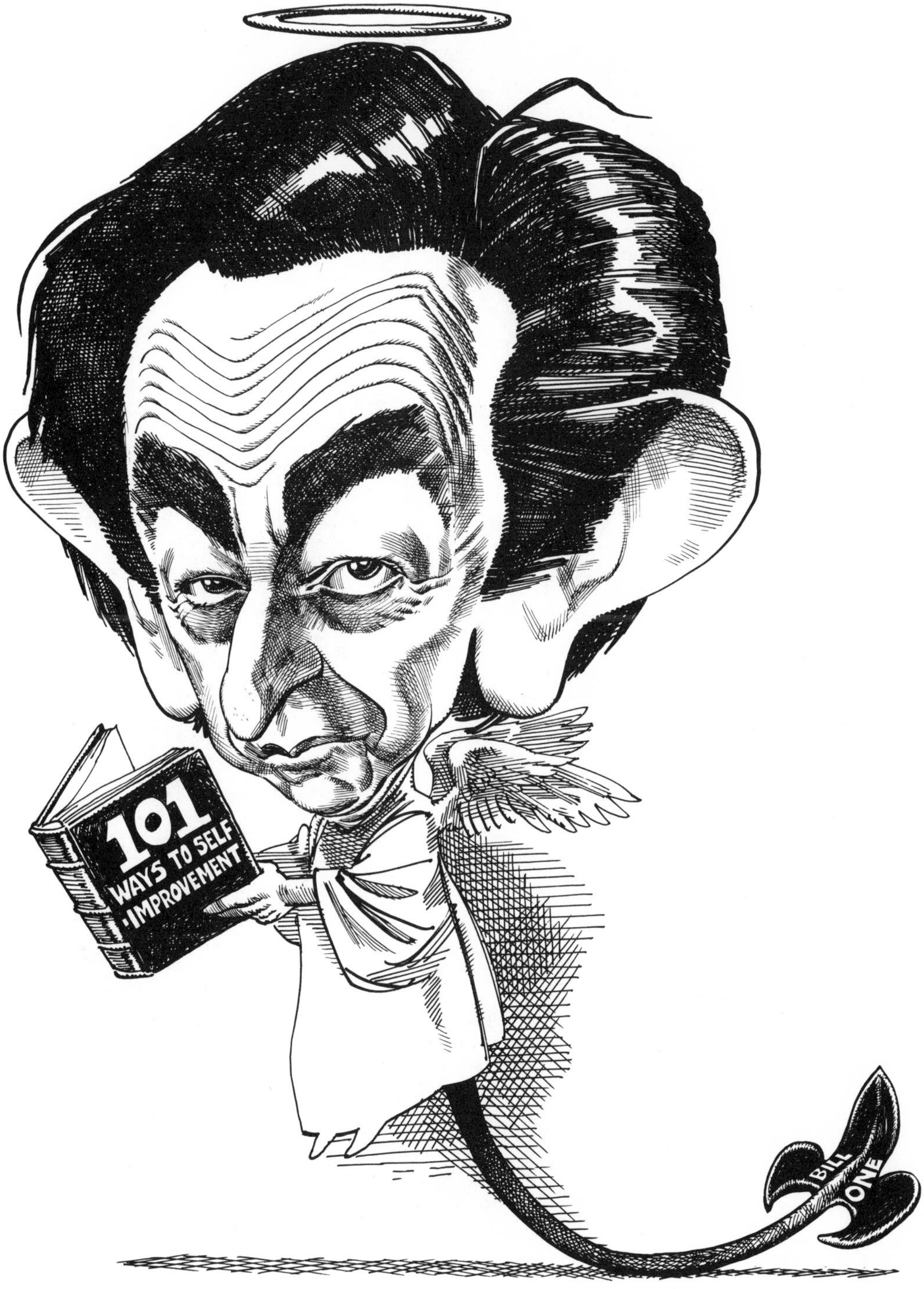
101
WAYS TO SELF
-IMPROVEMENT
BILL
ONE

Camille Laurin

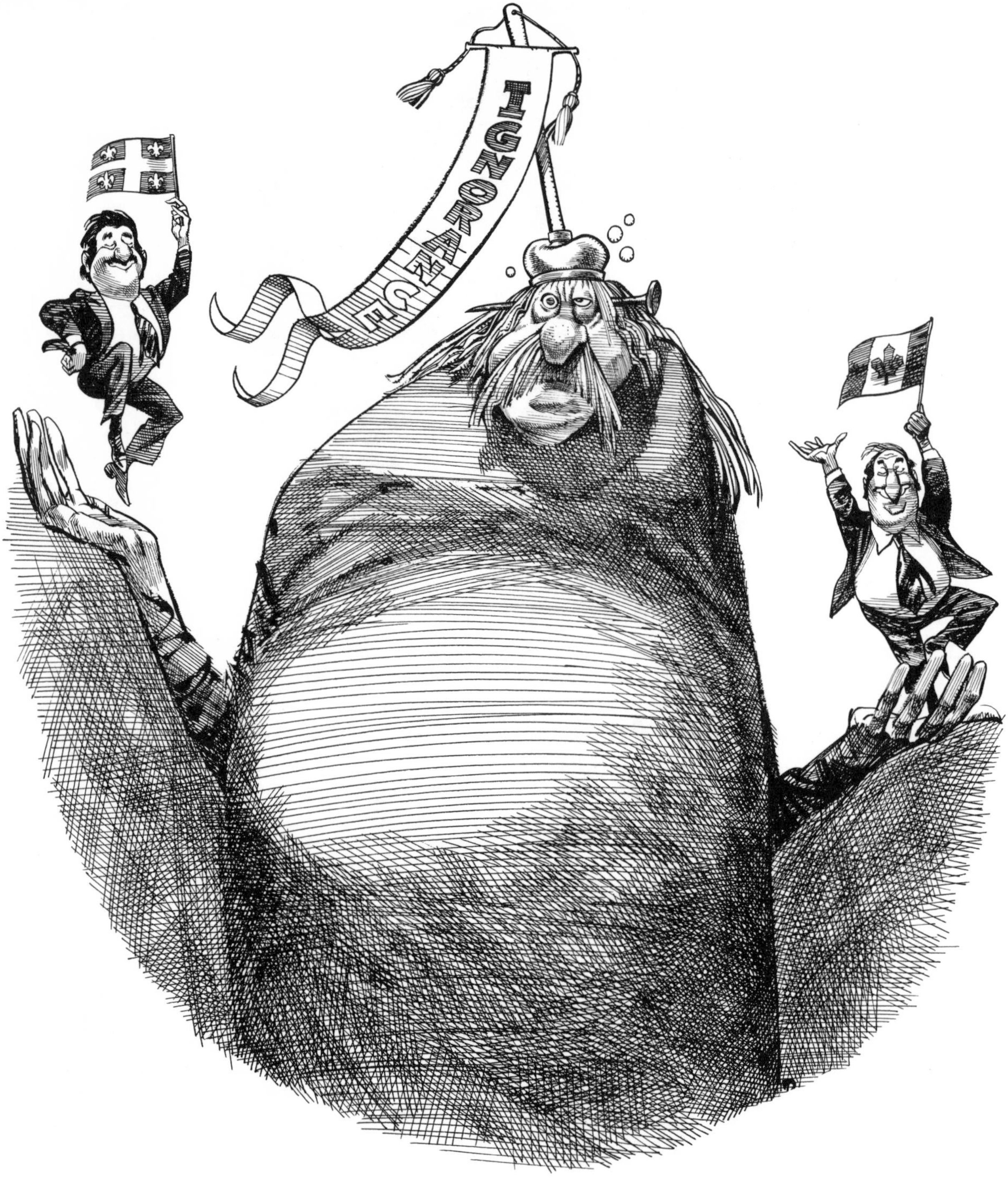
IGNORANCE

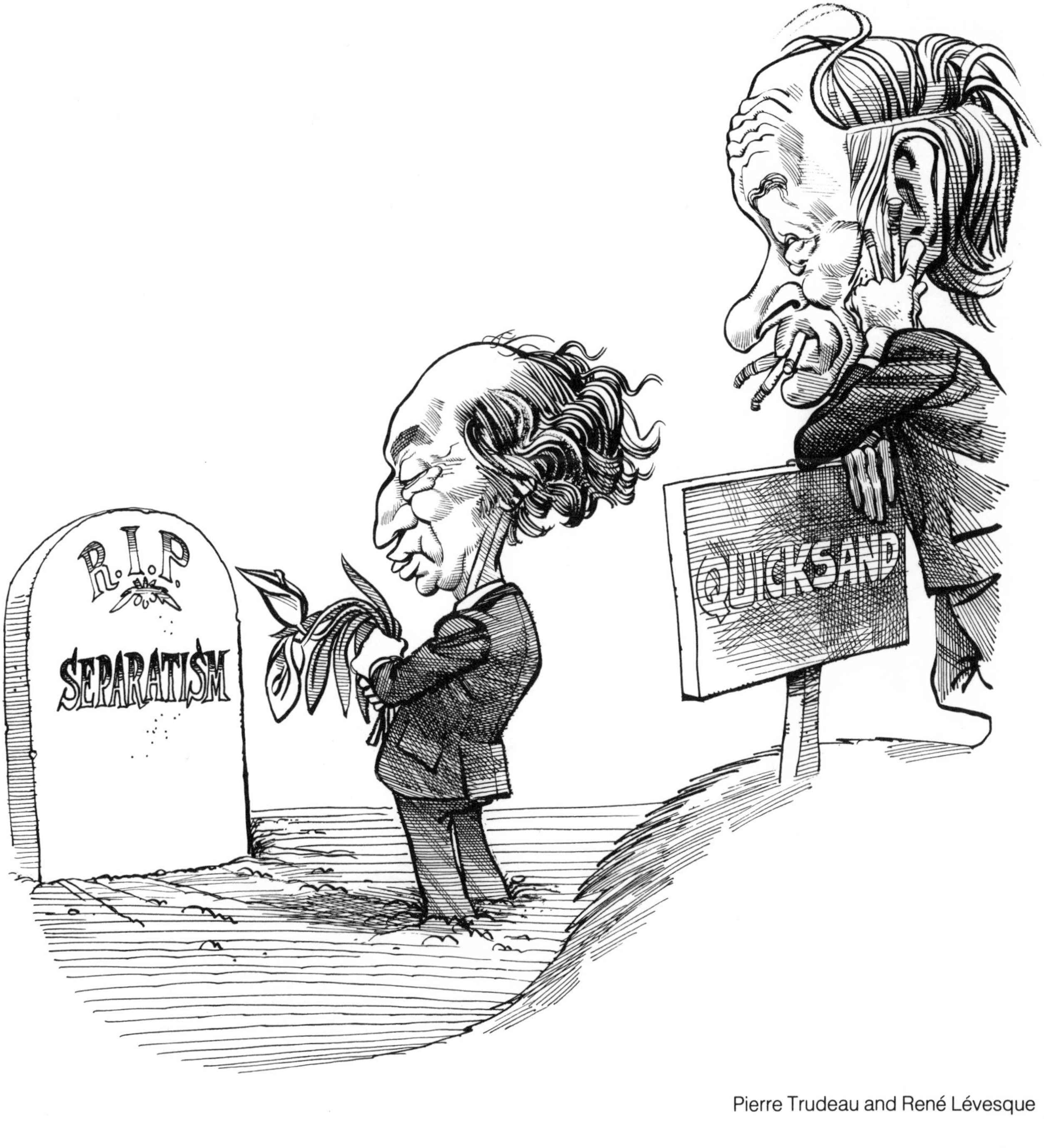
R.I.P.
SEPARATISM
QUICKSAND

Pierre Trudeau and René Lévesque

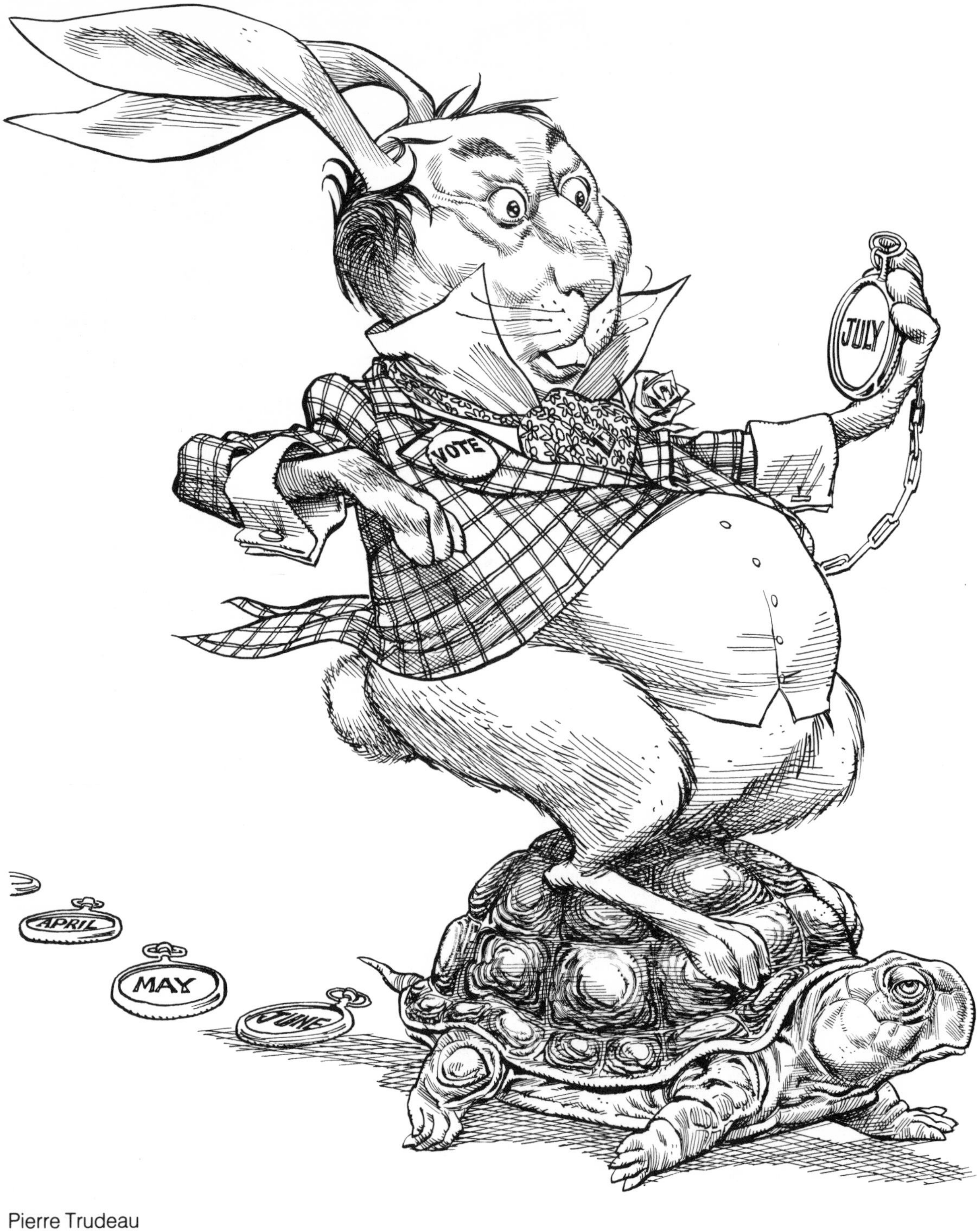
JULY
VOTE
APRIL
MAY
JUNE

Pierre Trudeau

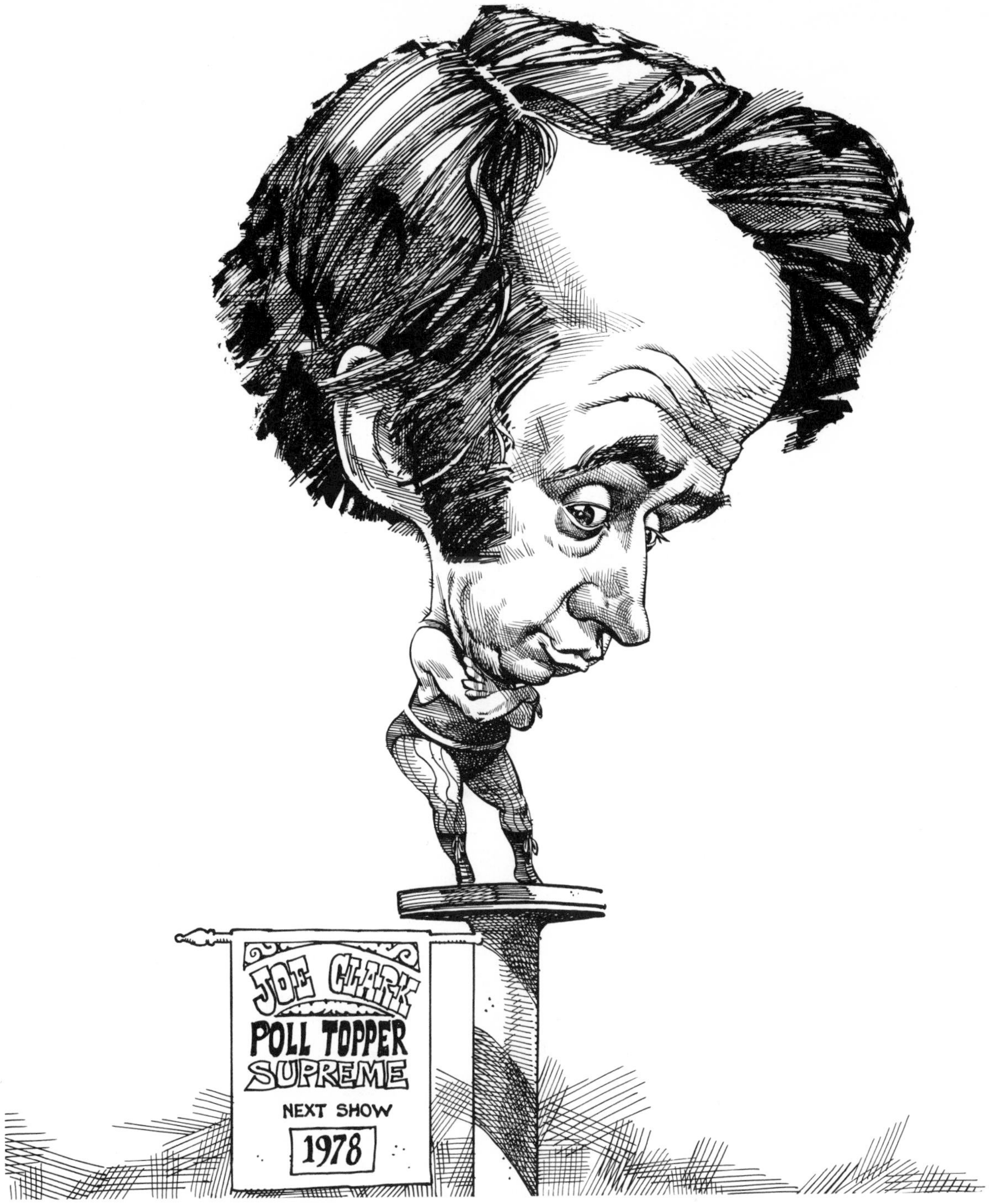
JOE CLARK
POLL TOPPER
SUPREME
NEXT SHOW
1978

Joe Clark

The Chronicles of the Swamp

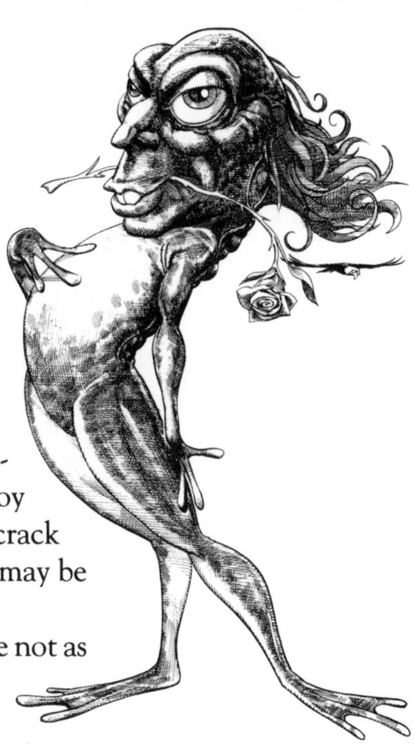

Everyone else has failed to explain this ungovernable land. Not the political scientists, nor the historians, nor the journalists—let alone the CBC, that ponderous electronic organ—have been able to interpret Canada to Canadians. Since all other methods have fizzled, Roy Peterson (accompanied by his lyricist, Stanley Burke) has taken a crack at it. So far, the results have sold 200,000 copies. So far, these two may be closer to the truth than anyone.

Perhaps we are not as advanced as we presume. Perhaps we are not as sophisticated as we would like to think, nor as subtle, nor as complicated. Perhaps we struggle in our national Swamp in rudimentary terms, childlike in our naive beliefs, fumbling in our insane desires. This is the thesis of the Burke-Peterson theory. We do not progress so much as we struggle. We are all residents of the Swamp, trapped in our territorial imperatives, prisoners of our native tongue, fearing the great Eagle that swoops from the south.

Burke, the worldly former CBC correspondent and newsreader, who now views life from the vantage point of a houseboat in Vancouver, six years ago evolved the theory that the problem in the Swamp was the existential struggle between the Beavers and the Frogs. The first of four books on the problem, *Frog Fables and Beaver Tales*, explained why Rene Terrifique, down at the Frog end of the Swamp, would come to power (as he did, three years later).

The Beavers, you see, "took long hours off from their important work on the dam and from cutting down trees and running the Swamp. But they couldn't talk Frog." Peter Waterhole, of course, was mortified. He had been marching about telling everyone that "the Swamp is strong." Oh dear. The Beavers had let him down.

Peterson, through all this romp, is in exuberant form, his fantasies loosened by Burke's imagination. Has there ever been a shrewder evisceration of Peter Waterhole than this sleek amphibian with the rose between his aristocratic teeth? Or Lugubrious J. Standfast, the lobster from Halifax? Peterson is simply brilliant, casting our characters in a regional frieze, reducing our personalities to the vertebrates (or crustaceans) that are their closest cousins.

The quiet man on the West Vancouver slope, egged on by Burke, does in most everyone in the country who counts. In one of the books—*The Day of the Glorious Revolution* (supposedly published for children but with images that wound only adults)—there is the Peterson view of famous journalist Pierre Bullion, author of *The Bug Minority* and *The Last Dike*. There, too, is Gordon Carborundum, who loves to rub people the wrong way; John Diefenboomer; Charles Grynch of the Depressed Gallery and the celebrated guru, Marshall McCosmos.

In *Blood, Sweat & Bears* the hobbled Bobby Ore appears along with Clarence Cowbell and Alan Eagleclaw in the great Canada-Russia struggle on ice, imprinted on our soppy brains so long ago by the oracle of our age, Fossil Spewit. Peterson, in his gentleness, reveals the force that is the secret soul of the nation: the Jockstrap Mothers, shrews in pin-curlers and bandanas, each Saturday morning at the rink, urging their cute little Beavers to kill. Cowbell and Eagleclaw reap the rewards of hired flesh; the Jockstrap Mothers—chilled suburban Witches of Macbeth—are the key.

Peterson ventures one step beyond Walt Kelly's Pogo fantasies. In a way, these books are history in drag. As well as Civil Serpents, there are in the latest book, *Swamp Song*, devastating cameos of William Lyin Mackenzie Sting, the Gliberal Party, Sir Charles Tippler, Sir Wilfrid Laureate, Sir Robert Boredom, Arthur Mean and R. B. Bandit. Senator Keith Gravy is there, along with the Unity Task Farce and the capital of Nottalot. There are, in a magnificent group portrait, the Fathers of Conflaburation.

There is also in this little book of prophecy, published in 1978, the first appearance of Joe Hoo, the Befuddled Owl. "Elect me," he pleads: "I'll think of something."

How prescient. How ominous.

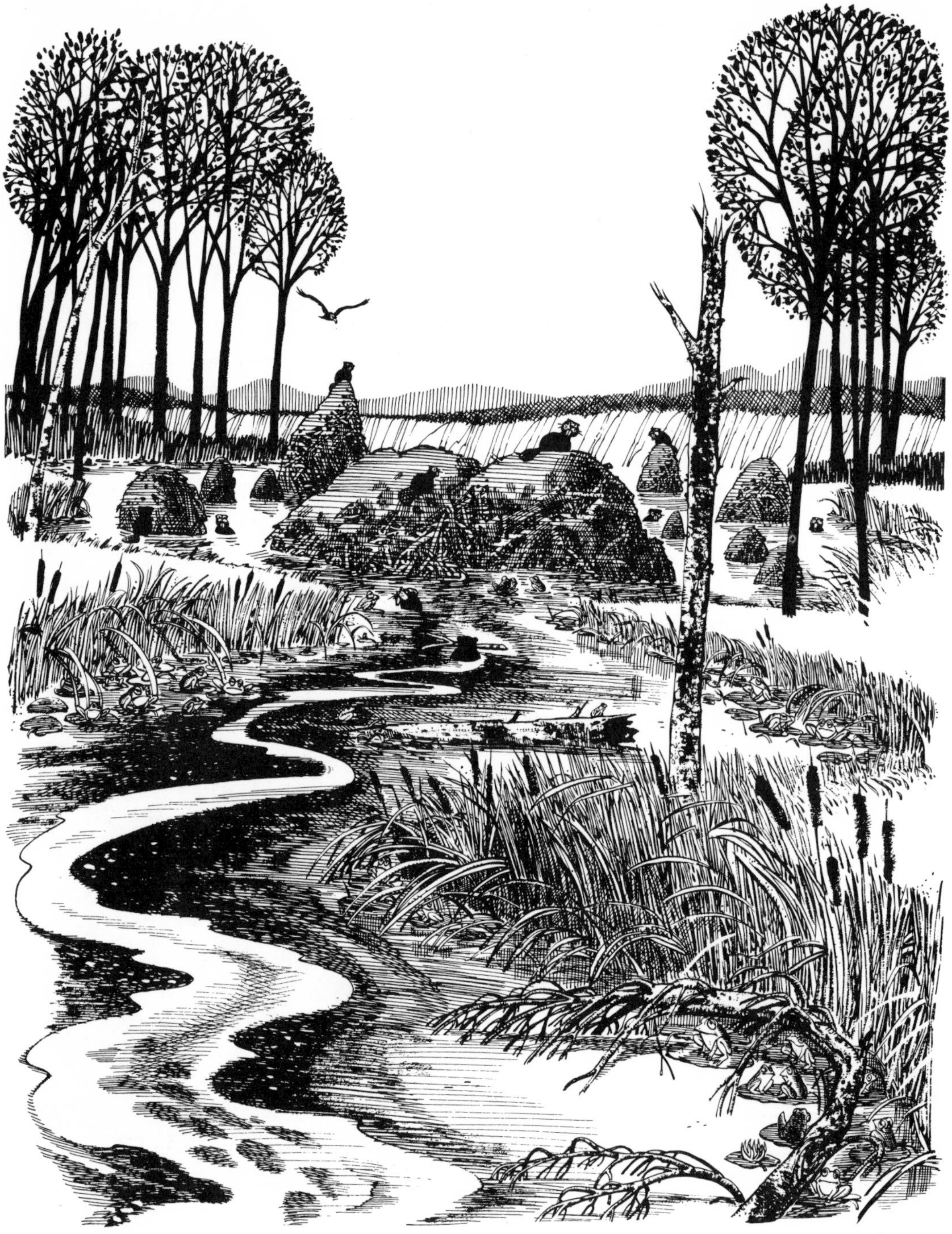

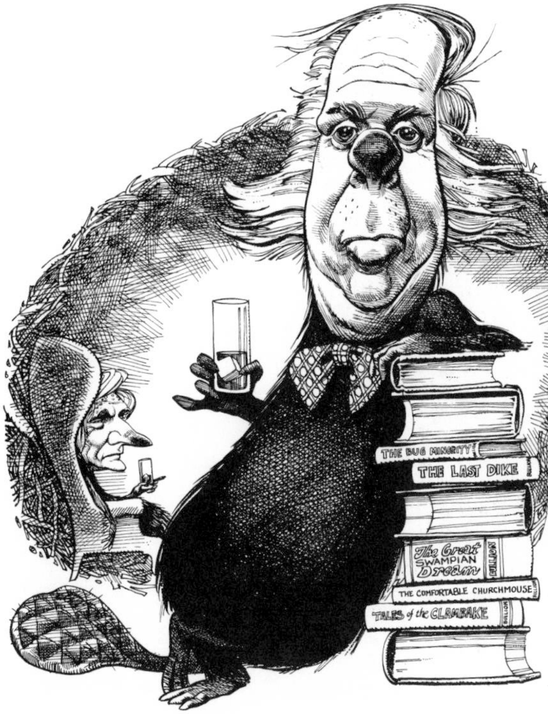
THE BUG MINORITY
THE LAST DIKE
The Great SWAMPIAN Dream
THE COMFORTABLE CHURCHMOUSE
TALES of the CLAMBAKE

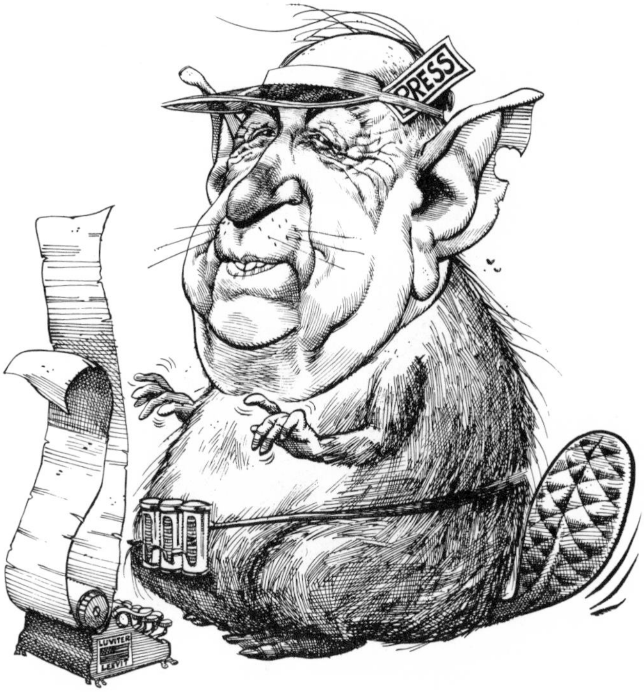
PRESS

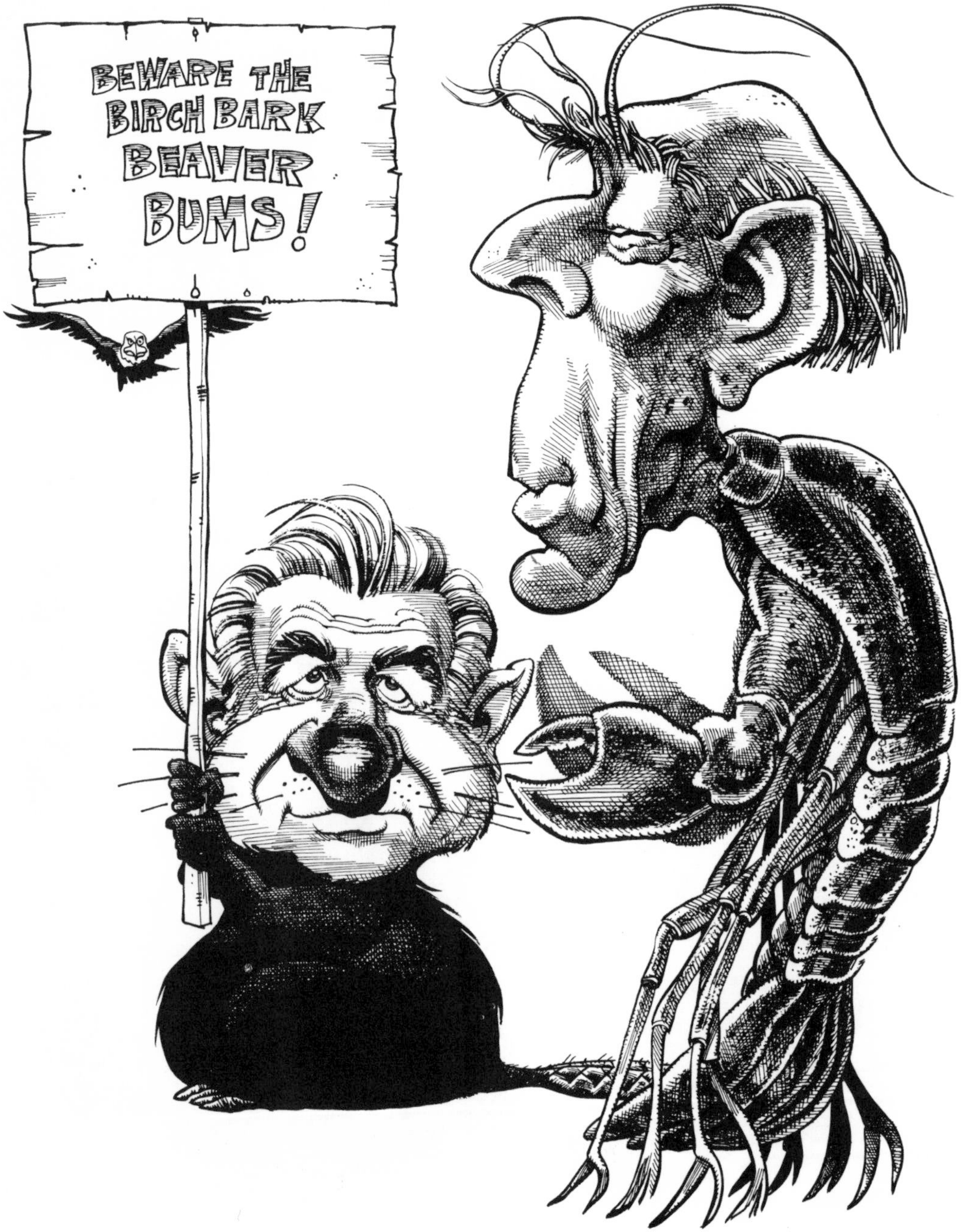
BEWARE THE
BIRCH BARK
BEAVER
BUMS!

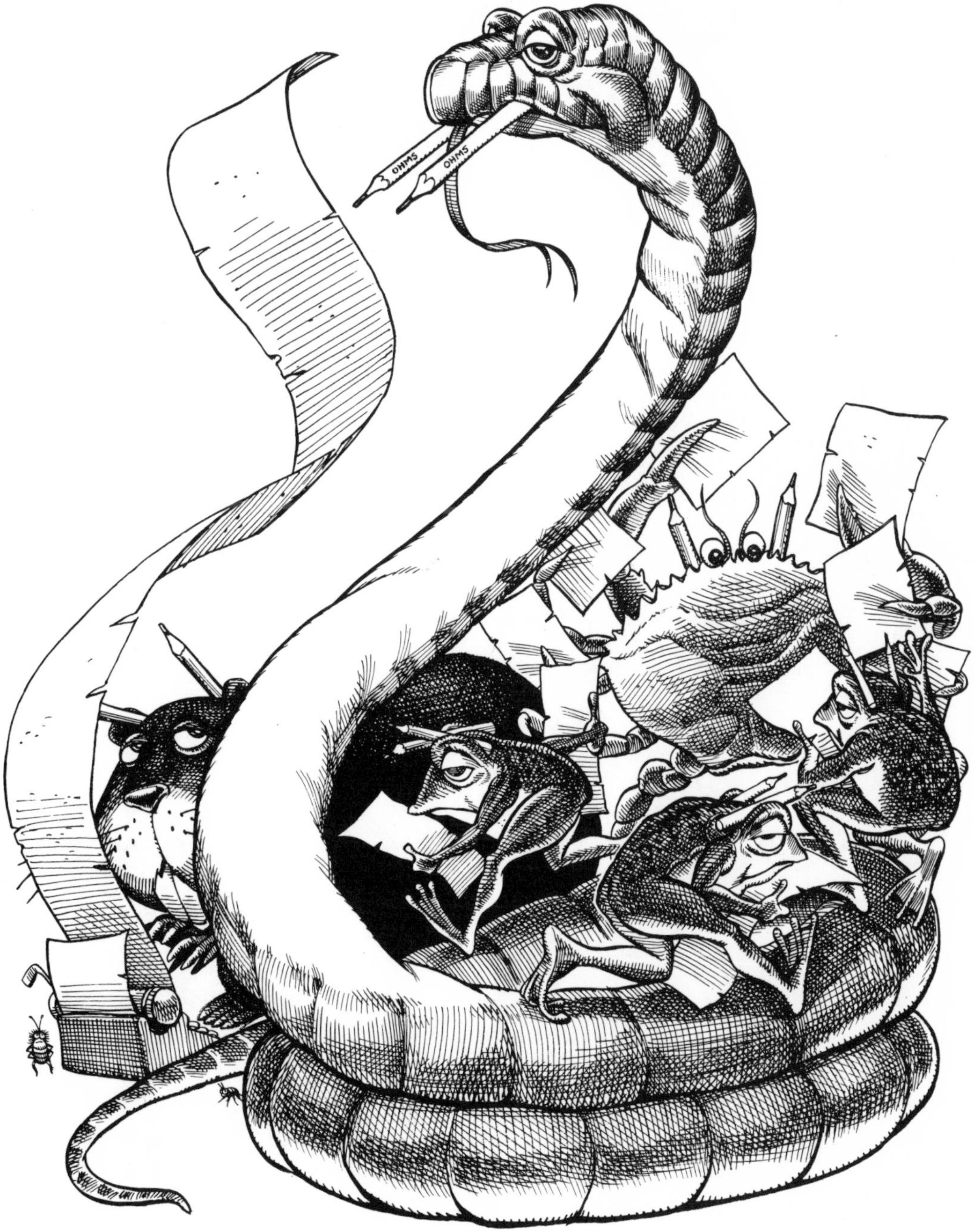
OHMS
OHMS

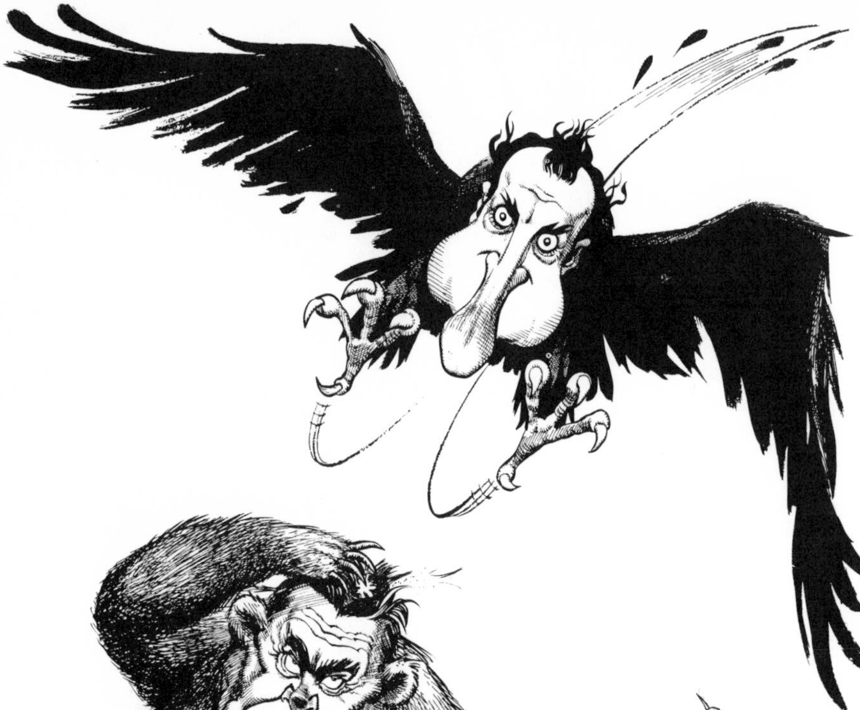

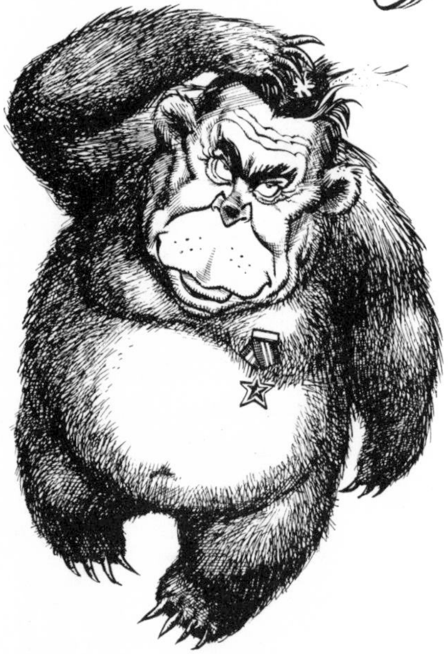

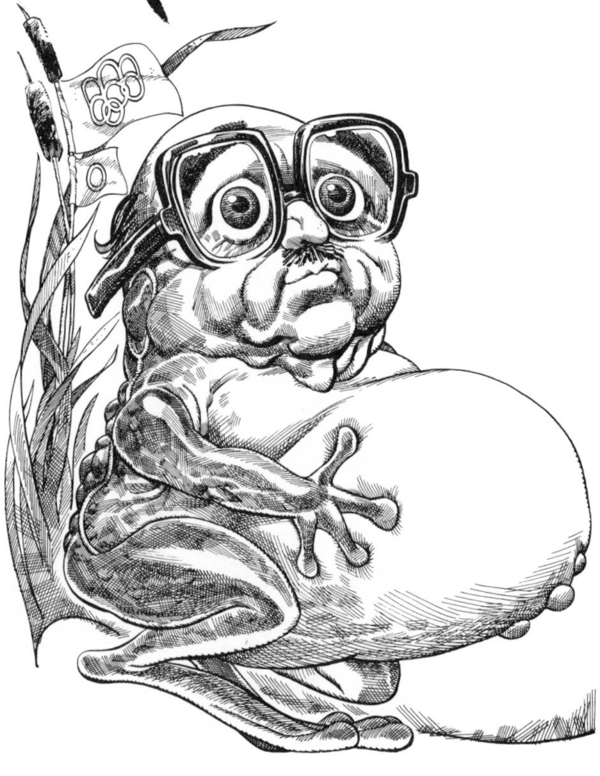

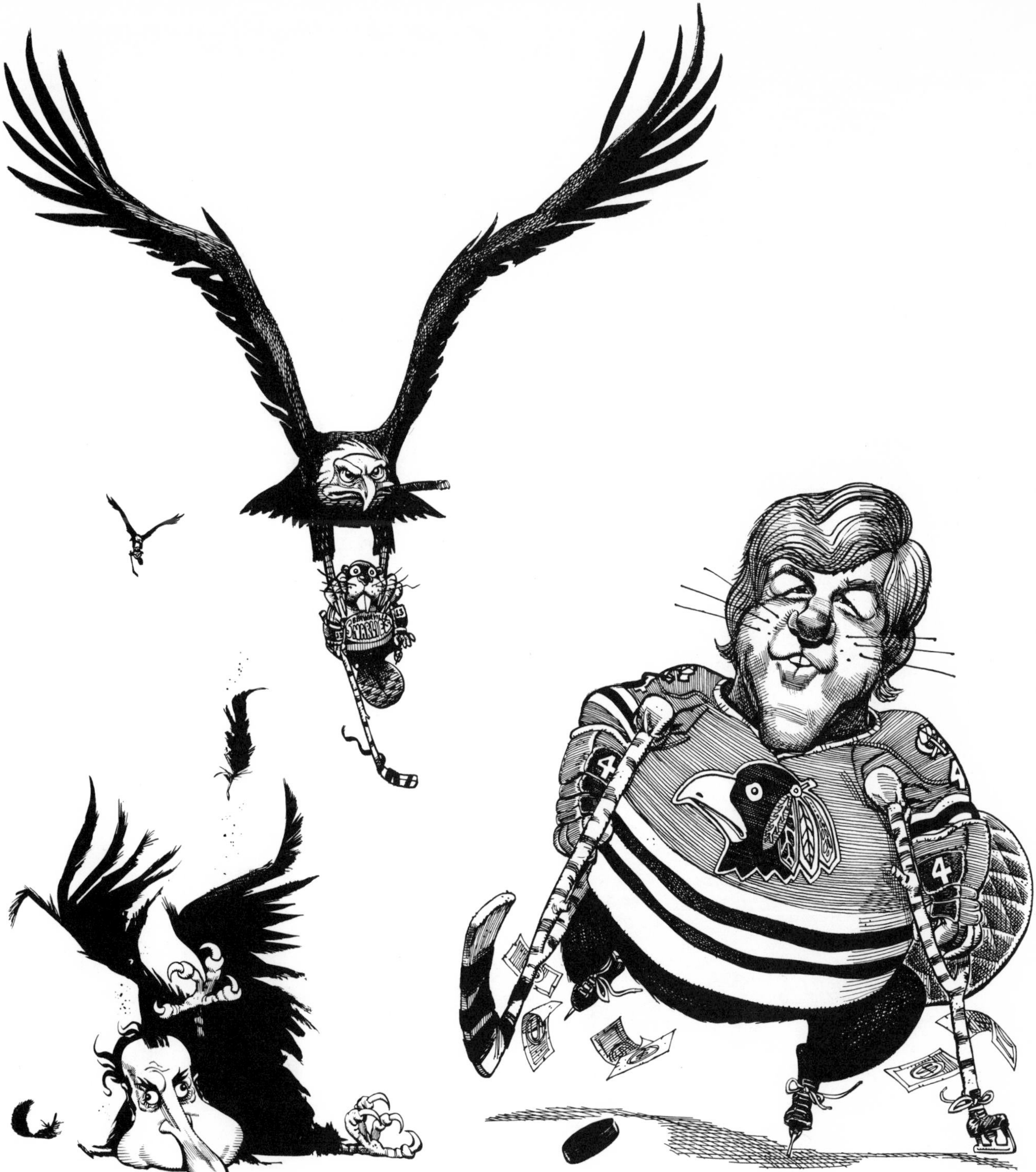
SNARLIES
4
4
4

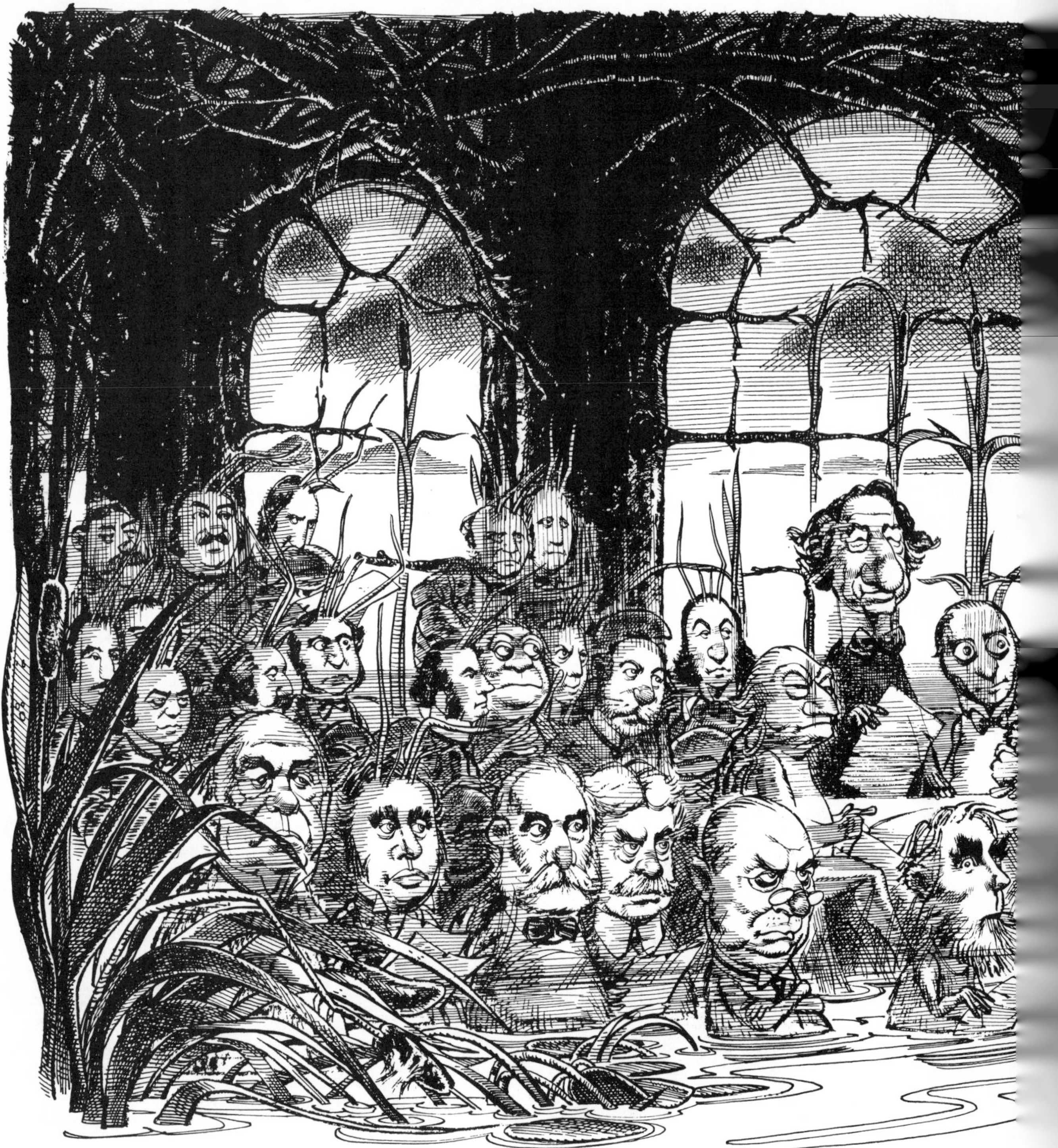

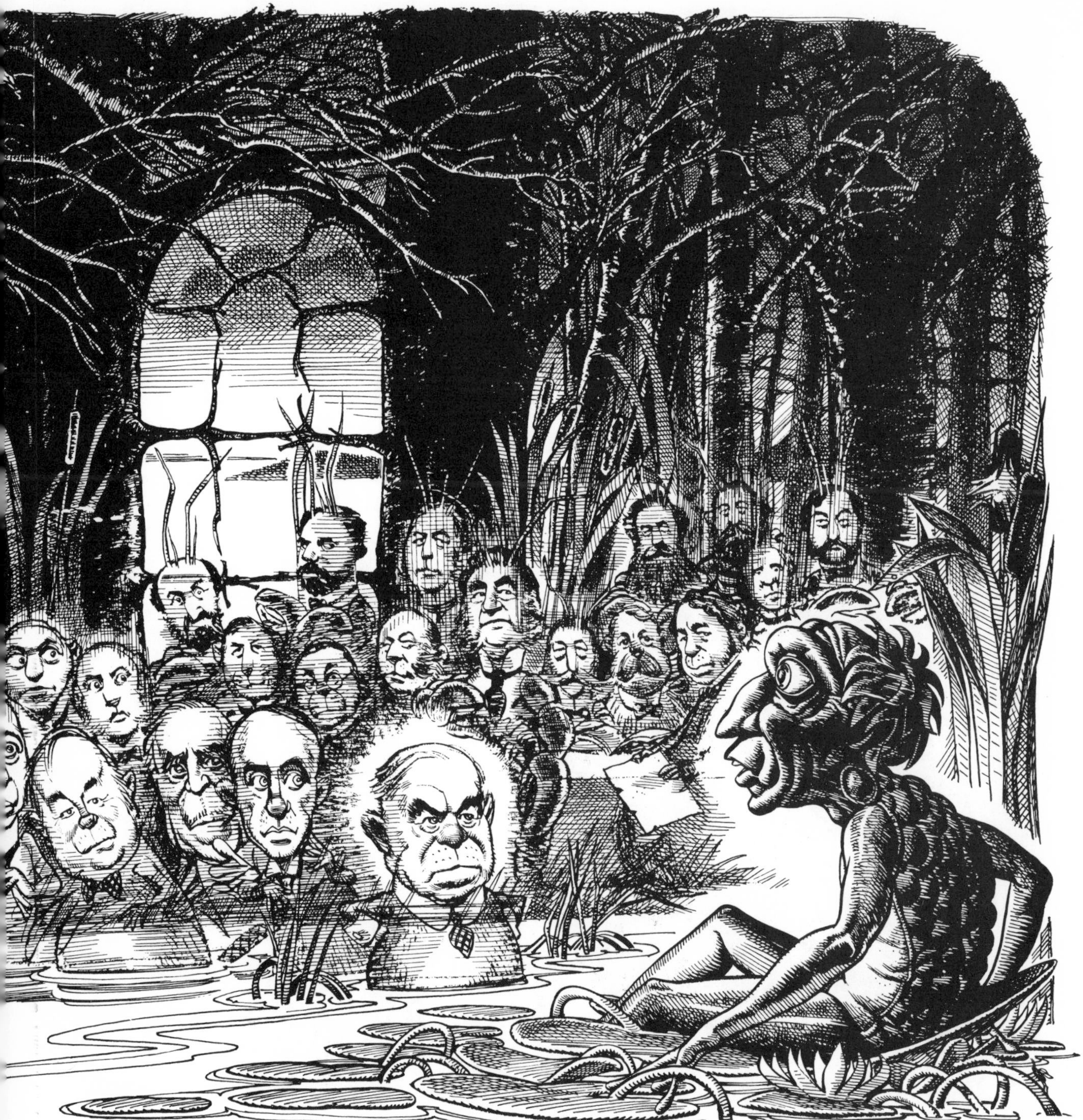

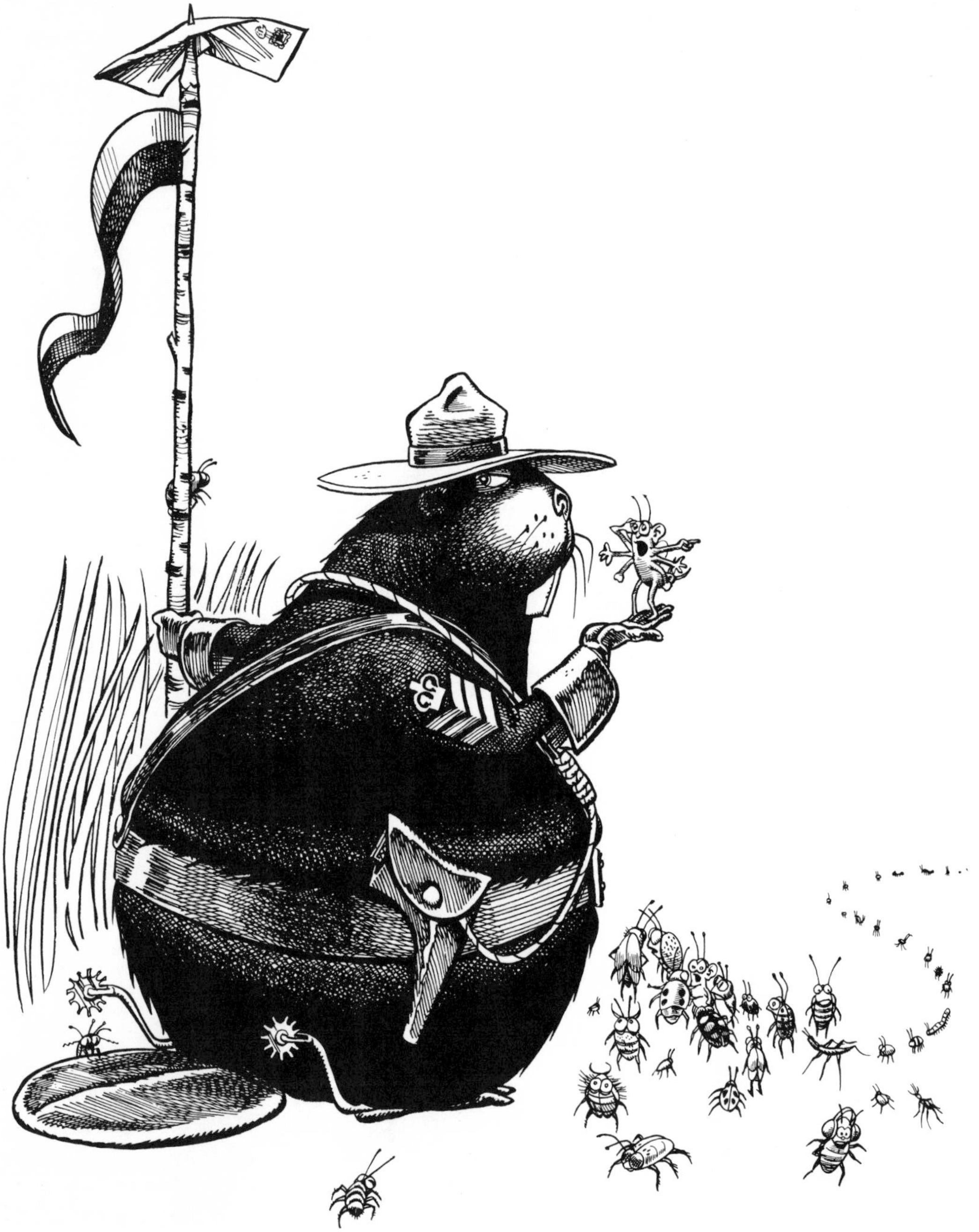

ON STRIKE
EN GRÈVE

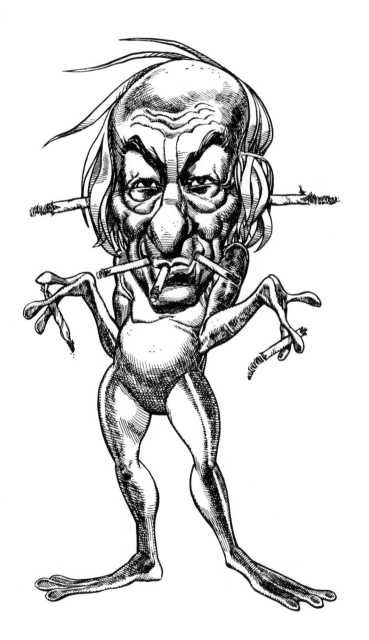

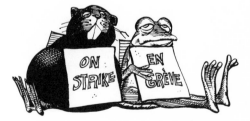

Acknowledgements

The illustrations in this book, found on the pages listed below, first appeared in: *The Vancouver Sun*, pp. 18-30, 32-57, 59-60, 62-71, 73-74, 76-79, 81-86, 88-110, 112-118, 120-155; *Maclean's*, pp. 7, 15, 58, 72, 80; *Frog Fables & Beaver Tales* (Stanley Burke and Roy Peterson), pp. 156, 158, 160, 162, 163, (reproduced courtesy of James Lorimer & Co.); *Swamp Song* (Stanley Burke and Roy Peterson), pp. 161, 164-165, 166, 167; *Weekend Magazine*, pp. 2, 10, 11, 14; *Blood, Sweat & Bears* (Stanley Burke and Roy Peterson), pp. 162, 163; *The Day of the Glorious Revolution* (Stanley Burke and Roy Peterson), pp. 159 (reproduced courtesy of James Lorimer & Co.); *Time*, p. 16.